Going It Alone

Going It Alone

The Family Life and Social Situation of the Single Parent

ROBERT S. WEISS

Basic Books, Inc., Publishers   NEW YORK

Library of Congress Cataloging in Publication Data

Weiss, Robert Stuart, 1925–
   Going it alone.

   Includes index.
   1.   Single-parent family—United States.   I.   Title.
HQ777.4.W44   301.42′7   78–19936
ISBN 0–465–02688–5

For my mother, Bessie Marcus Weiss

CONTENTS

Contents

PREFACE

WHAT IS LIFE LIKE for someone raising children alone? Sometimes stressful. Sometimes lonely. Sometimes—perhaps not often enough —rewarding. Always, it is a different way of life from that of people who have partners in their parenting.

This book is based on interviews with over two hundred single parents, some of them seen several times, and with about forty children of single parents. In a few chapters, interviews with a small sample of married couples provide comparative data.

The first section of this book describes how people become single parents. It outlines the transition from marriage or from a childless single life to life as a parent whose responsibilities are unshared.

The second section of the book describes the household of the single parent, the way it is structured and the way it operates. This section also describes single parents' relationships with their children and, for those single parents who are separated or divorced, with their former husbands or wives.

But single parents are not only parents; although their responsibilities as parents complicate their other relationships, they are also single adults who need friends, family, and intimates. The third section of the book describes the way they organize their social lives.

The fourth and last section considers two related issues: the strengths and the vulnerabilities that can be found in parenting alone; and the ways in which single parents manage.

The first section of the book presents mainly background materials. Readers who want simply to understand the experience of single parents might skim through this section and treat the book as beginning in earnest with Chapter Three.

Parenting alone is becoming ever more common in our society. The proportion of children living with only one parent more than doubled from 1960 to 1978. In the single year from 1977 to 1978, the number of one-parent families increased by 9 percent. By 1978, of the 30 million American families with children, 19 percent were headed by a single adult.[1]

A study of the sources of increase in single parenting, in which information to 1970 was examined, showed that although about a fifth of the increase was due simply to population growth, most of the increase was due to a larger proportion of our population moving through the pathways to single-parent status: especially, more couples with children separating and divorcing; secondarily, more unmarried women having children, together with a new reluctance among unmarried mothers to relinquish their children to grandparents or give them up for adoption. Meanwhile, the proportion of parents whose marriages were ended by the death of the husband or wife remained about the same.[2]

At the present time more than one American child in six lives with only one parent.[3] But this statistic grossly understates the proportion of American children who will at some time live in single-parent households. Children who are now living with remarried parents at some earlier time were in single-parent households. And many children who are now living with both parents will yet, before they become adults themselves, experience a parental separation or lose a parent to death. At our present rates of parental separation and parental death, almost one in two children who are now infants will, before they reach the age of eighteen, live in a single-parent household.[4]

The proportion of children who will for some part of their developmental years live within a single-parent home is a good deal larger than the proportion of adults who at some point in their lives will be single parents. Right now about 70 percent of Americans marry and have children. A significant separation (which may not actually proceed to divorce) can be expected to occur in about half these marriages before the children are grown. Putting these two proportions together, we would estimate that about a third of Americans will at some point be in the position of having still-immature children while they themselves are not living with the children's other parents. If we assume that one parent has custody of the children when there has been a separation, then half the parents who are living separately would be single parents in the sense of parents taking care of their children alone. This would mean that about a sixth of American adults can anticipate at some point being separated or divorced parents responsible for the care of their children.

Single parents are created by the death of the spouse and by unmarried parenthood as well as by separation and divorce. If we include together the chance of becoming a single parent through any of these events, then the likelihood of an individual's becoming solely responsible for his or her children at some point—becoming a single parent—is much greater than one in six. It may approach one in four.

But the chance of becoming a single parent is very different for a woman and for a man. Among all children who now live with either their mothers alone or their fathers alone, 93 percent live with their mothers. This comes about because of three phenomena: among children one of whose parents died, about two-thirds lost their fathers; among

Preface

those whose parents separated or divorced, about 90 percent live with their mothers; and of those children whose parents were not married, almost all live with their mothers.[5] Therefore, while the likelihood that an adult, sex unspecified, would become a single parent approaches one in four, the likelihood of a woman's becoming a single parent approaches one in two. The likelihood of a man's becoming a single parent might be less than one in twenty. When we discuss single parents who are living with their children we are largely discussing women.

The likelihood of becoming a single parent is at this writing much greater for Americans who are black than for those who are white. About 40 percent of black children are in single-parent households; only 12 percent of white children live with single parents.[6] Nevertheless, because there are so many more white Americans than black Americans, the great majority of children in single-parent households—84 percent—are white. Almost all the parents and children quoted in this book are white.

It is time for a definition. How do we know whether someone is a single parent? Let us take the term to mean someone who is raising his or her children alone, without the presence of the sort of substitute second parent that would be provided by a new spouse. A single parent, in short, is someone who has unshared responsibility for the care and direction of his or her children.

When the children become old enough to do without parental care and direction, their mother or father would no longer be acting as a single parent. However, we should not disqualify someone as a single parent if that person's household included, in addition to his or her children, an adult who might be a sister, brother, mother, father, girlfriend, or boyfriend. For the purposes of this book, an individual is a single parent so long as that individual retains sole responsibility for his or her children. Remarriage would bring about an end to single-parent status because it would provide a partnership in parenting, even though it would be a different kind of partnership from that of two natural parents.

The rationale for this definition is that unshared responsibility for children imposes special demands and constraints on people's lives. The structure of the one-parent household is different from that of a two-parent household. And the social and emotional situations of single parents are in many respects more nearly like those of other single people than like those of married parents.

To anticipate one argument of this report, many aspects of single parents' household situations can be understood as consequences of understaffing. As in an understaffed office, much of the time there is no problem. But now and again demands on those within the office exceed their capacities. Then everyone must pitch in as needed, no matter what the person's title and official position. Some tasks must be done hurriedly; others cannot be done at all. At the end of the day the people within the office are likely to be exhausted: they may feel that too much has been asked of them; they may be resentful that they have had to do so much. And yet, simultaneously, they may be pleased with themselves, think better of themselves, because they have, after all, kept the enterprise going. The great majority of single parents, I think, will recognize their own lives in this analogy. To be a single parent is to head a family that is often understaffed.

Being a single parent is not quite an either-you-are-or-you-aren't condition. Rather, it admits of more or less. The wife of a salesman whose business trips take him away from home for days and weeks may function in her household as a single parent when her husband is away, although her social world would very likely remain that of a married woman. In contrast, in the course of interviewing for this report, we encountered a woman raising children alone whose former husband lived only a few doors away and participated actively in her family life. In most cases it is clear whether someone is a single parent; in a few cases it can be hard to decide.

Is it good or bad to be a single parent?

It has been argued that the nuclear family consisting of two parents and their children in a home of their own suffers from having cut itself off from the supportive network of grandparents and aunts and uncles. As this argument goes, parents cannot call upon their relatives for help and so are burdened by their children and at times exhausted by them. Conflict between a parent and a child is maintained within the parent-child relationship rather than being diffused within a larger network, and so parents and children more often get on each other's nerves. Because the children cannot call on parent figures who are not actually their parents for the understanding their parents are too emotionally involved to display, the children too often feel themselves entirely bereft of adult support and sympathy. Finally, in addition to everything else, the children can draw only on the resources their parents possess. They cannot learn carpentry from a skilled uncle or storytelling from a wise grandmother if they see uncle and grandmother only at the Christmas family reunion.

In this view, the nuclear family is contrasted, to its disadvantage, with a more extended family of three generations under one roof, or with a family in which the mother's unmarried sisters help with child raising, keep the mother company, and give the children someone to talk to when the parents are busy. Family historians now question whether such families ever were common. But the underlying idea remains: two parents, all by themselves, are too few to raise a child.

If two parents are too few, what about one? The ills associated with the two-parent nuclear family should be all the more evident with only one parent in the house. There should now be even more for that parent to do. The children should have even fewer resources of adult sympathy and understanding. There should be even fewer opportunities for the children to learn skills and outlooks from a variety of adults.

Is the single-parent family necessarily defective? Certainly it is not new. A significant proportion of our children always have spent some part of their developmental years in single-parent households. Until recently, most of these households came about through the death of a parent, generally the father, rather than as the result of parental divorce, but they were single-parent households, nevertheless. If the worldly success of the children can be taken as evidence, these single-parent households were not inferior to two-parent households. Among the children of these single-parent households have been some of the most distinguished men and women of our time. Indeed, there is evidence that the children of these single-parent households have contributed more than their share to the roster of outstanding scientists and artists.[7]

But what of the parent? Is parenting alone a desirable way of life?

Compared with parenting as a member of a well-functioning parental couple, parenting alone appears to have more problems and fewer gratifications. Such compensations as it may have—for example, the ability to make household decisions without having to consult another parent—are of value only when the other parent is more nearly an antagonist than an ally. All survey studies that have examined indicators of happiness report that single parents are more likely than married parents to describe themselves as unhappy. However, far from all single parents are unhappy. And, in any event, it is worth remembering the principle attributed to Maurice Chevalier. Asked on his eightieth birthday how it felt to have become old, he is reported to have said, "When you consider the alternative. . . ." The way we evaluate single parenting depends on the alternative we have in mind.

When the alternative to being a single parent is to be a member of a thoroughly malfunctioning parental couple, much may be said for single parenting. It is certainly better for the parents. I would not agree with those who claim it is always better for children to be members of a happy one-parent home than of an unhappy two-parent home. It is possible for individuals to be unhappily married and yet to function well as parents. But if conflicts between the parents absorb so much of their energy that they have little left to give to the children, if the efforts of one parent to support and direct the children are systematically frustrated by the contradictory efforts of the other, if angry quarrels keep the home in constant turmoil—if the parents' marriage is so bad that the parents are totally preoccupied by their troubles with each other, or so depressed that they cannot attend to their children—then the children as well as the parents are likely to benefit from parental separation.

When people who are now single parents, no matter how they reached that status, consider that one alternative would have been a childless single life, they often are grateful that their lives are what they are. There are problems in single parenting, often severe problems. But parenthood under any conditions can bring problems. If the alternative were not to have their children at all, it would be a distinct minority of single parents who would choose it.

Sources and acknowledgments

This is a book based on interviews. The interviews were collected in a series of studies conducted at the Laboratory of Community Psychiatry, Harvard Medical School. The studies included the following:

1. A longitudinal study of social ties among nineteen single mothers and six married couples living in stable low-income areas. All respondents in this study were interviewed at intervals of two weeks to a month for a period of six months. The interviews focused on respondents' relationships with others, the problems that arose from these relationships, and the contributions the relationships made to the respondents' functioning.

2. A study of recovery from bereavement among fifty-two recent widows and nineteen recent widowers, all living in the Boston metropolitan area, all under the age of forty-five. These men and women were interviewed about the course of their recovery from their bereavement. Three interviews were held with each participant in this study during the first year after the loss and a fourth interview was held with most of them two to four years after the loss.

3. Discussions held with approximately one hundred fifty separated individuals in groups of from five to twelve. These discussions took place as part of a program of education for marital separation.

4. Interviews held with fifty single parents and four married couples who had children. Some of them were seen several times.

5. About two dozen meetings held with members of the Framingham chapter of Parents Without Partners to discuss conclusions presented in this report.

6. Interviews with about forty children living in single-parent homes

Preface

as part of work for a study of the impact on adolescents of parental separation, and perhaps a dozen meetings with members of a group of high school students, all of whom lived in single-parent settings.

Other sources of information that have contributed to this book include informal interchanges with single parents that took place in connection with a course at the University of Massachusetts on the single parent, work with the Divorced Catholics group of the Paulist Center of Boston, and work as a counselor to individuals attempting to cope with the problems of marital separation and single parenthood.[8]

Each source of data for this book has been, in its own way, non-representative of single parents as a whole. The group of mothers with whom repeated interviews were conducted were residents of low-income neighborhoods. The widows and widowers were that minority of a much larger number whom we contacted who were willing to talk with us despite their grief. The newly separated individuals we worked with were largely, although not solely, middle-income. The sample of fifty single parents interviewed specifically for this book was developed by a kind of snowball approach, beginning with a few individuals known to us and then proceeding to their friends and friends of their friends. The others with whom we have talked, adults and children alike, have been similarly nonrepresentative.

To some extent the samples compensate for one another, since each sample is nonrepresentative in a different way. Yet it would be unjustifiable to suppose that our materials provide a base for statistical generalization. We may hold that issues that are intrinsic to the single-parent situation will of necessity appear within our materials. But the primary use of our materials is not as a basis for asserting that such-and-such a percentage of single parents do this or that. The primary use is as a basis for understanding the single-parent situation: for identifying what is special in the structure of single-parent life and in the single parent's functioning. We and the single parents who have worked with us have become collaborators in the task of developing a theory that is grounded in real experience of the nature of the single-parent situation: what it is and why it is that way.

When this report notes that "some single parents" do this or "most single parents" do that, it is only partly to communicate to the reader a rough idea of the proportions we have observed. More, it is to introduce the reader to a phenomenon of importance that we will then try to explain by going deeper—with the help of those with whom we have talked—into what it is to be a single parent. The difference between "some" and "most" is that I ascribe an experience or behavior to "some single parents" to suggest that it is one alternative among many in a relatively unconstrained situation and ascribe an experience or behavior to "most single parents" to suggest that it is fostered by the single-parent situation. Thus I might note that most single parents experience a reduction in income after the ending of their marriages, and that some use day-care centers as providers of substitute child-care.

A number of the interviews on which this book is based were conducted by me, but the great majority were conducted by others. I would like to thank Roz Gertner, Dr. Elizabeth Hartwell, Beatrice Hurwitz, Mary McCrae, Claire Mitchell, Dr. Charles Nathansen, Gail Plotkin, Dr. Nancy Shaw, Emily Sullivan, Richard Vittitow, Natalie Webb, and Joan Weiss. I am especially indebted to Claire Mitchell, without whose many contributions this book could not have been written.

Dr. Carole Joffe and Claire Mitchell helped organize and interpret the data. Other friends and colleagues who discussed specific points with me or reviewed sections of the manuscript include: Dr. Susan Anderson-Khlief, Dr. Mary Jo Bane, Phyllis Belford, Dr. Dorothy Burlage, Dr. Arlene Daniels, Elizabeth Hormann, Dr. Jacqueline Jackson, Dr. Teresa Levitin, Michelene Malson, Mary McCrea, Arthur Norton, Gina Prenowitz, Dr. Lee Rainwater, Dr. Martin Rein, Dr. Kristine Rosenthal, and Diane Vanden Beukel. Midge Decter of Basic Books read an early draft of the manuscript and encouraged the preparation of the present book.

The studies underlying this book were supported by: a grant from the Social and Rehabilitation Service, Department of Health, Education and Welfare, A 294; National Institute of Mental Health Grants MH 31716, and MH 12042; a small grant from Harvard's Milton Fund; and, most important, a contract, No. 100-76-0135, with the Department of Health, Education and Welfare. Part Two of the book and a portion of Part Four are based on work supported by this contract. Some of the statistics in the book are derived from data collected by others but analyzed by Dr. Mary Jo Bane and me. Our work has been supported by National Institute of Mental Health Grant MH 27261. Joyce Brinton has administered all these projects. She has been superb: responsible, conscientious, and, above all, helpful.

Mary Coffey typed and retyped materials for the book, as she has for books that preceded it. In this effort she was joined by Carolyn Arend. Each, to my good fortune, has also functioned as colleague and editor.

My wife, Joan Hill Weiss, participated in most of the studies that underlie this book. She and I together led single-parent groups for the Paulist Center of Boston, where many of the ideas of the book were first formulated. She has conducted interviews, transcribed tapes, and reviewed drafts of the manuscript. She has also sustained my spirit.

I am grateful to everyone I have named. I am grateful, too, to the single parents who agreed to be interviewed despite their already crowded lives and then, often, agreed to be interviewed again and yet again. I hope this book speaks for them as well as to them.

PART ONE

Single Parents:
Who They Are
and How They Begin

CHAPTER 1

Becoming
a Single Parent

OUR LIFE SITUATIONS are products of choice and chance. Always there is choice, although sometimes it is unsteady and ambivalent, or an acceptance of what appears to be the least unsatisfactory alternative rather than a grasping of an attractive prospect. Always, too, there is chance: both good luck and bad, both unforeseen opportunity and unanticipated reverse.

Entrance into some situations—into marriage or a good job—tends to be a happy choice from among desirable alternatives. Other situations, however, are most often a matter of making the best of things, of accepting what cannot be avoided. The situation of the single parent is almost always an instance of the latter.

There are three primary routes to the single-parent situation: marital separation, widowhood, and parenthood without marriage. There are less-often-taken routes as well: adoption of a child by an unmarried individual and informal adoption of a child by the child's grandparent or older sibling or other relative. In the latter instance the children's care-takers may not identify themselves as single parents. Also not identifying themselves as single parents but nevertheless functioning as such are married men and women whose partners are away indefinitely in the armed forces, working in another community, or hospitalized with a chronic illness.

The route that, at present, is by far the one most frequently taken to the single-parent situation is that of separation and divorce. Almost

70 percent of single-parent households are created by the voluntary separation of parents. The death of a spouse ranks next: 14 percent of single parents are widows and widowers. Another 10 percent of single parents had never been married to their children's other parent. About 6 percent of single parents define themselves as only temporarily alone; many of these are women whose husbands are in the armed forces. Other routes were taken by less than 1 percent of single-parents.[1]

The route taken to the single-parent situation makes for great differences in the situation's emotional coloring. Let us first consider a separated parent, then a parent who is widowed, and finally two unmarried parents.

Mrs. Alpert had for years felt her marriage to be unsatisfactory. After the birth of a retarded child, the marriage became worse.

> We were a typical couple who got married right out of college. Richard became the head of the household, took care of the money, and made all the decisions. I took care of the children and the house. When Richard came home at night there was a definite schedule. He would read the mail and take his shower. And it had to be quiet in the house, and the children had to be well behaved, and I wasn't to look like I had been taking care of children or cleaning all day. Then we had Shirley, who is retarded. With Shirley's demands, because of her problems, and Richard's demands, it was too much.

Nevertheless, despite her deep dissatisfaction with the marriage, Mrs. Alpert could not end it. Like many others in troubled marriages, she felt that the children needed her husband as well as her. In addition, the thought of being on her own frightened her. She worried about managing financially without her husband's help and about taking care of a big house alone. Other separated and divorced single parents describe still other reasons for clinging to insupportable marriages: fear that loneliness and social isolation would follow separation, unwillingness to admit to failure, and hope that somehow things would improve.

For all those who take the initiative in ending their marriages, justifications for inaction at some point no longer suffice. A particular event may precipitate the break; new figures may enter their lives, or their spouses'; with the help of counseling they may become aware of their deep dissatisfaction. They may ultimately decide that their children would suffer less from the separation they have been contemplating than from continuing to live in an unhappy, tension-filled home.

But the marital bond can be extraordinarily tenacious. Mrs. Alpert complained, became ill, became depressed, blamed her marriage for it all, and still remained married.

> I got an ulcer and was in the hospital for a while. And that same winter I was in for pneumonia. And after that I developed bronchial asthma.

4

> That's really psychosomatic, asthma. Finally, a couple of months before we separated, I was in bed for weeks because it was just too much. I was seeing a therapist and he said, "It's going to continue like this unless you do something."

In this instance it was the husband who made the break. Mr. Alpert took to staying away evenings. At first he said it was work. Then he rented an apartment and just stopped coming home.

As is common among separated parents, Mrs. Alpert and her husband continued to see each other despite their separation. And, as is also common, their relationship deteriorated still further. They argued about the division of their property, about the level of support Mr. Alpert would provide, about Mr. Alpert's rights of visitation, and about which of them should have custody of the children. Each retained a lawyer for defense against the other. Two months after they finally obtained their divorce, Mrs. Alpert said:

> It has been a very nasty, nasty divorce. And it has been a very expensive divorce. I was divorcing Richard on the grounds of desertion, and he was divorcing me on the same grounds. He wanted the house. And he had a custody suit going. Until a couple of weeks ago we weren't sure how that was going to come out.

There can be many variations on these themes of separation. The break is usually long foreshadowed, as it was here, but occasionally a separation occurs in which one of the partners is entirely unprepared for the other's departure. In such unforeseen separations, the abandoned partner must first deal with a fundamental disruption of life for which there was no preparation—which often can hardly be believed—and then, later, after the shock has abated, must wonder not only at the spouse's capacity for deceit, but also at his or her own blindness. Sometimes separated couples are locked in continuing combat; sometimes they contrive to minimize their conflicts at least insofar as the children are concerned. Occasionally the noncustodial parent will disappear instead of remaining on the scene. But despite these variations, separation and divorce almost always are attended by feelings of having been misused and by the wariness and self-doubt that are the residues of an unhappy marriage. The separated and divorced parent generally carries an image of the children's other parent as someone who is disparaging, critical, and untrustworthy.

Quite different are the feelings brought to the single-parent situation by those whose husbands or wives have died.

After the death from leukemia of her husband, an architect, Mrs. Lorimer was left to raise their two boys, aged eight and six and a half. Mrs. Lorimer was then thirty. She remembered her marriage as having become a happy one, after a rocky start.

> We were at first very stormy, but the last three years were very happy for us. I think of all the times that we went blueberry picking and went on picnics and on drives and things like that.
>
> Greg loved to garden and work outdoors, to fix up the house, paper, and paint. And he loved taking the children places, like the science museum or the beach. As far as taking care of them in the house, that was an entirely different story, until I said, when the boys were small, that I just had to be able to get out of the house some time, to go shopping, just to go out. He was very good after that. He'd make supper on a Saturday night occasionally.
>
> Once, when we first got married, I got mad and I wouldn't talk. Greg yelled at me, "What do you expect to solve by not talking? I don't know why you're mad at me, so how can I apologize?" Which was exactly right. And I never did that again. When something was bothering me, I told him.

Mrs. Lorimer organized her account of her marriage with the positive elements in the foreground. The tensions and disputes were of secondary importance—minor incidents, problems that had to be dealt with on the way to achieving a happy marriage. Because she was bereft, her feelings required that she give attention to what she had lost. Without misrepresenting any particular event or suppressing her memory of any event, the way she organized the events had the effect of idealizing the relationship.

There is another reason for idealization: remembering the relationship as happy made it a little easier to accept its loss.

> We were fortunate in having a happy marriage. I think if I didn't have that, I would feel very cheated. But where we had that, I think it's easier to take.

For months after bereavement widows and widowers are constantly burdened by their awareness of loss. Briefly they may forget, imagine their partners are still with them, perhaps think about sharing with them a story or an observation, but then almost immediately they return to full awareness. Three months after her husband's death Mrs. Lorimer said:

> Yesterday I was reading the paper and a picture of one of the fellows in Greg's firm was in there and I thought, "Gee, Greg would like to see this." And another time, I heard about a friend who was having trouble with her husband and I thought, "I'll have to remember to tell Greg about this." And I went shopping to the store that we always went to, and it was the first time I was alone, and I just got in the store and I just all choked up. I ran right around and bought what I had to and got out in the car, and I cried and I cried and I cried.

The widowed, more easily than the separated and divorced, can turn to their children for solace. Separated or divorced parents can find it difficult to talk with their children about the events leading to the breakup of their homes. Their conflict with their former partners often feels to them like a private matter they really should not share with their children. In the homes of the widowed there is greater likelihood that grief will be shared. Mrs. Lorimer described the following incident as happening about a month after her husband's death:

> Saturday morning, a couple of weeks ago, the boys were fighting about some crazy thing—somebody had said something—and one of them said to me, "What are you going to do about it, Ma?" And I said, "You know what I'm going to do? I'm going to sit here and cry." And I sat on a chair in the corner of the room and I cried. And I told them, "Join me." So we all had a good cry. And it cleared the air.

When a spouse dies others rally to the side of the new widow or widower to express sympathy, to help, to offer as solace their own grief. This support from their community, even though some widows complain that it proves short-lived, is sustaining for a time. Certainly it is dramatically different from the feeling, reported by many among the separated, that their neighbors and some of their friends are embarrassed by their troubles.

In marital separation anger and guilt are intense. In bereavement, though they occur, they are much less deeply felt. Surviving partners may blame themselves for not having fended off the fatal event, their dead spouses for not having cared better for themselves, physicians, or fate or God. But a widow's or widower's feelings of guilt or anger are soon muted, and what remains, usually, are memories of a marriage in which there was mutual affection and support. The widow or widower can draw strength from knowing that the partnership remained firm to the end. A woman recently widowed offered the following contrast between the way she felt and the way those of her friends who were divorced seemed to feel:

> The bitterness isn't there that my friends who went through divorces have. I have a lot to hold onto. I don't mean I can live on that love forever. But the first year after my husband died I could still live on his love. And the hurt is not there that my friends who went through divorces have. I think it would be really terrible, it would be really awful, to look back and to think that you loved someone very dearly and that you were really hurt by them.

Widows and widowers differ from each other in the manner in which they display continued commitment to their marriages—widows appear more reluctant, during the first year of bereavement, to contemplate new attachments—but both define themselves for some time as still representing a partnership, although one from which the other partner is permanently absent. One widow, alone for several years, said that at first she regularly consulted what she thought would have been her husband's wishes:

> In making decisions for the kids and what-not, I used to think, "Now what would Lennie do?" I still considered myself Lennie's wife.

While separated and widowed parents become single parents through loss, unmarried mothers become single parents through accession. The new situation of the unmarried mother is produced not by painful marital dissolution but by the birth of a child. And while for all but a few the *pregnancy* was unwanted, for most the *child* is not.

This is not to minimize the troubles associated with becoming a mother outside marriage. Decisions must be made under the pressure of time: the time to the end of the first trimester, after which abortion becomes difficult; the time to the completion of the pregnancy, when the issue of adoption must be dealt with. The dilemma may be painful—to give up the baby or to accept a thoroughly constraining responsibility. But almost always there is opportunity for choice.

This opportunity for choice tends to be dealt with differently by older women already on their own from the way it is dealt with by younger women still living with their parents. Older women are likely to be both more realistic and more self-reliant. A woman in her late twenties, for example, described a process of decision that moved fairly quickly from confusion to certainty:

> I just couldn't figure out what to do when I had all the options open to me as far as abortion. I just couldn't make up my mind. The baby's father never, never said anything to me one way or the other about anything. I finally decided after about a month and a half that I was going to have the baby and I didn't care what anyone thought, what anyone felt, or anything else. I would have it and that was that. And I'm very glad I made the decision.

A much younger woman's account of becoming a mother without marriage, while displaying awareness of alternatives, suggests a kind of naïveté regarding their implications. Her account suggests that her attention was very much directed to immediate events and very little to the future.

> I dated Marty for about three years and we were always doing things together and we got along good. And this weekend we went away with another couple, his best friend and his best friend's girlfriend. And I had just had an infection so I wasn't using anything and I was susceptible to getting pregnant and I couldn't do anything about it. So I found out that I was. And my alternatives were to keep it, give it to my parents, or have an abortion. Marty asked me to get married because we were going to do it anyway. But I said, "No," because I wanted to wait. I was into being pregnant. It didn't bother me. I loved it. I had a job working after school, but I had to leave school because I had to work full time. That was the only bad thing.
>
> Well, I decided I wanted to keep it. Marty said he would pay for the hospital and he stuck by me and everything. But, more or less, Marty and I just drifted apart.

Becoming a Single Parent

Most important for this young woman was her parents' willingness to have her bring her baby into their home. Her mother looked after the baby during the day while the woman worked, and although the young mother complained that her younger brothers sometimes teased the baby, the arrangement seemed to be a good one. For the young unmarried mother still in her parents' home and still dependent on their support, her relationship with her parents may be more important in deciding how she deals with her pregnancy than her relationship with her boyfriend.

There is a special vulnerability in the situation of the single parent who was unmarried at the time of her child's birth. No other single parent can so easily identify the child as the cause of whatever troubles are later encountered. The widowed parent can blame fate or medicine or God; the separated or divorced parent can blame the other parent; the very few adoptive single parents can blame their own need to nurture. The mother whose child came unbidden can too easily blame the child. More than other single parents, she may remain unreconciled to the child's existence. Nicholas Zill, on the basis of a national sample study, reports that 30 percent of never-married mothers—compared with 20 percent of separated mothers, 15 percent of divorced mothers and 10 percent of widowed mothers—say that if they had to do it over again, they would not have children. Zill also reports that never-married mothers are more likely to admit that at some point in their dealings with their children, they lost control and may have hurt their children: 27 percent of never-married mothers admit to this, compared with about 15 percent of separated or divorced mothers and only 5 percent of widowed mothers.[2]

There are still other differences among the separated and divorced, the widowed, and those unmarried at the time of their children's births. Chief among these is the role of the other parent in their lives.

There are many ways in which a separated parent's relationship with the other parent may develop, yet almost always that relationship has aspects of discomfort. The other parent almost always continues to have rights and responsibilities to the children that the separated parent must acknowledge. The other parent can be regularly intrusive, telephoning or appearing at unexpected times. Furthermore, the children of separated and divorced parents are likely to be loyal to both their antagonistic parents and to search for some method by which they can preserve their identifications with both parents despite the parents' criticisms of each other. Insofar as the children attempt to defend their relationships with the absent parent, they may enter into conflict with the parent with whom they live.

Single mothers who are not married to the fathers of their children rarely allow the fathers equal standing as parents. The unmarried father may keep in touch with the children and mother and may even visit regularly, but he lacks the legitimized relationship with the children possessed by the separated or divorced father. Some unmarried fathers are nevertheless extremely important to their children and play nearly the same role in their children's lives as might be played by a separated or divorced father. Other unmarried fathers are more nearly shadowy figures in their children's homes, their appearances rare, their names seldom spoken. Should the mother live with a man other than the children's father, the children may feel closer to the man with whom they live. Adolescent children of unmarried parents have been known to assert that they cannot bring themselves to address their fathers as "father," even when they see them fairly often.[3] The absence of parental marriage may strain the child's linkage to the father's family. One adolescent girl with whom we spoke said that her father's mother, her grandmother, never was entirely comfortable with her. "She keeps acting like she doesn't know my name," she said. "She knows my name all right."

For widows and widowers the other parent is a memory, often cherished, whose wishes are still considered and whose internalized support is relied on. Children of widows and widowers have been made bereft just as the parents themselves have been, and the shared sorrow—and shared idealization of the absent parent—provide an important basis for a sense of community within the bereaved family. Separated and divorced parents often become targets for their children's anger over the disruption of their homes. Unmarried mothers may have to deal with questions about the fathers' absence from their children's lives, and about how it happened that their children are different from other children in so significant a respect. Widows and widowers are spared these experiences.

The separated and the never-married must sometimes deal with others' unthinking disparagement. Bereavement is clearly tragedy. Separation and divorce have their tragic elements, but they suggest something in addition: failure, or at least bad judgment. Unmarried motherhood seems to elicit searches for explanation in the mother's personality. The mother who never married tends to be seen as unfortunate or thoughtless or easily misled, perhaps a disorganized member of a disorganized family or a rebellious member of an organized one.

The views held by others are likely to be encountered by single parents whenever they must present themselves to strangers. One such occasion is application for credit. A divorced woman in her thirties told the following story:

> I went into a store one time and I was looking at some beds for my son. I spoke to a salesman and he asked me, "Is this going to be cash or charge?" I said, "Well, I don't know yet," because I was thinking of starting some credit on my own. And he said, "Well, what does your husband do?" And I said, "I'm divorced." And he said, very cold, very distant, "Oh, well, I'm terribly sorry. Are you working?" I went back

the next day and I got another salesman. And the same thing, "What does your husband do?" And I said, "I lost my husband six months ago." "Well," he says, "I'm sure we can work something out." Boy, I got all the sympathy in the world.

The financial situation of widows is in general somewhat better than that of other single mothers, since widows' husbands are likely to have carried insurance and most widows are also eligible for Social Security. Social Security payments to a widow and her children far exceed the typical level of child support. In addition, many separated and divorced mothers do not receive support payments at all. Although there seem to be no good estimates of the proportion of separated and divorced *mothers* receiving child support, one recent estimate has it that fewer than half of all separated and divorced *women* receive either child support or alimony payments from their former husbands.[4] It seems to be the case that the lower the income of the formerly married pair, the less likely is postmarital support. The financial situation of the unmarried mother is even worse; almost no unmarried mothers receive support from the fathers of their children. Unmarried mothers are dependent for income almost entirely on their own resources together with the help they receive from their families and from the government.

Other differences among single parents

The primary difference among single parents is the route they have taken to the single-parent situation. But there are other differences among single parents as well. Let us consider some:

Single fathers versus single mothers

Single fathers often feel themselves not entirely prepared for the role of custodial parent. In keeping with this, they are more likely than single mothers to bring into their homes housekeepers or sisters or mothers or mothers-in-law to help them with housekeeping and child care. On the other hand, single fathers appear much less likely than single mothers to feel guilty about working as well as acting as a parent. Only rarely do single fathers consider the alternative of remaining at home with their children.

Single fathers and mothers who had subscribed to traditional divisions of emotional responsibility when married may have to make complementary modifications in their parental style. Single fathers who were distant and directing during their marriages, following the model of traditional heads of families, may have to become softer and more nurturant. Single mothers who made few important decisions in their marriages will almost certainly have to become more self-reliant. Those single mothers who left discipline to their husbands will have to learn how to be firm with their children.

Length of time as a single parent

Other studies have shown that during the first year after a marital separation or the death of a spouse a single parent tends to be preoccupied with problems of loss and reorganization.[5] The persisting problems of single parenting become dominant concerns for most single parents only after they have been in their new situation about a year. But thereafter, as long as they remain single parents, their concerns are apt to be like those of other single parents.

Family income level

Lack of money is a nagging, painful worry for many single mothers and some single fathers. In the northeastern United States, because of a comparatively generous welfare schedule, inadequate income gives rise to a special sort of deprivation, not one in which there is an absence of food, clothing, or shelter, but rather one in which the kind of food, clothing, or shelter that can be afforded is much less desirable than that available to others. There may, in addition, be inability to provide a child with the small sums necessary for a school picture or a snack during recess, without which the child must feel marginal to the life of the classroom. It will be difficult to run an automobile, and it may be difficult even to repair a refrigerator in which food regularly spoils. To someone who is poor in an underdeveloped country, for whom hunger may be a frequent experience and whose children may suffer from chronic malnutrition, these are hardly serious deprivations. Yet the underfinanced single parent in our society may be wracked with worry over unmet bills . and humiliated by a periodic need to borrow money. Because it' costs money to go places and to entertain friends, inadequate income also produces a restricted social life.

Single parents with fully adequate financial resources can live where they choose, send their children to private schools, and purchase tutoring or therapy if their children are in trouble. And yet it appears that single parents on every income level report constant worry about money. As we will show in the next chapter, the assumption of sole responsibility for children brings with it worry about income, irrespective of the parent's objective level of income.

Becoming a Single Parent

Race

There are grounds for speculation that single parenting may mean something different for blacks than for whites. We have already noted that a greater proportion of black families are single-parent families than of white families. It is far more common for young black women to become single parents by way of motherhood without marriage than for young white women, although white women seem to be in the process of catching up. What is responsible for current disproportions we cannot say. The differences may be due to somewhat different courtship practices among young black people, to greater acceptance of the single-parent role, or to a lesser attractiveness of marriage, although many black single mothers later marry the fathers of their children.[6] In any event, the few black single parents we interviewed did not describe life situations significantly different from those described by white single parents at the same income levels.

CHAPTER 2

A New Life

THE SINGLE-PARENT SITUATION begins in disruption. Separation, bereavement, the birth of a child to an unmarried woman all disrupt relationships with intimates, kin, and friends. In separation and bereavement there is loss; in unmarried parenthood there are apt to be changes in relationships with critically important figures. For all, kin are likely to become more important and friendships are likely to become more difficult to maintain—because of time constraints, if for no other reason. For the previously married, the premise on which their lives had been based, namely participation in a marital partnership in which there was shared responsibility for children, is now invalidated. Their concerns become different. Indeed, their very self-definitions change; they become different people.

Imagine a woman, a mother of two children, who has just agreed with her husband to call an end to living together. The husband has taken a studio apartment only a few blocks away. Now, nodding to a neighbor, the woman wonders if the neighbor is aware that her husband is no longer at home. Her mother, on the phone, is annoyingly solicitous. The children, when they arrive from school, are as noisy as ever (that, at least, does not change). But supper without the husband, while less tense, is strangely incomplete. And when the husband later calls to talk with the children, or to ask the woman how she is doing, the woman is confused and upset.

A New Life

The problem of finances

The woman and her husband had earlier bought a modest house in a suburban community. It cost a little more than they could afford, but the neighborhood was good and there were other children for theirs to play with. And, besides, it wasn't as though housing costs were so much lower anywhere else they would want to live. Now the woman must meet the same monthly costs from much less money.

Her husband sends a check every month. Let us say that he is generous or responsible or guilt-ridden and sends 50 percent of his net pay. And let us say that his net income is about $1500 a month, so that he contributes $750. How far does the $750 go? Mortgage payments and taxes and heat and light amount to $650 a month. There is $100 left for food and clothing and transportation and fixing the television set. It can't be done. (And the woman will almost certainly be worried about how long even this contribution can be counted on: what if her husband remarries?)

What can the woman do? Move to a cheaper place? That might well require moving from the children's school district and would inflict on the children the loss of still another island of stability. What are the alternatives to moving? Obviously, finding a job. But will anyone hire a woman who has for nine years done nothing other than care for children and manage a home? And who will then care for the children?

This is the predicament of the separated mother living in middle-income circumstances who, when married, had relied on her husband to provide the family income but who, with separation, has become responsible for meeting the family's bills. She may have absolutely no idea of how to manage. One woman remembered how she had felt:

> We had a fairly high standard of living and I wanted to maintain it. But I didn't know what I would do. One option was, I would starve to death.

Marital separation almost invariably leads to a sharp reduction in family income. Suppose both the woman and her husband had been working and had earned the same income. And suppose the husband, after leaving, contributes half his income as child support. Then the drop in household income is 25 percent. If the wife's income has been less than her husband's, the drop in household income would be greater than 25 percent. If the wife has not been working at all and the husband contributes half his income, the drop in household income would be 50 percent. If the husband should contribute less than half his income, as usually is the case, the drop in household income would be even greater.

While the husband's departure assuredly reduces income, it does not reduce expenses by very much. To be sure, there is one less person to be fed, and there no longer are charges for the husband's clothing and laundry and transportation. But there are likely to be new expenses: the cost of kitchen equipment or a television set or a radio to replace whatever the husband took with him; almost certainly new expenses for baby-sitting; perhaps the cost of a wardrobe suitable for a job search; and perhaps carrying costs for a second car, if the husband took with him the one the family owned. The following observation was offered by a woman whose husband had been a successful salesman:

> My husband got a good salary and when he went on trips he made bonus money. I'm living on less than half of what I used to get. I have the same responsibilities with less than half the money.

A recent survey showed it to be generally the case that the ending of marriage imposes on mothers a decided drop in the ratio of their income to their needs.[1] It hardly matters what the income of a couple was before separation: if they were like other American couples, they had established a standard of living that used most of it. The departure of the husband from the home and the consequent reduction in household income means that the parent left to care for the children is severely pressed for money. Indeed, the dollar amount of the discrepancy between income and commitments will be greater for women whose income level when married was higher.

Two groups of separated and divorced women may be exceptions to the rule that marital separation brings with it a sharply reduced household income for mothers left to care for the children. The first group would be those mothers who had not worked before their separations but afterwards found jobs whose pay, when added to the support payments they received from their husbands, equaled the husbands' previous contributions to their households. The other exceptional group is made up of women whose husbands had contributed little to their household incomes even when they lived together: those whose husbands had been unemployed or had spent what they earned on themselves. With these exceptions, separation requires that a mother with custody adapt to a lower standard of living.

Many women are, for a time, constantly worried about money. One woman, looking back at the first months after her marriage ended, said:

> I would worry so much that I would worry myself sick. I needed the security of having the money to buy what I need, food and stuff for the house and kids. And when, like at the beginning of school, the kids would normally go out to buy new school clothes, and I just couldn't afford it, it would really overwhelm me.

A New Life

An attempt after separation to maintain anything resembling the previous standard of living inevitably leads to unpaid bills. The newly separated mother then finds herself, perhaps for the first time in her adult life, cadging and dodging:

> You have more bills at the end of the month than you have money to pay them. You never catch up. You pay $5 to the department store, $10 to the hospital bill. You put off bills that can be put off, and you pay the bills that are going to come after you. Twice I've gotten notices from the telephone company. "If you don't pay this in the next ten days we are going to cut off your service." I said, "I lost the bill. I'll put the check in the mail."

The widowed whose husbands had for some years worked steadily at low-paid jobs often are spared this precipitous drop in their household incomes. For in place of the divorced woman's troublesome and often inadequate support payments, the widowed generally have Social Security. Social Security provides a monthly income for widows with children under eighteen, with supplementary benefits for each of the children. The schedule of payments is such that if a man had worked steadily at a low-paid job for some years, the family income of his widow would remain virtually undisturbed. Widows of men who had higher levels of earnings would not be able to maintain their standards of living on Social Security, but very likely they would have received insurance income. Some widows, of course, are left with neither Social Security nor insurance. Their financial situation is then identical to that of the separated woman whose husband provides no support.

The unmarried mother is likely to be in the worst financial position of all, since she rarely receives support from the father and is eligible for no form of insurance. Yet she may not at first feel herself to be so badly off, insofar as she has not established a standard of living she can no longer maintain.

Previously married mothers who had relied on their husbands to deal with household finances may have to learn new skills—skills that may, to be sure, turn out to be fairly elementary: how to review a bank statement, how to plan for future purchases. But the most unsettling aspect of the new financial arrangement almost certainly will be the assumption of sole responsibility. In financial matters, as well as elsewhere, partnership provides a certain measure of security.

> In marriage there is more security. What's lacking for me is the feeling of security. I mean, I work and I'm getting along all right and so forth, but if I were ill or something, if I went a couple of months without working, I'd have problems. I really don't feel that secure.

The financial responsibility of the single parent, whether mother or father, is unlimited. When parents are separated, there is a distinct difference between the responsibilities of the custodial and the noncustodial parents. The noncustodial parent is responsible for a certain amount each week or month and, very occasionally, for some part of the children's medical or dental or educational expenses in addition. The custodial parent is responsible for everything else, no matter what it might be, and for whatever the noncustodial parent fails to provide, as well.

Money from the other parent

The money the husband sends his former wife for her support and the support of their children is not only much less than he contributed when he was a member of the household, but it also is a contribution of a different kind. No longer does the husband share responsibility for the household's financial security. Now he functions only as an income source and, like any other income source, is responsible for a certain amount and no more.

A separated wife may at some point let her husband know that she considers his financial responsibility more open-ended—as is hers. So she might ask her husband to buy a coat or sweater for one of the children, or tell him that the children need medical or dental work that the separation agreement hadn't anticipated, or that the children should be sent to a summer camp or enrolled in a special course. The husband may in response insist that he is responsible for nothing more than the sum called for in the separation agreement. The mother has in mind her husband's unlimited moral obligation to provide for his children, while her husband is apt to have in mind his limited moral obligation to provide for her.

Some husbands, just because they want to feel like fathers and not income sources, are willing to give money or gifts directly to their children but not to help finance their former households. Separated and divorced mothers tell stories of the children's father buying bicycles or typewriters or portable radios for their children or treating the children to expensive dinners while refusing to help the mothers with a mortgage payment or a doctor's bill.

Separated husbands rarely contribute more to their former households than they are required to by the separation agreement. Their former wives are unlikely to share in any new good fortune; unless there is an escalation clause in their separation agreement, a husband's salary increase will not lead to an increase in the wife's support payments. But separated husbands frequently contribute less than they agreed to; their former wives may very well be required to share their reverses. The husband who has been laid off, who has encountered a business reverse, or who has an unexpected bill may decide that this month he cannot manage full support:

> When Ollie went in the hospital he told me that he had bills. He had charged a lot of things plus he bought another car. His old one quit on him, so he bought a new one. He's got bills to pay on that and excise tax and so forth and so on. And they are dunning him. So, with what he has to pay out, he doesn't have anything left for me and the kids. He said he would give it to me if he had the money, but he doesn't have the money.

Nor is it only those husbands who experience financial reverses who reduce their support payments. One man who had agreed at the time of separation to continue to pay for his family's housing, including utility bills, simply stopped doing so after a few months, although there was no change in his financial situation. To be sure, the man felt he had justification: the phone bill included the costs of his former wife's calls to her boyfriend. The electric bill went unpaid just for good measure.

Another woman first learned that her husband was not meeting her mortgage payments when the bank sent a notice of foreclosure. She had sent earlier letters from the bank to her husband unopened, assuming they were the regular mortgage statements. This one, however, had a different return address; she opened it and discovered that she was about to be dispossessed.

Dependence on the husband's support makes for constant anxiety. The separated wife is likely already to be financially pressed. Especially if the separation has been acrimonious, or the husband has his own financial worries, she may have little faith that her husband can be counted on. One woman said:

> If my husband misses one payment, I'll be down the tubes. The last one was late and I started to get nervous. If it hadn't shown up in the mail the day it did, I was going to call.

For most women whose husbands have been delinquent in providing support, taking the husband to court is an unsatisfactory solution. The procedure may appear difficult to manage without a lawyer, and a lawyer is costly. And how can a woman enforce a court order once she obtains it? Not many women are willing to threaten their children's fathers with jail. The result is that most women whose husbands refuse to honor their separation agreements simply give up, believing that chasing the men is difficult and unpleasant and ultimately without profit.

Women on welfare, however, are often required to cooperate with agency action against nonsupporting husbands, whatever their own wishes. They too comment on the ineffectiveness of the procedure:

> The divorce decree can say anything, and if the man doesn't want to pay, forget it. It gets to be a financial burden to get the money, and it gets involved too, and you wonder if it is worth it. I'm getting welfare, and my husband is supposed to pay the welfare, but he hasn't paid in years. The welfare did go after him one time. They sent a notice to the court where he is living. But the court didn't do anything about it for a year and a half. Then they got hold of him and told him he was in default of payment. And they haven't done anything since.

Some women do find it worthwhile to go to court. But then, for their husbands' support to be maintained, they may have to be willing to go back whenever necessary:

> My husband cut back what I was getting to where it was impossible to do what I had been doing. So I went into court and I was awarded $175 a week. Then my husband gave up his job with the firm he worked for and set up as a consultant and stopped giving me anything. And I had to go into court again.

If one problem with relying on a former husband for support is insecurity, a second problem is the continuation of some aspects of the unhappy marital relationship. The continued financial connection makes it possible, for example, for a woman who had been a nagging wife to become a nagging ex-wife:

> My husband has been fine lately. He knows that as long as he pays me every week, I'll not bug him. But I can be a miserable son-of-a-gun.

A husband who had been a bully in the marriage may use the threat of withholding support to continue as a bully after the end of the marriage. One separated mother said that to get money from her ex-husband she had to agree to spend the night with him. Another separated mother was required by her former husband to justify every one of her expenditures:

> The one thing my husband has got under his control is money, and so he has this cute little thing going on where I have to list down everything, what my car costs to drive, when the plumber came and the man to fix the washing machine. I have to list every dollar. When we were married he used to make me itemize everything down to the last toothpick. And he is still doing this.

Although it is most unusual for a separated or divorced husband to continue to dominate his former wife in this way, many women feel that as long as they are dependent on their husbands for money, they are not truly free. Far from being grateful for the contributions they receive from their husbands, they are angry at having to remain dependent:

> The only thing about money that upsets me is that I have to be dependent upon my ex-husband, that I have to wait for his check to come

in, and that it is *his* money. I wish I could make my own money and wasn't dependent on him. What I'd really like to be able to do is tell him to take his money and put it where he has the most room.

To work or not to work

Recent census data show that about 55 percent of women who were single parents were working and another 12 percent either were only temporarily laid off or were actively looking for work.[2] These women worked because they needed the money. If we except the very few adequately supported divorced mothers, only the widowed among single parents—and not all of them—can have anything approaching an adequate income without working. But a great many of these women also worked because they needed the work itself. As one of our respondents put it:

> I went to work because I needed the money. But partly I went to work for the sake of my sanity.

Results from a national sample survey suggest that single mothers, more than other working women, need the nonfinancial contributions work makes to their lives. The survey asked working women, both married and unmarried, whether they would continue to work if they had enough money from other sources to support themselves comfortably. Of single mothers who were working, 73 percent said that they would continue to work even if they didn't have to. Only 57 percent of working *married* mothers said that they would continue to work if they didn't have to.[3]

Why is work so important for single mothers quite aside from the very necessary income it produces? Primarily because it provides them with a social world alternative to that of home and family, often one that demands less of them emotionally and offers more support for self-esteem:

> The finances were the number-one consideration in my working, but the job really does help. You know, you are away from your house and your children and you're coping with a different situation altogether. Your job is therapy.

Some single mothers, especially those who had worked throughout their adult lives, feel that they just are not suited to staying home. As one said:

> If I were at home alone, not working, I would probably slash my wrists. I don't enjoy polishing and cleaning and baking and all that stuff. I'm not the housewife type.

Most single mothers find that the ending of their marriages makes household tasks—cooking and cleaning and caring for the children—peculiarly unrewarding because the tasks no longer contribute to an enterprise they share with another adult. Whereas the married mother who stays home can feel herself to be a participant in the marital enterprise, just as is her husband, the single mother who stays home is likely to feel herself a participant in no enterprise beyond her own. Worse, she may feel herself dominated by her children's needs and desires. In any event, with her household tasks emptied of meaning, the single mother who does not work is likely to find her days becoming formless and dull. Work, tiring as it may be, improves matters:

> I have been tired where I couldn't put one foot in front of the other. But I found tiredness was worse if it was boredom, and if I had been staying home, it would have been.

To point out that work is important for many single mothers quite apart from its role as the source of their income is not to minimize their financial dependence on their jobs. Nor is it to deny that single mothers frequently give time to work that they would far prefer giving to their children. Most working single mothers are troubled by their inability to be with their children as much as they feel they should be. Some report that there have been times when a child has been ill or simply at home alone and lonely, when they could not concentrate on their work. Then, instead of being sustained by their ability to hold down a job, they might see themselves as inadequate in all their roles. One single mother, a social worker, described feeling this way:

> I was in a really bad way at work the other day. One of the other social workers came in and I said, "I feel bad about working." And she said, "You feel like you're doing a lousy job both here and at home." And I said, "Yeah."

One woman who went to work immediately after she and her husband separated could not tolerate always feeling that she was neglecting her children. She decided to quit her job and remain home full time:

> I worried too much about home. If the children were sick one day—they might have a small fever or they might just not feel good—and I had pushed them to school, I would feel very guilty about that. I might have sent them to school even if I had been at home, but the fact that I was at work and pushed them to school, that would make me feel guilty. I would work all day feeling guilty, wondering whether my son is going to see a school nurse, if the school nurse is trying to contact me.

Another woman felt that her children had displayed, in unmistakeable ways, a need for more attention than she had been able to give them when she was working full time. Her children included two boys not yet in their teens and a girl aged five. When she made the following comment she had given up her job and was receiving welfare:

> When I was working a forty-hour week, it was bedlam after supper because everyone wanted my attention. The baby constantly demanded my attention until she went to bed. The older two boys were trying to get my attention. And by the time I could settle down to give them a little counseling on their homework, it was eight or nine o'clock and we were all tired and irritable. When I stopped working, within a month their school work went up almost 50 percent. It is hard, but I decided to get money a different way.

Mothers of preschool children are sometimes unwilling to be separated from their children for even part of a day. They may fear that if they were to send their children to a nursery school both the children and their relationship to the children would suffer. A divorced mother of two preschool children explained in this way her decision to stay home and live on welfare:

> To me these kids are my life. They are what I have to love and to take care of for the rest of my life. And I'm going to take no chances. I'm just not going to mess up that relationship by going to work.

Some jobs are easier for single parents to manage than are others. It can be important that the job not be far from home. A commuting time of half an hour on each end of an eight-hour day may be manageable; a commuting time of an hour would very likely mean too little time with the children.

It can be important, too, that the job provide easy access to a telephone. The telephone is a link to home. The single parent can check that the children have arrived from school on schedule, or warn them that the parent will be late. The children can reach the parent if they feel uneasy. There are drawbacks in accessibility, to be sure: one mother despaired of telephone calls that went, "Mommy, tell Joey to stop looking at me." But not being able to keep in touch by telephone can mean worry through much of the day.

Flexible hours are valuable because they permit the parent to remain with a child in the morning, until the child leaves for school or to return home before the child returns. Also of value is the freedom to take time off should a child be sick or should the parent think it important to confer with a teacher.

Part-time work, if it is paid well enough, may be an answer to the dilemma of how to be both a parent and worker. One widowed mother had gone from full-time work to work that occupied her mornings so that she could be home when her youngest child, an eleven-year-old boy, returned from school. While regretting the drop in her income, she felt that the change was important for her son:

Alvin likes having me around when he comes home. He felt a very big loss when his father died, and he likes having me around. He just feels secure, having me here. He likes to come home and tell me what he did, or sometimes he doesn't even talk to me, but at least he knows I'm here. And I don't think that's too much to ask.

It may not require a reduction of many hours below the traditional forty for working to be made manageable for single parents. One woman who taught school and so had a schedule that matched the schedule of her ten-year-old son experienced little stress in working. A widow whose uncle had given her a job in his restaurant partly to distract her from her grief liked being able to begin work at eight-thirty and end at two. She could see her children off to school, meet them when they returned, and get the house in order before beginning the evening meal.

But part-time work is not easy to find. In addition, it often carries a lower hourly rate than full-time work and so results in appreciably smaller pay checks. Fringe benefits, including critically important family medical insurance, may not be extended to part-time employees. Full-time employees may treat a part-timer as less than a full member of their group. Yet to a mother overtaxed by full-time work, part-time work, even if it seems impractical, can be appealing:

If I had a profession where I could get paid well, maybe I wouldn't have to work so many hours. Maybe I could work part time and be able to be the mother I should be, but I can't be, working full time.

The issue of what would constitute the right kind of job may seem academic to previously unemployed mothers whose marriages have ended and who feel themselves to be in urgent need of both income and occupation. For them the first issue may be how to obtain any work at all: how to convince any prospective employer to hire a woman who has for some time done little other than raise children and manage a home and who will continue to have the responsibilities of children and a home after she begins working.

Many women have little sense, at first, of what they can do. Some fumble through a succession of jobs, trying one sort of work after another, until they happen on something they feel happy with. Some obtain additional training—in vocational rehabilitation, in shorthand and typing, in law—perhaps prevailing on their former husbands to provide temporarily a higher level of support as an investment in their eventual self-sufficiency. And some never do find work that suits them:

I have done an awful lot of things. I've worked in offices and I've tended bar; I've driven emotionally disturbed children. I was a substitute teacher for a few months. I've done a lot of things. Everything I've done has been to survive. Any time I did go to work it was because I had to, financially. I haven't enjoyed any of them.

A New Life

In addition to deciding on a line of work to try, the mother just entering the labor force may have to fashion a method for convincing an interviewer that her responsibility for her children will not reduce her reliability as an employee:

> When I applied for jobs, the first thing they wanted to know was who's going to babysit and am I sure that I have a stable babysitter. I got to the point of telling them that if I didn't have a babysitter I depended on, I wouldn't even be looking for the job.

Some single parents invent a mother or sister who lives with them and cares for their children while they are away. Some try their luck with honesty, aware that not all interviewers will be understanding:

> I have been very honest and said that my children come first, and when one of them is sick, I will be with that one. A guy like my present boss can say, "Yeah, I appreciate that, because I want my wife to be with my child when he is sick." But what if you are sitting across from some guy who doesn't give a rat's ass about your problems at home?

Occasionally a single mother feels so uncertain of her acceptability to the job world that she agrees to a dubious arrangement with an employer or an employment agency. One woman agreed to repay an employment agency two months' salary if she quit the job within the first year; later she felt she had entered into indenture. In contrast, another woman, recognizing how little she knew about the work world, became an office temporary so that she might look around. When she was eventually offered permanent employment, she was confident that the job was one she wanted.

Child care

It appears that the great majority of separated and divorced parents whose children are still young, along with a somewhat smaller proportion of widowed parents, at some point enlist others to look after their children.[4] Single parents whose children are small and who are themselves working have no alternative. But single parents who do not work also need times away from the children.

Theoretically, a parent has many possible sources of substitute caregiving: a relative who might come in or might look after the children in the relative's home; a teenager or older woman who would come in;

25

a neighbor who might, for pay, look after the children in the neighbor's home; a college student who might exchange help with the children for housing; a day-care center or an after-school program. But despite these many alternatives, it is the fortunate single parent who can find an arrangement that works for both the parents and the children, that does not require its own long trip, that is not forbiddingly expensive, and that proves reliable over time.

Survey findings suggest that many single parents put up with their current child-care arrangement only for want of something better. One large-scale study asked single parents who had already said they used child care: "Assuming you could have any type of child care you wanted, would you prefer to use some other type?" About one in four said that they would. Least likely to say they would choose another type of arrangement if they could were those who had relatives who could come to their homes to care for their children and those who used formal child-care programs such as day-care centers.[5]

There are several advantages to having one of the children's relatives look after the children in the children's own home. Relatives are inexpensive; they have a stake in the childern; the children know them and are likely to feel comfortable with them; and the children remain in their own setting with a caregiver who has some right, based on kinship, to supervise their activities. Relatives can, in their own way, also be troublesome. They can burden the parent with feelings of indebtedness; they can be intrusive; they are more likely than someone not related to the children to compete for the role of number-one parent. And, like other babysitters, they can be unreliable. One woman said, when a brother who had agreed to stay with the children called at the last minute to beg off, "What you get for nothing isn't worth much more." But these arrangements, when they work, appear to be good ones.

Day-care centers provide reliable care immune from the sorts of vagaries that occur with individual caregivers, both relatives and nonrelatives. In addition, there are other children in the center for the children to play with, and there may be a variety of toys and equipment. But day-care centers may well be inconveniently located and are likely to be expensive. And there is a wide range in quality: in some centers the staff are sensitive and attentive; in other centers the staff are impatient with children's demands or have too many children to care for to be able to respond to the needs of any one child.

Every child-care arrangement has its own potential difficulties. The college student who lives in the home will eventually move away, and if the student has become important to the children, the departure will mean a new loss for them. The neighbor who provides care for other mothers' children will have her own schedules, her own priorities, and her own approaches to childraising, none of which may be exactly what the single parent would want. And relatives, while they generally do not ask for recompense in money, do require acknowledgement that it is a great favor they are doing for the single parent.

Most single parents hope that, in addition to protecting their children and caring for them, the substitute arrangements they make will in some way be enriching for the children—that because of them their children will gain socially, become more independent, or be more ready for school. The belief that they are especially well equipped to provide enriching experiences is one attraction of day-care centers. A babysitter who is not only reliable but also caring and inventive is a treasure:

> My babysitter picked the kids up at school and took them to her home. And she was an outstanding person. She loved kids. And she was just so inventive: they did this thing and they did that thing.

Because child care can be hard to find, issues of cost and convenience often force single parents to make do with arrangements that offer little more than surveillance:

> I have a sitter that comes in and she's twenty and she's good to the kids. She feeds them and stuff like that. But I don't think she really does anything for their emotional needs, and that really bothers me. There's not much that I can do about it, basically. I have to work and I have to have somebody watch the kids. I've talked to her and told her to sit down and color with them and take them for walks and all that stuff.

The comparative advantages of having a neighborhood person as a babysitter are often persuasive. The children need not be delivered and picked up. They remain in their home, where they feel comfortable and where their things are. An adolescent babysitter can act as an older friend to the children; a mature woman can be a kind of maternal figure. And entirely avoided are the tensions that can develop when the children's grandmother or aunt looks after them: a babysitter is unlikely to question a single parent's approach to childraising.

Yet working single parents who have used neighborhood babysitters, particularly those who have relied on adolescents, often have a repertoire of trouble stories. Some of the youngsters were inattentive to their children. Others were simply inept. It was then a further frustration that they had to pay for so little help. One woman, mother of boys aged ten and six, said:

> I was paying $15 a week for child care. That's $65 a month, a lot of money. An older woman would have charged more, so I had to hire high-school-aged kids. I had one sitter that was like another child along with them. Then I had a boy who was good with my kids but still and all, half the time he didn't know where they were. I'd call up and say, "How are things going?" and he'd say, "Oh, fine. I haven't seen the kids." He was inside, watching television.

One time he called me at work and said, "Mrs. Chalmers," and I said, "Yes," and he said, "I was out playing football with Joey," and I said, "Yes," and he said, "I tackled him. . ." By this time I know that all of Joey's teeth are chipped and I don't have the money to take him to the dentist and what am I going to do; these are his second teeth! So I said, "Tell me, Bobby, what happened?" And he said, "His pants are dirty. What should I do?" I said, "Have him change his pants." I don't need this sort of aggravation. I mean, Bobby was very nice to call me, but common sense would say he should change the muddy pants, right? I could save $15 a week.

Other mothers report that babysitters have had friends in to listen to their records or that they took to fixing themselves food and leaving the dishes for the parent to wash:

When I moved up here I had my landlord's daughter in to babysit. I never came home to such a bloody mess in my entire life. I could hear the stereo long before I got home and smell the popcorn in the hall. It was more work for me to clean up after the babysitter than for me to clean up after my daughter. One time my daughter got out her Betty Crocker cookbook and decided to bake a cake from scratch and I came home to the babysitter sitting there watching television and flour all over the kitchen.

But it may be worse if there is no one to babysit at all. Single fathers new in a neighborhood may have particular difficulty in obtaining sitters. They may first have to establish themselves with the parents of their neighborhood's teenage girls:

Moving into a new neighborhood, trying to find a babysitter that would come into my home was very difficult. I think it was because I was a single man. There was some prejudice against me as a single man. I would have a sitter and I would call her up and she would say she was busy. And I would say, "Do you have some phone numbers of other people who sit?" And she would give me names of some of her girl-friends. And I would call a girl and she would say, "Just a minute, I'll have to ask my parents," which to me indicated she wasn't really doing anything that night. And she'd come back on the phone and say, "No, I can't," without any explanation. Parents wouldn't trust their daughters to come into my house. It took some convincing that I was an okay guy, that I really did have kids and that when I came home the daughters left.

Many parents explore a succession of child-care possibilities, perhaps beginning by asking friends or relatives for help, and then moving on to babysitters or day-care centers or still other arrangements, searching for one that will work. Here is a report by a mother of an only child, a seven-year-old girl:

For a while you can depend on your mother or a friend, but you can only do that for so long before they say, "Oh, oh, here she comes again." And you feel it. You feel you are being a burden. So I had a few young girls come in, two or three; it didn't work out and I had to get rid of them. I had one girl who came from a big family and she was low on the totem pole, so when she came here she was a boss. She would say to my daughter, "Get me my cigarettes. Make me a sandwich. Go watch television, I'm busy." My daughter wasn't happy with her. And then another girl would just sit on the phone and talk, and regardless of what my daughter wanted it would be, "Go to your room." And I had a few young girls come in and they ended up wanting to work themselves, so you lose your babysitter. Now I've found a woman, through another girl that works for me, that does babysitting professionally. It's a set fee, $5 a day, and she has four or five kids that come over plus four of her own. She has a house full of kids, and they are all equal; they all have to pitch in. So we'll see if that works out.

Single parents tend to be uncertain about the age at which children can look after themselves. In working out a policy they may consider not only the child's age but also the sex of the child, whether the child has siblings, the child's competence, the apparent safety of the neighborhood in which they live, and, not least in importance, the standards of the neighborhood. For they would not want the neighbors to think them neglectful.

Sometimes parents are forced by the absence of a babysitter to leave children to look after themselves, even though they think that the children still need the presence of a caregiver. For want of any alternative, a parent may leave a child of six or seven unattended between the hours that school ends and the time the parent can return from work. The parent may first alert a neighbor and ask whether the child can call on the neighbor should there be an emergency, then caution the child to remain at home, then at work keep in touch by telephone, and finally, the work day over, rush home as quickly as possible. Children of nine or ten are often required to care for themselves in the after-school hours, especially if the parent's job permits use of a telephone. But only when children approach adolescence, ordinarily, do single parents feel entirely comfortable in letting their children remain alone. And some single parents would prefer that not even adolescents be without supervision. Indeed, some single parents fear that adolescents are especially likely to get into trouble if left to their own devices.

Summers and school vacations present special problems to working parents. Even those who do without babysitting for the two or three hours after school are likely to be reluctant for the children to be on their own throughout the day. New arrangements must be made: perhaps the children can stay with grandparents; perhaps they can attend a day camp. Or there may be nothing that can be done other than to ask the children to stay in the neighborhood, and to keep in touch by phone.

Work or welfare

Not all single parents are able to find work or to find work that pays enough to maintain their families, and single parents who have small children may be unwilling to leave their children to the care of others. For those single parents who are receiving adequate income from Social Security, insurance payments, child support, or alimony, absence of employment will not mean destitution. But for others, for widows left without insurance and ineligible for Social Security, for separated and divorced mothers whose husbands contribute little or nothing, and for virtually all mothers who were not married to their children's fathers, absence of employment means absence of income and, with few exceptions, leaves no alternative but welfare.

A substantial minority of mothers who become single parents receive welfare assistance at some point. Not quite a third of all formerly married women who become single parents receive at least some welfare assistance during the first four years after the ending of their marriages.[6] Utilization of welfare is particularly likely in the first year after marital disruption, when about a fourth of single mothers receive welfare assistance.[7] Those who do not receive welfare assistance in the first year are unlikely to receive it at all.[8] Furthermore, of those single parents who *do* use welfare in the first year after the ending of their marriages, only about one in eight continue to receive welfare for the two years following.[9]

Of special interest may be the experience of single mothers who, when married, might have counted themselves among the middle class. Let us consider single mothers whose family incomes, when they were married, averaged more than $8,000 a year from 1967 to 1969, and thus were at the national median or above it. In the first year after the ending of their marriages about 12 percent, one in eight, received some welfare assistance. But by the third year after their marriages had ended, virtually none were receiving welfare.[10] These findings suggest that some women who, when married, would never have thought of themselves as potential "welfare mothers" discover that one consequence of marital separation is that they, too, are required to present themselves to a welfare office. But they also suggest that for those mothers whose family incomes had been average or above average when they were married, welfare is at most a temporary expedient.

It should be noted that giving attention only to previously married mothers leads to an underestimate of the proportion of single mothers who rely on welfare assistance. Mothers who had not been married to the fathers of their children are the group, among single mothers, most likely to receive funds from welfare. Although they constitute only about a seventh of all single parents, they are a third of the single parents who receive welfare assistance.[11]

The form of welfare encountered by single parents is Aid to Families with Dependent Children (AFDC). AFDC is largely federally financed, but each state works out its own payment schedule, and payment schedules vary widely from state to state. Policies regarding who is eligible vary less, but since administration of the program throughout the country is in the hands of local offices and particular social workers, single parents can encounter quite different treatment in different places.

Establishing eligibility for welfare can be made easy or difficult by the rules of a particular office and the style of a particular intake worker. Some offices and workers will accept, at least tentatively, a mother's report that she is without income and in need, although almost always a home investigation must follow to corroborate the woman's report. Other offices and workers may require that mothers document that their children are indeed theirs by bringing birth certificates, and that they show that their rent is what they claim by bringing rent receipts.

Any single parent receiving AFDC must cooperate with the agency in securing support from the other parent. Many offices require a separated or divorced mother to file charges for nonsupport against her husband and require a mother who was not married to the father of her child to bring a paternity action against the father. Some offices bring nonsupporting husbands into court, move to garnishee portions of their wages, and stand ready to seek criminal charges against those they believe to be stubbornly uncooperative.[12]

Most welfare offices are indifferent to applicants' comfort and convenience. It is not uncommon for an applicant to arrive early in the morning and first talk with an intake worker in the afternoon. The rules of the agency may then limit the worker's ability to respond quickly— or at all—to the applicant's need. Furthermore, some workers seem to have become callous to distress that they are largely helpless to remedy and may appear aloof and insensitive. One former applicant said:

> I had to bring my rent, heat, light, doctor's bills, dentist's bills, my last five paychecks, and explain what happened to my support check. My ex had had a very bad winter and he wasn't sending anything. And I had to bring my bank account and say if the children had a bank account. They destroy any pride, any dignity that an individual would have. You have to plead poverty, say you are starving to death, before they'll give you anything.

Whether someone is finally ruled eligible for welfare can turn on which of a large number of rules is thought to govern the case and how that rule is applied. Different welfare workers may treat the same situation differently:

> I was living with my sister, but she was off and on again with her boy-friend, which meant that I really couldn't stay there. So I went to welfare and I said, "I have a son and I'm living with my sister and I can't stay with her any longer." This is to the first social worker, the woman downstairs who takes the initial report. She said to me, "All I can say is for you to go to a temporary hostel for women and put your son in foster care." So I said, "Well, that won't do." Then I got to talk to another social worker who was very sympathetic. She said, "If you can get an apartment, even if you don't live in it, just get an apartment, then I can get everything started for you." And I said, "Well, how do I pay the first month's rent?" And she said, "If you can prove to me that you have an apartment, I can get you on the rolls. Borrow the money for the first month's rent or get your landlord to wait. Then we'll get you started."

The experience of applying for welfare can be disastrous to a single mother's self-esteem. She can hardly avoid feeling humiliated by a long wait to be seen or by insensitive workers. Her helplessness to defend herself against arbitrary interpretations of rules completes the attack on her feelings of worth. One woman, particularly bitter, had endured the application procedure only to be ruled ineligible:

> Even before you go there it's heartbreaking to have to say to yourself, "Oh, God, I'm going to have to apply for welfare." It breaks your heart. And then you go there and the way they treat you is awful. They demean you. Last year was my one and only experience. My husband cut me way down and I couldn't take care of the house and the kids. I finally gathered up my courage and went. And they said that with what I made I was making $90 a month too much. I said, "You've got to be kidding." "Sorry." They don't care.

Once a single parent is accepted for welfare assistance, things are usually better. Some offices send workers to clients' homes to review their current situations, but the clients may be pleased, all in all, to have a chance to talk to someone about their lives. Very occasionally a client may be selected for a thorough review:

> I have gone through a spot check. They came to my house. They checked everything. They checked savings account, checking account, they checked my registration on my car, my insurance, my mortgage, everything I had. Two weeks before I had to do it with my own social worker, and then they pulled a spot check, and I had to do it with the district supervisor. It is quite demeaning, when you might have a couple of extra bucks and they see it in your checkbook and you have to explain to them how you got that extra $10.

But welfare departments are usually understaffed and their workers burdened with more cases than they can keep up with. If the client doesn't take the initiative in contacting the worker, the worker may very well never contact the client. The following comment was made by a woman who had received welfare for several years.

A New Life

I was never even visited by a social worker. I never bothered them and they never bothered me. I just got my check every two weeks. That was cool.

Investigations aside, the welfare program acts toward its accepted clients like a rich but extremely stingy uncle. It ensures that they will not starve by providing food stamps in addition to the basic grant, ensures that they will have housing by standing ready to prevent evictions for nonpayment of rent, and ensures that they are able to obtain needed medical services by providing medicaid or paying for clinic visits. The program, in short, ensures that its clients will have whatever it believes the clients really need. But it gives its clients very little cash:

I couldn't stand the way I was living when I was on welfare. Welfare was $62 a week, just enough for the rent and some food. It was very tight. Sometimes it was a toss-up whether to buy cigarettes or a half-gallon of milk.

Even in states that provide generous welfare schedules, cash beyond that in the basic grant is often needed for items not included in a mother's budget: furniture for the apartment, babysitting, transportation to a relative's home, movie tickets, school lunches, a hamburger at McDonald's. Some welfare departments, recognizing this, issue periodic supplements to their basic allotments; but these are small and usually inadequate to recipients' needs.

It was September and my kids needed shoes for school. I went to my social worker and I said, "They need shoes for school. They need back-to-school clothes." And she said, "Well, you have a $90 flat grant that comes out four times a year." And I said, "Big deal. I've got to get a stove repaired and I've got bills and I need clothes myself."

A widespread response by welfare clients to being kept cash-poor is to work a bit and not inform the welfare department. Some departments permit clients to earn small amounts of money without penalty, but anything more than a few dollars of earnings will result in a deduction from the monthly grant. While very few welfare recipients engage in massive fraud—such as holding down a well-paying job while receiving welfare—minor fraud appears extremely common. Indeed, agency workers may collude in it:

They almost teach you to be crooked. They really do. I was getting $285 a month and my three children and I were supposed to live on that. And one social worker told me, "We know you can't make it. See if you can find something under the table."

One welfare recipient complained to her social worker that she was unable to meet her bills. The social worker said that there was nothing the agency could do. The recipient then raised the possibility of obtaining unreported income:

I said, "Well, you might see me on the corner downtown at night, wearing high-heeled shoes and swinging a big purse." So she started laughing. And I laughed and said, "With my luck, I'll probably only make fifty cents." And she said, "Surely you're worth more than that." And I said, "I take that as tacit approval of my working." And she sort of shrugged when I said that, which to me said, "If you want to work, it's okay with us; just don't bother us." And from that point on, I worked. I got a job as a waitress a couple of nights a week. The hours were good, the pay was good, and the tips were all under the table.

Sometimes a woman can take a low-paying job without entirely relinquishing welfare aid. A department may, for example, pay for child care for a woman who has gone to work after having received welfare or may continue her medicaid eligibility. With this kind of assistance, working can distinctly improve a woman's financial situation. On the other hand, working at a low-paying job without augmentation from welfare, child support, or Social Security may not be preferable, financially, to one of the more generous welfare schedules augmented by under-the-table earnings. One single parent who worked as a secretary compared herself to a neighbor who had chosen to stay at home and receive welfare:

I'm getting almost $9,500 a year. After taxes, my check comes out to $800 a month. The woman that lives next door to me is on welfare and she gets $295 a month. And I'm having a harder time than she is. Of course, I'm running a car and she isn't. But she gets food stamps and I don't. And she can work a little under the table. She cleans people's houses and she makes about $50 a week. And there's no taxes because it isn't reported to anybody. Well, she is getting $300 a month from welfare and another $200 from her work, that's $500 a month. That's not a lot of money, but she has no expenses. I have to keep my clothes up, and in our office we have collections every week for one thing or another—somebody's getting married, somebody's leaving—and if you go out to lunch with people, well, that's two dollars, even for the special on the menu. And then I have the expense of a babysitter.

When the children are small, and the alternatives are either one of the more liberal welfare plans or a low-paying job, then, despite its inadequacies and indignities, welfare can look pretty good. Nevertheless, welfare holds charms for few of its clients. As has been noted, many treat it as a temporary expedient only, something to help them meet the financial emergencies of the first postmarital year or, later, to get them through an interval of joblessness or of diminution of a former husband's support. And although some mothers may hesitate before entirely relinquishing welfare—may, perhaps, try to get their children's dental work attended to while it is still free to them—many intensely dislike the sense of dependency and personal inadequacy they experience as clients, and leave the welfare roll as soon as they can.

A New Life

Turning to kin

When a marital partnership fails, for whatever reason, kinship bonds can provide a safety net. The separated or bereaved partner can apply to kin not only for help but for relief from isolation. There may be latent tensions in these relationships with kin, but nonetheless, mothers and fathers and sisters and brothers are generally helpful:

> Before my husband left, my mother and father never really said any-thing to me. But when I decided to take the bull by the horns and put him out, they stood behind me 100 percent. In fact, my father paid for the lawyers and stuff. And when my husband's checks would bounce, my father would give me the money. I don't like to borrow from any-body; I want to stay within what we've got without having to borrow, but I have had to, and my father has helped me out. He's been terrific.

Often a marital separation comes as a shock to relatives. It is one of the unspoken understandings of marriage that a seamless surface must be maintained, especially with kin. The anouncement that a marriage is ending can then require a good deal of explanation:

> My family lives down the coast, so there's a distance there. And I never told them that we were having problems. My mother didn't know if things were good or bad. I never told her that things were going wrong. When I did, it was a big shock to her.

In most instances relatives quickly adapt to the changed situation, although there may be muted criticism for breaking up the children's home, and a flurry of attempts or at least gestures toward fostering a reconciliation:

> I went home this summer to stay with the folks for a while. And at one point Mom said to me, "You know, maybe if you had both come we could have talked to Larry and could have done something about it."

Having relinquished the status of a married member of the family, the new single parent may experience some loss of standing. Relatives may treat the parent as someone needing solicitude, almost an object for good works:

> They are loving and kindly, but they don't understand that you want them to act as if it is a pleasure seeing you. You know, that you are not a poor relation, that you are not an emotional cripple. You want to feel that they know that you are as capable and as adult as anyone else.

But despite all this, relatives ordinarily stand ready to help as they can, both financially and in the management of the children. One woman, for example, who worked part time and received support from her ex-husband, could rely on her mother to help out when an unexpected bill proved more than her budget could manage:

> It bothers me, my mother helping me out, but I know I can count on her for money. I just did for taxes. I don't get enough to put away money each month, and she gave me the money to pay my taxes.

Some single parents, recognizing how valuable their parents could be for them, may move simply to be nearer to their parents:

> I moved to be closer to my mother. Now it is no problem for her to babysit. She doesn't have to leave the house. If the kids get home and my car is not there and my door is locked, they just go to Nana's house. It's about two blocks away. They cross the boulevard and go down a block, and it takes them two minutes.

Even in-laws may be supportive, especially to the widowed. But without the spouse to serve as a link, much depends on the relationship with the in-laws that had been established when the single parent was married. And, for the separated and divorced, it is always necessary to respect the in-laws' loyalty to their blood kin:

> At one point Freddy's parents thought I was this really wonderful, wonderful person, and they were very protective of me. They were embarrassed by Freddy, by some of his actions. Then, when I didn't receive support from Freddy, I wrote his parents. That was my only alternative. And he told them that I was crazy, that he had been sending me money. I got this letter from Freddy's father: "It sounds to me, Helen, as though you're having problems, but Freddy is certainly sending you adequate money for the children's needs." And he was sending me nothing! I no longer maintain any contact with Freddy's parents.

Relatives sometimes are so helpful that single parents wonder about moving in with them. Most often it is their own parents that single parents consider joining; their brothers and sisters are likely either to be not yet settled, or else to be entirely too settled, with families and family responsibilities of their own. And doubling up, even with the single parent's own parents, seems reasonable only when there are no more than two children. Parents of three or more children are likely to feel themselves too large an order for the children's grandparents to cope with.

Single parents who have tried living in their own parents' homes for more than a very few months almost uniformly found the experience to have been either of mixed value or mostly unhappy. Younger mothers report having been treated as though they had returned to adolescence:

> It was difficult to get my mother away from my being her little girl again. I had to be home at a certain time, just the same as when I was a teenager.

There may be conflicts over direction of the children. The children may observe that while mother can tell them what to do, grandmother can tell mother what to do. Some measure of confusion regarding whether the mother or the grandparents represent ultimate authority seems almost inescapable when mother and children live in the grandparents' home. One little girl said to her mother, "You just think you're big, but wait until I tell Grandmother." Occasionally the children's mother feels thoroughly displaced:

> When I was living at home and working, my son was with my mother more than he was with me, and it was kind of like I would come home and he would be asking her, can I have this or can I have that? I kind of felt rejected, almost. I wasn't his mother. I was more like his sister. And if he fell down and hurt himself, he wouldn't run to me; he would run to my mother!

Still other problems arise when single parents move in with their own parents. The grandparents may grumble about being asked to live with small children again. There may be conflicts in styles of childraising and styles of living. But the most important issue seems to be that so long as the single parent lives in the grandparents' home, the single parent is not fully in charge.

> My mother took a lot of responsibility away from me. At times I resented it but at times I didn't. Sometimes it was really nice. You know, I had all the freedom in the world. But after a while, you don't feel too good about yourself, because you're not living up to your responsibilities.

Having a grandparent move into the single parent's home creates less trouble for the single parent. In the single parent's home it is clear to all that it is the parent who is head of the household. Even so, there may be tensions. One woman reported that soon after her separation her mother, who had been widowed for just a year, moved in with her. The arrangement seemed on the whole to be a success, but each found it trying, at times, to have to adapt to life with the other:

> When I was married, we were like sisters, and it was great. We still get along. We never have really out-and-out fights. But lately I really seem to be watching everything I say. She thinks I have a terrible disposition and I think that she's nobody special to live with either. The best thing is that we both have activities that take us elsewhere. Stay away from each other and we are fine. We get along marvelously if we stay away from each other.

Living near the children's grandparents, as opposed to living with them, seems almost entirely desirable. The auxiliary home to which the children can go provides the single parent with a kind of back-up childcare facility and gives both children and parent an additional measure of security:

> My mother lives close by and she is a big help as far as taking Walt overnight when I have to be at work at seven the next day. And I went

to Florida the last week in March and she came and stayed right here with the children for the week, which was a wonderful help for me.

So long as the relatives live in another household, the single parent is protected from their intrusiveness and is able to retain some privacy. The ideal arrangement is to be close, but not too close: not too far for the children to walk, with no heavily trafficked street between, but not next door and certainly not in the same house—about a block away, and around a corner.

Moving

The single parent who can stay put is fortunate. But it appears that, sooner or later, many single parents find it necessary to move. The house is too big or too expensive; or it no longer is comfortable living in a neighborhood of two-parent families; or jobs or schooling or the possibility of living near the children's grandparents make moving advisable.

But moving, regrettably, means resettling not only oneself, but also the children. It means the children must adapt to a new school and make new friends. And, for the parent, it means once again finding babysitters, once again developing good relationships with neighbors, and once again painting walls and fitting furniture to rooms and learning who to call to fix the plumbing or to deliver fuel.

Often the new home turns out to have been poorly chosen: it is too small, or too far from friends or relatives or jobs, or not right for the children. Then there is a second move to a place that corrects the errors of the first but that may turn out to have its own discomforts. And so single parents may engage in two, three, or more moves, each move a correction of a previous mistake, until they find something satisfactory. The following history is, in outline, a common one:

> After my husband left I had to sell the house. I had a whole bunch of furniture, and I had to figure out what I was going to do. The real estate broker told me about this apartment complex that included some three-bedroom town houses. I just assumed that it would have some married people with kids, but it turned out to be a singles' complex. At first it was fun, because it was just parties constantly. Maybe I needed that right then. Immediately after I moved in, somebody was knocking at my door, "Come on out and have a good time!" I thought, "Gee, this is terrific." But after a while the place really got to seem like a zoo. I mean, people just assuming that everything was on a walk-in basis for everybody, because it was all singles. So I decided to move.
>
> I found this woman who was in a similar situation to mine, and she

had a ranch house and was moving down to her basement and was going to rent out the upstairs. It was in a super single-family residence neighborhood. Well, it had no soundproofing, and my kids made a lot of noise. And she was not a very pleasant person. She got very picky. I was running my fan too long and she came up to inspect. And the garbage disposal broke down and she was convinced it was something that I threw down there. I had put artichokes in there. "Artichoke leaves broke my disposal! You owe me $300 for a new garbage disposal!" Little, picky hassles. I stayed there only a few months.

I found this place because I knew some people who lived up here. I hadn't heard anything terribly favorable one way or another about it. But I knew there were children. There was a pool. And there is a play area: they have swings and a slide and all that type of thing. And I could have a dog. I don't have the maintenance here that I would have if I lived in a duplex or rented a house. I don't have to shovel the snow; I don't have to cut the grass or prune the shrubs. And I don't have to deal with a landlord on a one-to-one basis. I pay my rent and I'm not bothered. There are no personal hassles over anything.

In areas in which there is a strong demand for apartments, single mothers who were not previously married or who are separated or divorced may encounter discrimination; some landlords and agents may be reluctant to rent to them. The mothers may be told that there is a risk they will bring strange men into the apartment house or will be unable to supervise their children or will prove financially unreliable. Or they may not be told anything directly but still be made to feel that they are not desirable tenants:

You go to people and you say, "I'd like to rent a two-bedroom apartment." And they say, "For how many?" And you say, "Myself and my two children." "Are you a widow?" "No." "Oh. Are you divorced?" "Well, yes. Does it make any difference?" And—it's just a few of the people—"Well, gee, I think the rooms would be too small for you." All kinds of stuff like this. And I really can't stand it.

The primary problem in moving, however, is that the dislocation of life produced by the ending of marriage can so complicate the process of search that the single parent accepts a house or apartment whose defects, although at first overlooked, after a time turn out to be intolerable. It is the fortunate single parent whose first move is good enough.

The process of reorganization

New arrangements, some carefully thought through, some arrived at by trial and error, occupy much of the first year of single-parent life. Repeatedly, decisions must be made under duress, despite uncertainty, despite emotional unreadiness. Eventually a new coherent way of life is established, bringing with it a new stability. It may take two or three additional years before this new stability has entirely crystalized, before it is resilient enough to withstand questioning, the single parent's own, as well as others'. But usually the new way of life is largely in place before the first year has ended.

The account of one single parent suggests how short-term solutions may be adopted, only to be recognized as unsatisfactory and then rejected in favor of new short-term solutions, until ultimately an acceptable way of life is established.

Mr. Buscaglia is a widower. When we talked with him he was about thirty, a former construction worker. He had been married for about five years and was the father of two children: a boy about five, a girl not quite three. His wife had been killed two years earlier by a car that hit her as she was crossing a street. Like others overtaken by totally unanticipated loss, Mr. Buscaglia was at first both grief-stricken and bewildered. The painfulness of his loss was almost overwhelming. In addition, the assumptions on which his life had been based were now destroyed. Mr. Buscaglia's sister offered to take his baby, then about eight months old. Mr. Buscaglia and his three-year-old son went to stay with a friend.

> I thought about suicide. I was walking across the street and a big truck was coming down and I thought how easy it would be to just sort of stand there and let myself be hit. It would be all over. My son had gotten over across the street and was standing there waiting for me. And then I decided that I was either going to be a turkey and do that or I was going to do something with the kids. And the kids didn't have anybody else but me.

Mr. Buscaglia returned to his home, called his sister, and said she could bring back the baby. For about a week Mr. Buscaglia tried to care for both children himself. He received constant advice, especially from his mother and his sister.

> I was getting phone calls, maybe seven a day, from my sister, my mother, from friends. All sorts of things about the care of the baby. "Are you doing this?" "Are you doing that?" "Do you want me to come by and do this?"

During this week Mr. Buscaglia stayed home with his two children. He worried constantly about how he could continue to keep his children. He had only limited savings. He called the welfare department and was told that if he were capable of working he would be ineligible for welfare. Yet he felt that the children needed his constant attention. If he left the house on an errand he would ask a neighbor to keep an eye on the children and would hurry back. He worried about whether he would be able to continue to devote himself to the children. He became depressed and then began worrying about his depression and what it might mean to the children. Finally, he called his parents and asked whether he could move in with them.

> I didn't like being by myself in the house where I lived with my wife. I wanted to get the hell out of there. And I didn't have any money at all. I was already thinking about going to my parents' house, for economic reasons. And if I moved in with my parents, there would be no problem about somebody watching the kids.

Mr. Buscaglia hoped he could ask his parents to look after the children only in the evening, when his parents would be at home anyway. He therefore looked for a job whose hours would permit him to be with his children during the day. He found one as a doorman and bouncer in a nightclub. He went to work at ten, stayed until the club closed at two, and was home by four. Except for times during the night when the baby awakened, the children were asleep when he was away.

But Mr. Buscaglia's parents were used to being by themselves. Their home felt crowded by the presence of their grown son and his two small children. Both Mr. Buscaglia and his father were irritated by the other's way of doing things. After a few months Mr. Buscaglia decided that he had to move again.

> I got an awful lot of understanding from my parents, but I found that their patience was growing thin after maybe two or three months, and they found mine growing thin too. My father and I are so much alike it is incredible. It was two bull elephants crashing into each other.

Mr. Buscaglia was lucky enough to find an apartment only a block away from his parents' home. Once he had his own place, the tension between him and his parents subsided. His parents continued to be helpful.

> I moved into my own place right up the street from my parents. There is a lot of room up there for the kids to play. And there are a lot of kids in the neighborhood. I know an awful lot of people up there. I had access to my parents' house for whatever I wanted; I had a key. I often walked down to my parents' in the morning and sort of spent the day there.

But the night job, which had worked so well when Mr. Buscaglia was living with his parents, no longer worked at all. Mr. Buscaglia could not ask his parents to come to his home to stay overnight with the children, and bringing the children to his parents' home was awkward.

> Either I had to bring the kids down to my parents until I got back from work or else I had to have somebody come to the house and watch the kids. If I brought the kids down to my parents, I got back so late from

work it was impossible to pick them up. So sometimes I had my brother or my younger sister come up to my house. But they didn't want to do it regularly. There are other things that somebody their age wants to do.

Mr. Buscaglia found a day job as a playground director. Now he had to arrange for daytime child care. His mother was willing to help out once in a while, but he couldn't ask her to give all her days to caring for his children. A neighbor offered to look after the children, and, briefly, this appeared to be a good solution. But within a few weeks Mr. Buscaglia decided he had to find something else.

> There was this lady who lived a couple of doors over from me who said she would watch my kids for a certain amount of money per week. So I dropped the kids off in the morning and then I'd go to this job of being a playground director and I'd come home and Paul would be talking about the old bread that he ate for lunch and saying that the milk smelled funny. And once I found the baby with spaghetti sauce all over her face and all over her chest. And then, when I would drop the kids off in the morning, the fights between the husband and wife were already starting, and I didn't want the kids to get that every day. So I looked around and I looked around. I think I called every agency in the state. I couldn't find anything.

Finally, Mr. Buscaglia's widowed mother-in-law arrived on the scene. She was willing to move into Mr. Buscaglia's house on a five-day-a-week basis, and to adapt as best she could to his way of doing things. With some accommodation on both sides, the arrangement proved practical.

> The kids' grandmother, my mother-in-law, stopped out to the house to see the kids and in the course of the conversation let me know that she felt that the kids needed a more secure sort of looking after, which I agreed with entirely. So we made an arrangement to have her live with me and take care of the kids while I was at work.
>
> It has worked out much better than I thought it would. It's really kind of interesting. I think my mother-in-law and I like each other basically, but we don't want to let the other one know that we do. There isn't any question about the fact that my mother-in-law would rather have me dead and her daughter alive—which is fair. But once you admit that and handle that, I think it is kind of easy to deal with. It is a big one to get over, but it is manageable.
>
> I have no fears at all now, when I leave the house, about the care the kids are going to get. I have total confidence in her. And I work a lot of evening hours. She is there Monday through Thursday night, and out of the four nights she is there, I'm probably home late twice. Friday afternoon I come home and she leaves when I get there. Then she comes back Monday morning.

It took Mr. Buscaglia just about a year to work out a reasonably satisfactory way of life. This is not to say that he will not make further changes as time goes on. But gone is his feeling that his arrangements are only temporary, that his life has yet to settle down. He is no longer constantly improvising solutions to urgent problems. His life is no longer in transition. Now his concerns are those of all single parents: raising his children, though he is without a partner, and maintaining a satisfactory social and personal life, though he is responsible for his children.

PART TWO

A Parent, Though Single:
The Single Parent
at Home

PART TWO

A Parent, Though Single:
The Single Parent
at Home

CHAPTER 3

Managing a Household as a Single Parent

THE SINGLE-PARENT SITUATION is described as burdensome by most of those within it. When its specific demands are examined, however, it may not seem very different from the situation of the married parent. And yet, those single parents who were formerly married generally insist that parenting alone *is* more difficult than parenting with a partner. This chapter will examine why this is so.

In both single-parent families and two-parent families, hundreds of discrete tasks are required of the adult members if the families are to be maintained. These tasks, although they are as varied as calling the oilman to look at the furnace, preparing lunches for the children, and battling commuter traffic to get to and from work, can almost all be classified within one of three "task packages": clusters of tasks similar in aim.

Clearly distinguishable as a task package are the activities concerned with income production. Here may be included not only the job itself but also commuting to the job and maintaining the car required for commuting, and other such job-related tasks as maintaining clothes or uniforms in good repair, entertaining colleagues, and keeping up with an industry's literature.

A second task package consists of the cluster of chores related to home maintenance. Included here would be such things as buying furniture for the home, arranging the furniture once purchased, and making curtains and painting cabinets, along with the repetitive, constantly recurring tasks of cleaning and straightening and picking up. In this category, too, would fall the tasks associated with food preparation, from shopping for food, storing, cooking, and serving it, to washing the dishes and disposing of the garbage.

The third task package consists of the tasks of child care: nurturing and disciplining and responding to the children, listening to their enthusiasms and complaints, setting rules and settling quarrels, transporting the children to day-care centers and friends' homes and doctors' offices, helping the children with homework in the evening and reading them bedtime stories, laying out their clothes for the next day, and getting up with them in the morning to get them off to school.

In traditional two-parent households the husband takes primary responsibility for the task package of income production and divides responsibility for the task package of child care, although most of the actual work is done by the wife. The wife is responsible for home maintenance. This is, to be sure, only a first approximation. Certain aspects of home maintenance are ordinarily understood as the husband's responsibility: maintaining the outside of the home—painting the shutters or fixing the roof or seeding the lawn—as well as the handyman chores of replacing a rubber washer in a faucet and fixing a balky window shade. In addition, the husband may "help out" with cooking and cleaning, although these tasks would continue to be understood as being within the wife's domain. And, in roughly the same way, the wife may "help out" with income production by working part time or full time. In "symmetric" households, responsibility for each task package is more nearly shared.[1]

No matter how the three task packages are divided, however, husbands and wives view themselves as fully occupied by the three task packages taken together. Almost universally the three task packages are taken to constitute two full-time jobs. If this view is correct, the single parent is required to choose among three alternatives, no one of them entirely satisfactory: to take on responsibility for two full-time jobs; to accept that some necessary tasks will go unperformed; or to search for a way of augmenting the parent's own efforts. The last alternative may seem the most appealing, except that it often implies dependency on the goodwill of others.

But first, is it true that the three task packages together represent two full-time jobs? Let us take as a given that the usual eight hours of employment plus commuting time together constitute a full-time job. Do housework and child care, as they might be performed by a single parent, then also constitute a full-time job? One way of assessing this is to examine the workload of single parents who do nothing more than care for their homes and children.

Managing a Household as a Single Parent

The single parent without paid employment

Consider those single mothers whose income comes from pension plans and Social Security or from support payments from ex-husbands and occasional gifts from kin, together with welfare assistance. What are their days like?

If the children are very small, the activities of the nonworking single mother are restricted, since the children have to be attended to constantly. If the children are of school age, the nonworking single mother unquestionably will have a good deal of time that is free. Here is a description of a typical day offered by such a mother in her early thirties. She managed on her husband's support check supplemented by income from the welfare department. She had three children, twin boys aged nine and a girl aged seven.

> I get the twins up first. They have to go to school earlier. They eat and get ready while I'm getting dressed. By the time the twins leave, the little one is up and dressed. I take her to school. Then usually I go shopping. I go food shopping and I look around the stores. Once in a while I'll go up to my mother's. I visit my sister, too. I don't visit often. I'd rather sit in my own house and enjoy the peace and quiet while the kids are gone. I just go around straightening up the house. The kids come home about two-thirty. They show me their papers and all that stuff. They get changed and they go out. I watch a soap opera from three to four and then I start supper. And from four until seven, that's suppertime, between cooking it and eating it and cleaning up. Then I get the kids ready for bed. Everybody showers or has a bath. And that's it for the night.

The day begins with a morning rush but then settles down to several unhurried hours of shopping, visiting, and watching television along with doing a bit of housework. When the children return from school, there is again a flurry of activity, but it is brief and there is time before beginning supper for more television. Then follows supper, some supervision of the children's preparations for bed, and finally an idle hour or two before the mother herself goes to bed. Except for the morning rush, the day is without pressure.

Yet let us count up the time in this day that is given to task performance. Two hours or so in the morning are given to getting the children up and dressed, to preparing their breakfast, and to sending two to school and taking the third. An hour or so is given to shopping. There is an hour of child care in the afternoon. Three hours are absorbed by the evening meal—more than might be given to it in a more pressured day. Finally there is another hour of child care before the children's bedtime. Somewhere during the day an hour may be spent cleaning or straightening up or doing laundry. All this comes to nine hours of task performance. The same work might be accomplished, were there need, within eight hours. But still it would amount to what would ordinarily be thought to be a full day's work.

The answer to the initial question—"Do housework and child care, as they might be performed by a single parent, constitute a full-time job?" —is that they do. What makes the day of this rather typical nonworking single parent appear so leisurely is that the times given to task performance are spread across the whole sixteen waking hours.

What goes wrong with staying home, when you become a single parent

But now a second question: in the previous chapter going to work was described as appearing to women who had become single parents to be necessary not only because they needed the money but also to protect their sanity. What is it that is so discomforting about just staying home with the children, once a woman becomes a single parent? Why would a woman who seemed content to remain at home when she was married feel oppressed by the arrangement when the marriage ends? Just this seems regularly the case. One woman, mother of three children, had not objected to remaining at home so long as she was married. But later, after going to work, she described in the following terms the time after her marriage ended when she had no occupation other than home maintenance and child care:

> I used to sit around saying, "What am I going to do now? I'm bored silly." I used to go crazy some days.

What changes with the ending of marriage? To answer this, let us consider the situation of a married mother without paid employment.

Mrs. Sherman was in her early thirties. She had two school-aged children, Deidre, seven, and Laura, five and a half, and in addition a small baby, ten months old. Her husband managed a hardware store. Here is how Mrs. Sherman described her day:

> The baby takes an hour and a half of my time in the morning. I spend that time feeding her and bathing her and getting her back into her crib. And all of a sudden I find that it is ten-thirty or eleven o'clock and I've got nothing done, there's not a bed made. So I'll start in making the beds and doing the odds and ends, things I have to do, and it seems

like all of a sudden it is twelve o'clock and it is lunchtime. And Laura comes home at ten past twelve. She has gotten into the habit of having her lunch in a lunchbox because Deidre has *her* lunch in a lunchbox, so I make her lunch and put it in a lunchbox. Now it is time to go for Deidre. So I bundle the baby up and dress Laura and go to pick up Deidre. Then I stop in at my mother's for a while or do an errand or drop by my girlfriend's. Then I come home and it is suppertime. And I think what a fool I was to stay out because I left all this mess. So I race around like mad to get everything done before George comes home. George comes home about seven-thirty. And when he comes home I have my hair combed and lipstick on, and I act like I haven't had a thing to do all day.

There's a lot of bustle here, and in truth Mrs. Sherman, because of the baby, is constantly on call. She also has a child who comes home for lunch, and this introduces a new task. Yet the constant attention demanded by the baby, plus the few additional tasks her situation requires beyond those required of the single parent whose day was described in the previous section, seem insufficient to account for the much greater intensity of pressures Mrs. Sherman perceives. At a later point in our interview with Mrs. Sherman she remarked, "I feel sometimes that I'm so overburdened that I can't possibly cope with the situation." In contrast, the single parent, who had not that much less to do, felt the day to be too empty.

Housekeeping and child care for Mrs. Sherman appear to her not only to be required for their own sake but also to be responsibilities delegated to her by her marital partnership. Whereas the single parent can do those chores she wants to do, when she wants to, and to the extent that she wants to, Mrs. Sherman feels obligated to her husband to have the house in order and the children cared for and, by the time he comes home, the evening meal underway. Nor does Mrs. Sherman have the single parent's sixteen waking hours in which to complete her chores. To be sure, she need not accomplish her eight hours of chores within an eight-hour day; the comment "I stop in at my mother's for a while . . . or stop by my girlfriend's" shows she has free time during the day. But she still feels she must complete her tasks by the time of her husband's return. She has a deadline, as she indicates when she says, "I race around like mad to get everything done before George comes home."

The married mother may have somewhat more to do than the mother who is not married, in that she contributes to keeping her husband in good working order. The single parent quoted earlier said that when she was married:

I had to do certain things for my husband: make sure his clothes got to the cleaner's, make sure they were picked up, make sure I took care of the insurance, make sure that everything he wanted was done first. Then I did the other things.

The married mother, because she is responsible to a partner, may also set higher standards for her cooking and housekeeping. Another single mother, for example, contrasted her current cooking practice with that of her marriage:

> The meals I present to my daughter, I would not expect a guy coming home after a full day of work wanting to have. At the supermarket I happened to see something on sale, this soup mix: you buy one, you get one free—how can you miss? So I thought I would try it. Well, my daughter loved it. But no way would I present that to my ex-husband. No way could I present it as a meal.

Finally, the married mother may give time to helping her husband maintain his morale. Mrs. Sherman, for example, makes herself available, when her husband is home, to listen to him, to talk with him, to keep him company. Her husband does the same for her, of course. But attentiveness to the other's needs absorbs some part of each one's evening.

But while the married nonworking mother has deadlines and standards and some responsibilities that her single-parent counterpart does not have, she also has the feeling that what she does for her home and children contributes to the aims of the marital enterprise. This sense of contribution to a shared enterprise, to a partnership, gives to her daily tasks both structure and meaning. There are deadlines by which her tasks must be accomplished; her husband expects it. And the tasks are important; they matter to her husband.

Many nonworking single mothers are quite aware that the ending of their marriages freed them from the pressure of their husbands' expectations. The following comment was made by a mother of four children, the oldest now on his own, the others school-aged:

> When I was married—I don't know why—I would feel I had to do everything in the house, have all the beds made, the dishes done, and all that, because otherwise he might come in and say, "What have you been doing? Sitting down all day?" And then I would feel guilty about it. And it was constant: doing everything, never having anything out of place, trying recipes, always making good meals, desserts and everything—because I did not want him to have anything to say—worrying about being home at a certain time to make the meals, having certain things to eat, trying to please just him. When I would try to look nice it was always for him and never for me. Now if it's four o'clock and I feel like going over to someone's house for a cup of tea I don't have to worry about supper. My boys are old enough that if I leave something around they can cook. Or they can wait until I come back. I have a lot of freedom now, an awful lot of freedom.

Although there are benefits in no longer being responsible to a partnership, without a partnership the nonworking single parent must cope with an almost structureless day and with tasks unshared by another adult. Because there is no fellow adult to value the single parent's work, home maintenance and child care may easily become chores and nothing more. A divorced mother of two adolescents said:

> I didn't like housework, so I'll never say I was a good housewife in that sense. But when there is no man in the house, something in you dies. You don't care. Like when I first got married, I set the table, put a few flowers in the middle of it, that little bit of creative stuff. There's no man in the house and you've got the kids: it's like the kids are not enough. They are there, but they're not enough.

Even older children, though they may participate in the management of the household, do not provide the sense of partnership, of shared enterprise, that would give special value to home chores. The following comment was made by a widowed mother of four children, the older two no longer at home, the younger two now adolescent:

> I think if I had someone here to do something for, I would feel better. I think if I had someone here I had to cook for and sew for, I would have a different outlook on it all. But now I don't care. And I should clean the house. I know it's not that clean. But I say, for who? And for what? For the kids? I think you really need a need or a cause to do these things for. I don't have that, so I don't care.

To fill the emptiness of her days, a single mother without a job may search for activities that will structure her time and engage her with others. Joining another single parent for regular outings sometimes will do. Here, for example, is a report of a nonworking single mother whose life became less depressing once she began doing things with another single mother:

> Before, I didn't care if I got up or stayed in bed all day. It was just dreary. The kids go to what they call a social center after school and they are gone until, like, five o'clock, and then the bus brings them home. So by the time they come home it is time for supper. Do the supper, watch TV, time for bed. It was just dreary. Now I get up, drive the kids to school, do my housework, at ten o'clock my girlfriend and I are off for the day. We go to the store, maybe go out for lunch. We just stay out all day. And I have a different outlook now.

Some single parents contrive to fill their days with a round of activities. They keep themselves busy with meetings, programs, classes, and volunteer activity, in addition to housework and child care:

> I don't sit still for an hour unless I'm watching television or reading. I go to the library for the parents' class and for sewing. I shop, I go to bingo with the neighbors in the evening, I go to the Divorced and Separated Group at the church. I clean the house, not as good as some people do, but I try to keep it clean. On Fridays I have Cub Scouts. I keep very busy. That is the only way I can keep my sanity.

Married mothers, too, may find the roles of housewife and mother insufficiently satisfying. But housework and child care ordinarily have much more meaning for the married mother than for the single mother. For the single mother, work outside the home may be the only way of establishing relationships with other adults who value what she does.

The schedule of the employed single parent

Working single parents are responsible for two full-time jobs. In consequence, although they have no deadlines at home, their days are without slack. Indeed, the schedule of a working single parent is extremely tight. Here is a description of one woman's typical day. She was the mother of two boys, one eleven, the other eight, and held a nine-to-five job as a secretary in an office about twenty minutes from her home.

> I get up at seven, make my bed, and make the kids' breakfast. The dishes go in the sink—I don't have time to do dishes. I sort of prod the boys to get ready. If it's trash day, they take the trash out before they go to school. If their pajamas are dirty, they have to get them into the hamper. I make their lunches and I get them out the door by eight o'clock. I have a cup of tea, run my bath, get dressed, and leave for work about a quarter of nine. I get to work by nine.
>
> Sometimes I get home at lunch time and put a stew in the crock pot so it will be ready when I come home, which is really nice. It is nice to know that supper will be ready when I come home. By suppertime I'm frazzled because of what I've had to cope with at work. Sometimes I'm so tired I tingle.
>
> I get home around twenty past five. I put some supper on and at six-thirty we'll have supper. Then the kids do homework or watch TV or something. The smaller goes to bed at nine-thirty, the bigger goes to bed half an hour later. And then I have a cup of tea and maybe I fold some wash.

The day is made up of segments, some more demanding than others, but none, except for the very last, relaxed. It begins with a morning rush, an hour and a half in which to get everyone up and out, and goes on to half an hour or so of travel to work. Then follow nine hours, including the lunch hour, on the job; half an hour or so returning home; two hours for the evening meal, including its preparation and consumption and the cleaning up afterwards; and two hours before the children's bedtime devoted to supervising the children's homework, breaking up the children's quarrels, and watching television with the children, interspersed with minor chores, telephone conversations with friends or relatives, and brief diversions like looking at the paper. Finally, after the children are in bed, there is an hour or two during which the parent can relax, before the parent's own bedtime.

This is the basic schedule of almost all single parents who work full time. If there are preschool children, the parent may in addition have to take the children to the home of a relative or neighbor or to a day-care center before setting off to work and, later, have to pick them up again. If the commuting time to work is longer than half an hour, then the work day is extended by that much on each end and time with the children is accordingly reduced. If there is an older child, the child may have begun preparation of the evening meal before the parent's arrival home. But an older child will stay up longer and there will be no free hour or two at the end of the day.

A certain amount of housekeeping is often necessary during the evening hours after the supper dishes are put away. Mornings are too rushed, and the weekend may already be full. And so an evening hour will be given to straightening up a living room or washing a kitchen floor or doing a load of laundry. The result is a very long workday:

> You work all day and then come home and it's like another workday starts all over again. I mean, with three children, if you don't do a certain amount of wash every day, you know what it's like. And the house has to be kept up. So it's almost like two days in one sometimes.

Errands must be done on lunch hours or on the way to or from work or be left for Saturday. Saturdays are chore days, as tightly scheduled as normal workdays, devoted to shopping, housecleaning, and taking the car for service and shoes to the repair shop and overdue books to the library—whatever cannot be done during the week. A divorced woman said:

> Saturday is my running around day, doing all the chores, you know, shopping and all this kind of thing. Saturdays I go in six different directions, running around. Sundays I usually clean my house, do laundry, that stuff.

Sunday is a slower day. For many, it is something of a family day. The same woman said:

> We don't go to church. I just stay around the house. It gives me some time to be with my kids. It is the one day of the week when we have a whole day where we are all here.

Single mothers who do not work see nothing special in the brief interval between the time their children go to sleep and the time they go to sleep themselves. They have already had time enough without special demand; they are not pleased now to have more. Indeed, this last hour or two of the day may be felt by them to be especially unpleasant, because they could not get out even if they had somewhere to go; they are imprisoned by their sleeping children. One nonworking mother of three, a resident of a housing project, said:

> After the kids are fed and their homework's done and their things are ready for school and they're in bed, there's nothing. Your house is so noisy all day long: phone calls, people, kids, all kinds of action going on. Come nine o'clock, there is this dead silence. And you have this feeling of, "What happened?" Like the whole world had come to an end.

For the working single parent, the last hour or two of the day is virtually the only time in the week (Sunday perhaps excepted) when the parent need not attend to someone else's concerns. Instead of feeling the sense of isolation experienced by the nonworking parent when the children are in bed and the house is still, the fatigued working parent is likely to experience a welcome relief. But for working parents to have this time their children must go to bed before they do:

> My older boy has to go to bed at ten o'clock. I've been coping with things all day long, and I want that hour for myself. And I can't stay up past eleven now that I work. I say to him he has got to go to bed. "What are you going to do, Mom?" "I'm not going to do a goddamned thing. I'm going to sit here. And I don't want to have to talk to kids. I want to sit here by myself."

Another woman described the anger she felt when her only son began staying up beyond his established bedtime, so that she no longer had her accustomed two hours to herself:

> What happened was, it would get to be a quarter of eleven and he would still be awake. I began to figure out that my time went from nine o'clock till eleven o'clock, seven days a week, and that's only fourteen hours a week of free time. I was getting cheated out of that. I really got extremely upset about it. I felt deprived of my time and my life. I got madder and madder. I was really angry. I had never been angrier. I understood child abuse for the first time. I didn't do it, but I certainly felt like it. One night I screamed so loud that my voice got all choky and I couldn't really scream any more: "I need my time! This is my time. You have to go to sleep!"

The parent's discretionary time at the end of the day may be used to watch television, read a newspaper, putter around the house, or telephone a friend. Only rarely is it given to serious housekeeping. This last brief interval in the day is for attention to self.

Managing a Household as a Single Parent

How is the employed single parent's situation different from that of the employed married mother?

Are the demands on employed single parents very different from those on working married mothers? In particular, does having a husband make for a reduction in the task responsibilities of working mothers? By and large, it would appear, the answer is no. Time-budget studies of working wives demonstrate that most working wives perform the bulk of home maintenance and child-care tasks in addition to sharing responsibility with their husbands for income production. Pleck summarizes the findings of one such study as: "Husbands contribute about the same time to family tasks whether their wives are employed . . . or not employed."[2] Indeed, insofar as she has a husband to care for as well as children, the working married mother, just like the nonworking married mother, has somewhat more to do around the house than does her single counterpart.

Mrs. Desmond may be taken as an instance of a married working mother who retained responsibility for home maintenance and child care. The Desmonds had two daughters: Diane, aged eleven, and Claire, aged nine. Mr. Desmond was a heating contractor. Mrs. Desmond had worked as a secretary before the birth of Diane. She remained at home for seven years until Claire entered kindergarten, and then returned to work full time. She returned to work partly because she and her husband needed the extra money, but also because she preferred working to staying home:

> I get awful sick of going to a neighbor's for coffee or having neighbors in for coffee. I enjoyed it when the children were preschool-aged, but now that they aren't, I'm beyond it. I'd rather work.

Mrs. Desmond's schedule was virtually identical to the schedule of a working single parent. Her day began with the same breakfast rush. Her husband slept late in the morning, and Mrs. Desmond left a breakfast for him.

> I get up at seven, call the children, and get out their clothes. After I've gotten them awake I make breakfast. I don't get dressed or anything; I stay in my pajamas. Diane makes her own bed every morning and picks up her room, but Claire right now is using the excuse that she can't make her bed because it's up against the wall and it is hard for her to make. Usually they are downstairs by twenty-five minutes after seven and through breakfast by a quarter of eight. Then I do their hair and they're usually ready to go about eight o'clock. I come upstairs and from eight to a quarter past eight I get myself dressed. My husband stays out of the way in the morning. He doesn't get up until I leave. I leave his breakfast on the table and a thermos jug for his lunch. And then I leave for work about eight-thirty.

Since Mrs. Desmond's office was only about fifteen minutes from her house, she was able to be home by five-fifteen or five-thirty. She then immediately began supper. At one point Mrs. Desmond's close friend Lois offered to drive Mrs. Desmond home if Mrs. Desmond would first accompany Lois to a garage where Lois's car was being repaired. Mrs. Desmond thought of her husband's reaction to a late supper and declined the invitation:

> I said, "Gee, Lois, I'd be about forty-five minutes late getting home. I'll start supper at six o'clock and that will go over like a lead balloon." If I had done that it would have upset Ed, because he would have felt that he and the children didn't come first. He would have been darned good and mad. He might have yelled at me, "You have responsibilities! You're a married woman!" At the least he would mumble and grumble for maybe half an hour.

Mr. Desmond did not help with the housework. In fact, he seemed almost unaware of the state of the house. And so Mrs. Desmond did it all. Like working single parents she did the bulk of her housework on Saturday and, because she worked, she gave herself permission to reduce her standards.

> I let the housework go a little. I haven't scrubbed the kitchen floor for over two weeks and it needs it desperately right now. Pretty much I do the housework on Saturday. Usually I vacuum Saturday morning. Actually, I devote Saturdays pretty much to cleaning the house.

Although Mr. Desmond did not help with housework, he did help with child care. He did not assume primary responsibility—child care was clearly Mrs. Desmond's responsibility—but if he was around he was willing to play with the children and be a parental companion for them.

> My husband will look over and say, "Diane is a dope." And then we have a wrestling match going on. Consequently, the couch needs new springs. Both my daughters like to be with their father all the time. Claire goes everywhere with him. She stayed up with him last night. She asked him, "Could I stay up as late as you do?" He said, "If your mother says it is all right." I thought she might as well. She could sleep late this morning.

There were other, smaller ways in which Mr. Desmond also helped his wife. He did errands for her. He would now and again drive her to see friends or to shop. He made home repairs as these were necessary. The last, to be sure, was not of unmixed benefit for Mrs. Desmond:

> When Ed gets going on something in the house, I wish I was someplace else, because I automatically become the helper. "Go down the cellar and get some nails." "Go get this." "Go get me the tools."

But if we weigh against each other the ways in which Mr. Desmond helped his wife around the house and the additional work his presence

Managing a Household as a Single Parent

required, the balance is not heavily in Mr. Desmond's favor. On Mr. Desmond's side it can be counted that he helped out by making repairs in the home, running errands, and playing with the children when the spirit moved him. He also helped discipline the children and was available when there was the sort of special need that might be produced by a sick child. But on the other hand he imposed on Mrs. Desmond a time by which she had to be home and a deadline for preparation of the evening meal and, because of him, Mrs. Desmond imposed on herself higher standards in her cooking, if not in her cleaning. In addition, Mrs. Desmond accepted as her responsibility the preparation of Mr. Desmond's breakfast, care of his clothes, and maintenance of a home to which Mr. Desmond could invite his friends and his kin.

And yet Mr. Desmond's presence did help a great deal. Compared to a working single parent, Mrs. Desmond, though she had as many demands on her and though she had in addition to meet a husband's expectations, seemed more in control, less harried.

One part of the explanation is that Mr. Desmond could be called on for help whenever Mrs. Desmond felt overload approaching. Mrs. Desmond could ask him to take over surveillance of the children if she was tired of child care or had something else to do. Mr. Desmond was a sort of parent-in-reserve; a live-in substitute caretaker, ready to step in at a moment's notice, but better than any substitute caretaker could be because he was a genuine parent, already vested with responsibility, entitled to authority, able to provide a parental presence. Mr. Desmond functioned like a first-rate back-up player on an athletic team, taking over when the starter needed a break:

> Ed has a very even disposition. I'm the one that might be happy one minute and snarly the next. Ed will say, "Come on kids, I'll take you for a ride before your mother blows her top." Or he'll say, "Your mother is on the warpath. Let's go." They usually go out for an hour or two. And then I run around the house and slam things and curse up and down. Then I relax and pick up the house or clean it or something. I'm fine when they come back.

In addition, Mr. Desmond provided his wife with emotional support. As is true with most husbands and wives, the Desmonds were not unfailingly supportive of each other. Mrs. Desmond at one point complained to us that her husband was too easily upset, and that she could not tell him, for example, if one of the children had trouble in school. Nevertheless, she did share her concerns with her husband, even though this sometimes made him anxious. Doing so helped her to maintain her own emotional equilibrium. Her husband's role, often, was simply to listen sympathetically:

> Ed is usually pretty nice. I don't like to admit it, but he is. Sometimes, every now and then, I talk just to blow off steam. Today was a hard

day. I had to do the monthly statement, and that's an awful lot of figuring, and I was tired tonight. So I said something like, "I'm through with that place. I'm never going to go back to work. I'm going to give my notice this week. The heck with them." Naturally, I'm just blowing off steam. I'm fine ten minutes later.

There are other ways as well in which Mr. Desmond's presence sustained his wife's morale. Helping with child care was only one expression of Mr. Desmond's acceptance of equal responsibility with his wife for the management of their family. If he did not help with the housework, it was because housework was defined as not his domain. In the domains defined as his, primarily including income production, but also keeping the house in repair and maintaining its grounds, Mr. Desmond was very actively engaged. Mrs. Desmond did not have the single parent's burden of sole responsibility for meeting the bills, nor the single parent's need to worry alone about having the house painted or getting someone to reseed the lawn.

In addition, Mr. Desmond was a companion within the household with whom the evening's activity could be shared. And, as important as anything else, Mr. Desmond was a figure on whose commitment Mrs. Desmond could count, partly because their lives were so intermeshed, and partly because he had pledged himself to her, a pledge made the firmer by being recognized by all who knew them. Because she could take his presence in her life for granted, Mrs. Desmond could relax, be comfortable, and give her attention to other matters. Her husband was, for her, a true ally, whose capabilities were available to her not only in pursuit of their shared family goals, but also in her striving for her own security and satisfaction. One single parent described what it was like to be without such a figure:

> You know the kids love you, but they can't turn around and put their arms around you and comfort you and love you the way a husband could. And I think at the end of the day when you've had a really rough day, you wish you could just turn to somebody and be loved. Somebody who would say, "You're doing a good job, Hon, and I'm behind you all the way."

We have seen that the single parent who has paid employment cannot relax during the early evening hours because of the children's sporadic demands for attention; the hour or so after the children are in bed then provides an absolutely essential opportunity for relaxation. For the working married parent, the children's demands in the early evening hours are more manageable: there is another parent to absorb them. In addition, the evening hours, both before and after the children go to bed, are times for reaffirming the marital bond: for companionship and reassurance of mutual support. In consequence the evening, for the married parent, is not nearly so much a second job; instead it is a time for emotional restoration.

It is worth noting the contributions the marital partnership makes to parenting: help when help is necessary; support, understanding, and, in general, emotional sustenance; and a sharing of responsibility for the well-being of the family. Chapter Eleven describes the overloads to which single parents are vulnerable because of the unavailability to them of these provisions of marriage.

How does the working single parent get everything done?

Working single parents, like working married mothers, are doing about as much as they can. So long as they are required to cope only with their normal routines, they can manage, but they do not have time or energy for more. And yet, always there is more. A child becomes ill, the car breaks down, there are guests for dinner. The working married mother can say to her husband: "You have got to help!" What can the working single parent do?

The single parent may make someone outside the household responsible for some tasks: may hire someone to do housework; may send the children to grandmother's for the day. Or the single parent may make do with less; may learn to tolerate slap-dash housekeeping, may fix peanut butter and jelly sandwiches for supper, may give the children only a portion of the time and energy they require. Or the single parent may seek time-efficient ways of managing, like doing paid work at home.

Also, the single parent is not alone in the household; the children are there as potential helpers. The parent may ask a child of almost any age to help with housework, may ask an older child to look after younger children, and may encourage an older child to contribute to the household income through a summer job or work after school.

Home maintenance

Men who become single parents seem much more likely than women to contract out home maintenance tasks, to hire a housekeeper or cleaning woman or to enlist as volunteer help a mother or sister or mother-in-law. Men, more easily than women, can plead incompetence; they can claim that their wives have always dealt with shopping and cooking and cleaning. Or they can claim insufficient time, given the demands of their work. Women would have been responsible for home maintenance during their marriages, and although their work, too, is likely to be demanding, they may have much more question about giving the claims of work priority over those of home. In addition, a man who brings into his home a woman who will be a housekeeper can establish with the woman the same complementary relationship he had maintained with his wife; he remains responsible for income production, with someone else responsible for housework and child care. The woman who is a single parent, in contrast, would be relinquishing part of her accustomed role to whomever she brought in to help with housework. Men tend to express satisfaction with their relationships with the female employees or relatives who help them manage their homes; women, when they have help, more often comment on tensions.

A substantial minority of men consider a full-time housekeeper essential if they are to manage as single parents. Consider, for example, the urgency in the following description by one man of his search for a housekeeper. The man had been left by his wife to care for their three small children. He had no relatives in the city in which he lived.

> I went to every social agency in the city and the suburbs to find a housekeeper, to get some help. I got lots of sympathy, but absolutely no help. They would say, "We are sorry. It's a difficult situation. Can't you take off work?" And I would say, "Yes, I can. Will you feed my children?" It was a difficult situation for a man. I had a job; I could afford a housekeeper. Well, whether I could afford a housekeeper or not, a housekeeper was a necessity.

After a month of searching, this man did locate a housekeeper. He defined her job as caring for the children while he was away at work and, in addition, keeping the house in order. He shopped and prepared the evening meal on weekdays and looked after everything on weekends.

Almost all working single mothers, and those working single fathers who did without household help, learned to let some things go. Generally they skimped first on housework. As one woman said:

> You can't do everything. You can't work, cook, take care of the kids, and clean house. Something has to give. You just have to let something go. And, to me, letting the house go is more sensible than dropping the money part or the taking care of the kids.

The result is a less orderly and somewhat dustier house, and less frequently washed laundry. The single mother who, when married, had been a meticulous housekeeper has to learn to live with a lowered standard of performance. Another woman said:

> There's a lot of dust in my house, a lot of dust. You can write your name on anything. The living room is sort of picked up all the time because I don't let the kids play in the living room that much unless it's a quiet game. That's the only room I don't want messed up all the time. But the house is always a mess.

Managing a Household as a Single Parent

The tasks of home maintenance are highly elastic. When there is a great deal of time there is always something more that can be done: a room that needs painting, new curtains that might be made. When there is almost no time, the house can be kept going with an occasional sweeping and dusting. And, for those working single parents who have no help with home maintenance, this may be all they can do.

Child care

Some degree of contracting out of child care is implied when a parent of young children goes to work. The only exceptions are the single parents who work part time at the right hours or work at home. Bringing a housekeeper into the home contracts out not only a portion of the home maintenance package of tasks but also a portion of the child-care package. And, as was discussed in Chapter Two, there are a variety of other ways of obtaining substitute child care, all with both advantages and drawbacks.

Single parents sometimes feel guilty because they have had to give their children into the charge of other people during the workday. They may then feel doubly guilty as they recognize that when the workday is over and they and their children are at last together, they are too fatigued and too harried to be truly available to the children. One woman said:

> Working as many hours as I do, it kind of limits my daughter's time with me. And then when I'm home I have more to do than just sit around with her or run here or there running her around. I don't think I neglect her. It's just that she's feeling the cutback.

Working parents' relationships with their children are affected by the pressures of the job from the time they awaken in the morning. The parents cannot indulge the children's dawdling, for not only do the children have to get to school, but the parents must get to work. Later, in the evening, the parents will almost certainly be physically tired and may be emotionally depleted as well. A mother of two school-aged boys said that since beginning work she had discontinued evening chats with her children because she could no longer really listen to them. Another woman, mother of a seven-year-old girl and, ironically, a school librarian, said:

> Some days I come home and Annie will say, "Read me a book," and there is no way that I can read a book to her. I struggle with my guilt, because I haven't seen her all day, I've been away, and she is asking me to do something, and she is my child. And there is no one else around to pick up the slack, to read that book.

Mothers who do not work outside the home often give a good deal of time to arranging their children's activities: registering their children for soccer and Little League, transporting the children to birthday parties and hockey practice and after-school plays and then transporting them home again, and helping out as den mothers or members of a PTA. Working single parents have too little time for this. Particularly if there are several children in the family, working single parents may expect children of nine or ten or older to arrange to get to their activities themselves. Nor can the parent easily give time to den mothering or PTA.

A few working single parents try to be as available as they would have been were they not working. These parents are remarkable for their energy and organization, and for their devotion to their children. They are likely at times to find they have driven themselves nearly to exhaustion. One woman, a mother of five, with a full-time job as a secretary, described a noteworthy evening:

> I got in at twenty of six and from quarter of six on, it was like I was caught in a tornado. I had to get the two older to the drum and bugle corps, had to get the two younger to doing their homework, and then got the middle one to his religion class. And after that I had a PTA meeting. I was in bed after ten almost in tears, I was so tired.

Income

The widow who receives Social Security payments does not ordinarily consider herself to have asked the government to take responsibility for her support; the Social Security payments are hers by right. But welfare recipients may feel uncomfortable about having been required to request governmental assistance. And an uneasy feeling of continuing dependence is found among some separated and divorced mothers who receive support checks from their former husbands.

With paid employment, a single parent can have no question about being independent. Still, as we have seen, it can sometimes be difficult for the parent fully to meet job responsibilities and the responsibilities of child care. Single parents may find that they cannot get to their jobs on time if they stay with their children until the children are ready to leave for school, or that they must remain at work even though they feel their children need them.

Two women with whom we spoke solved these problems by working at home. One did computer programming; the other established a typing service. The latter often referred calls to other single parents who also did typing at home. Still another single parent about whom we were told arranged to do piece-work sewing in her home. Some single parents set up informal day-care centers in their homes; by caring for the children of other mothers they avoid contracting out the care of their own children.

There are disadvantages to all these cottage industries. The parents remain marooned within their households; their jobs, far from helping them get out, tie them even more securely to their homes. And if they are to give attention to their children during the day, then their work must be done at night. Yet for some being able to remain with their children through the day outweighs all else. Their work may not be what they would most want to do, but it is an arrangement that permits them to meet their other responsibilities. Here is an appraisal by the mother who did computer programming:

> I still have the whole day with the children, so I can still essentially be a mother. All I do is not go to bed at night until the job is done. Most nights I get to bed by midnight. Sometimes I don't make it until four in the morning. But right now it is the most reasonable thing for me to do until I get the kids into school, and then I can rethink the whole thing.

Income production appears to be the least elastic set of responsibilities. Housework may be let go with no damage except to the parent's internalized standards. Children may be given less attention, and although the parent may worry that the children are being deprived, the parent can argue that there is no help for it. But income production is likely to seem too important to take chances with, and jobs with the right kinds of flexibility are hard to find. If the single parent has a job that is good enough—not too far from home, with access to a telephone, among friendly co-workers, interesting enough and well enough paying—he or she may prefer to cut corners elsewhere rather than endanger the job by coming late, leaving early, or staying home with the children when they are sick.

Children as partners

There is still another way in which single parents can respond to having more to do than there is time to do it in, and that is by replacing their marital partnership with a partnership with the children. Almost all single parents do this to some extent. The way this develops and what it implies are considered in the next chapter.

CHAPTER 4

A Different Kind of Parenting

A special investment

All parents care about their children. But single parents who were previously married have special reason for devotion to their children: their children are all that remain of their families. In addition, single parents who are divorced may hope that success in parenthood can partially compensate for their failure in marriage, while single parents who are widowed can find in commitment to their children an opportunity to demonstrate continued fidelity to their marriages. Single parents who were not previously married will already have committed themselves to their children, first when they decided that they would not abort, and again when they refused to relinquish their children to adoption.

Children give meaning to the lives of all single parents. For many single parents, especially those with neither work they care about nor an adult partner, the children alone give meaning to their lives:

> I lived alone before I got married. I got married when I was twenty-six. And for all those years I made it on my own. One thing that I know very definitely about living alone is that after a while there is no reason to get out of bed in the morning. There is no reason to do a goddamned thing. And because of that, I think, I value the chance to be living for my kids. That is a reason to get out of bed in the mornings. It is a reason to care what my hair looks like. It's a reason to do everything. And that keeps me from committing suicide.

A Different Kind of Parenting

To be sure, all parents' feelings toward their children are ambivalent. A single parent may blame the children not only for the usual burdens of child care but also for the restrictions and distresses associated with raising children alone. This is particularly likely among those whose children remind them of a mistaken relationship. But ambivalence is often resolved by redoubled commitment, and parents who could find emotional justification for resentment of their children may end by displaying determined devotion to them.

Raising their children successfully—providing them with care, protecting them from danger, trying to ensure that their homes are happy —tends to become for single parents the most important goal. It is easier for single parents to focus their attention on their children's needs just because their familial obligations are obligations only to their children. As one divorced mother said, "I'm not a housewife any more; I'm a housemother." Some single parents take caring for their children as their lives' mission. Another divorced mother said:

> My children are my life. I have my own life, but everything stems from my children. . . . You could become anything you want to be, and if your children don't turn out well, it's lost.

Focus on the children's well-being sometimes expresses itself in over-protectiveness. Overprotectiveness may be particularly likely when the single parent has resisted other opportunities for emotional investment, and there is no other adult to whom the single parent is close. It may also occur when the single parent is, perhaps with justification, aware of the fragility of security. The following comment was made by a widowed mother of four children, the youngest a daughter, aged nine:

> I think I tend to be more cautious with the children since I've been alone. I'm more fearful for them. I'll think twice before I let them do things. I would rather take them somewhere than have them walk somewhere. Cecelia has these softball practices and I just have a fit and a half if she isn't home by a certain time. So I would just as soon go and wait.
>
> I just feel that if something ever happened to one of my kids it would be the end of me. I feel that I've gone through all the emotional strain that I can go through, and I don't think I could take any more than I've had. I can't remember being quite so overprotective when I was married, and I don't like to be so overprotective now, but I know I am.

Decisions are made with the children in mind. Often the children's needs, or what are thought to be the children's needs, are given priority over the parent's. Another divorced mother said:

> When push comes to shove and it's a financial thing, the kids come first. I moved into the neighborhood I'm in for the children, not for me. I probably would have been happier in the city where there are more

single people. And I joined a church for the children, not for me. I made a lot of decisions for my children.

After several years alone the single parent may be able to say with some pride "I've learned not to put my children's needs first all the time. I don't always put myself first, but I don't always put my children first either." But this willingness to give occasional priority to the needs of the self comes only after children have grown older and persistent self-sacrifice has begun to seem pointless. In the early years of parenting alone, especially if the children are small, single parents can rationalize their constant concern over their children by seeing their children as unjustly deprived. The children, after all, were not responsible for what befell them:

> It wasn't their fault that they came into the world. They didn't ask to come into the world. And it wasn't their fault that my husband and I split up.

Single parents may try to provide their children with whatever the children would have had under better circumstances, even if this requires sacrifice. One mother, for example, bought new clothes for her daughters rather than a needed new dress for herself, so that the daughters would not be penalized by her separation from their father. Another mother said:

> I don't want them to go without the necessities of life, not anything, shoes, a new winter coat. I don't feel that they should suffer for what has happened in our marriage.

Clothes, toys, and housing as good as that of their friends, and, in upper income brackets, private schools as well, can all be provisions to which single parents feel their children are entitled and that they will try as hard as they can to obtain for them. The sense of obligation to ensure that the children not suffer materially for their parents' errors increases the single parent's discomfort with reduced income and becomes one more motivation for the divorced mother's insistence that her former husband provide support at a high level. In addition, single parents are concerned that their children not be deprived of emotional security by the loss of one parent from their homes. Single parents who believe their children cannot count on their former partners may strive to assure their children that they, at least, can be counted on:

> I love my kids very much, and, while I don't try to make it up to them for not having a father, it is important to me that they know that I love them above anything else.

Like all parents, single parents become alarmed if their children seem to be troubled. But more than other parents, single parents may feel they have reason for concern. The children are likely to have been subjected to upset and stress in connection with the ending of the parents' marriages. Now the children live in households different from others'. The children may have been asked to assume unusual levels of responsibility for themselves and for younger children. For all these reasons the parents are alert to indications that their children are not doing well. Any questionable behavior—daydreaming, attention-seeking, unwillingness to go to bed at night—becomes a reason for worry. As one mother put it, "You are constantly looking for pathology." Some parents find themselves monitoring the extent to which their children display what could be interpreted as symptoms of loss:

> My son has really come out of it beautifully. He still, like when he goes to bed at night, he'll say he loves me three times, but it used to be ten times, you know.

Single parents find it profoundly reassuring to be told that their children seem no different from any other children. It was with the tone of having come through an accident unscathed that one single parent said, "You know, they are normal little kids." On the other hand, evidence that a child is troubled is deeply disturbing to the parent. One widowed mother of four, the youngest a boy of ten, said:

> My youngest might say something about somebody who was in the yard with his father. And he might make a remark, "I wish we had a Daddy." If I'm in the right mood, it's like a knife going through me.

Separated or divorced parents may examine their children's reactions for evidence regarding the soundness of their decision to end their marriages. One mother found that her son blinked repeatedly and worried that this was connected to her husband's absence: was her son, perhaps, holding back tears? Had she injured her son by insisting that her husband leave? Other parents find support for their decisions to separate if their children seem to be functioning well at home and in school, and even more if they seem to be functioning better than when the parents were married:

> He started his sophomore year just after my husband left, and his work at school just changed. I mean, all his school work was better. His grades are higher. Now whether that could be attributed to the fact that his father was gone and there wasn't any more conflict between them, I don't know. But he kept up his work and he is still keeping it up.

Often parents don't know whether they should explore the children's reactions to the new household situation with them or be tactful and permit the children to keep their thoughts to themselves. Some parents believe that children's memories are short and their attention easily distracted, and the less said, the better. Other parents ask leading questions—and, sometimes, encounter emotions for which they are not prepared. The following was reported by the mother of an eleven-year-old girl:

> I picked up something that was bothering my daughter. She looked very unhappy one afternoon. I said, "Are you upset about the divorce?" And she just looked at me. And I said, "Do you think if we had tried harder we could have made our marriage work?" And she sort of nodded. And I said, "You know, maybe you're right. I have to admit the possibility." And at that point she ran out of the room screaming, "Don't say that. Don't say that."

In any event, single parents tend to be alert, sometimes hyperalert, to their children's emotional states. They want their children to have lives no less secure, no less protected, and no less gratifying than those of other children. And since they feel their children may have been exposed to special stress, they monitor their children's responses. They may ask the children directly, perhaps hoping the children will say—as an adolescent boy said to his father after the father finally separated from the boy's alcoholic mother—"What took you so long?" Or they may only wonder what may lie beneath their children's apparently untroubled exteriors. A mother of a school-aged only son said:

> I am more aware of his emotional development that I am of anything else. I guess I'm very concerned about him, wanting him to be secure, to feel secure emotionally as well as every other way, and that just because he's without a father, it doesn't mean that he's a strange person or that there is something he did. I'm hoping that in years to come he will understand the situation, because I think it is difficult for him now. I think he knows we both love him. And yet he never questions, "Well, if you love me, why aren't we all together?"

Some single parents whose marriages have just ended believe it is helpful to their children if they inform the children's teachers. They may ask the teachers to join them in monitoring their children's responses:

> I've kept in close contact with the school because I figure even if I couldn't notice something at home the school would pick it up.

Other single parents, however, do not want their children to be stigmatized in the classroom and do what they can to discourage teachers and others from anticipating that their children will be different. One mother went to some pains to hide her status as a single parent from her children's teachers for fear that the teachers would begin to see her children as "products of a broken home."

Single parents who work may fear that their children are being hurt by their absences. Sometimes guilt for not always being accessible to the children persists, even though the children show no sign of having been damaged. One woman, older and with grown children, had worked from the time her children were small. Although her children seemed perfectly fine, she still worried:

> I should have been with them more. I should have participated more in Boy Scouts and Girl Scouts. They never said, "Why don't you? Every other mother does." They never said anything, even to this day. But there may have been a void there that I didn't see.

Another mother, separated for two years, worried that her small son had been deprived of something important by having spent his days in a neighbor's home while she was at work:

> It was a very hard decision to leave my son with somebody else before he was three. I wanted to go back to work but I didn't want to leave him at that young age. I feel sometimes as if he's been gypped. The other kids always had me here. I guess he's none the worse for it—not yet, anyway.

It is understandable that working single parents should choose jobs that make it easier for them to respond to their children's needs, jobs near their homes, especially. Indeed, mothers of small children, who had not been employed at the time their marriages ended may not seek employment thereafter because they are unwilling to be separated from their children for any part of the day. Their children, in their view, have already suffered the loss of one parent, and they will not impose on them the partial loss of the second.

Closer to the children

One compensation for being a single parent is that there is opportunity to be closer to the children. There is no second adult in the household with whom parenthood must be shared, to whom loyalty is owed, who distracts the parent's attention and discourages the development of separate understandings with the children. Now there is just the one parent and the children. A mother of three children, two of them not yet teen-aged, said:

> Dealing with another person in your life, your mind is going to that person, it's dwelling on him, so that you are not as close to the kids. I've gotten closer to the kids since the separation.

Another mother said, "When I was married I never felt any real relationship with my children, but now I do." A man whose two school-aged sons spent half the week with him said this about his relationships with his children:

> It's weird, but we are much closer than we would have been if I had stayed married. We just couldn't be tighter. It shows itself in lots of

ways. They are able to be more relaxed with me, more open with me, tell me about secrets, do things with me that show they are more at ease. And I'm much more open with them, more relaxed with them.

It is easier, when a parent is alone, for the children to win the parent's attention for their talk about friends and games. And, because it is only the children with whom the parent now lives, it becomes natural for the parent to discuss with the children what is to be cooked for dinner, what they will do on the weekend, where they will go on vacation. Now parent and children keep each other company, watch television together, provide an audience for each other's stories.

In a two-parent household, parents can bring their tensions and uncertainties to each other. In a one-parent household, the parent has only the children to turn to. And although the children's reactions are sometimes childlike, the children *do* react. Having them to talk to permits the parent to put words to a problem, to formulate it, and so to objectify it and make it available for examination. While talking to the children may not be the same as talking to another adult, it is better than talking to no one. And, as children become more aware of parental feelings, they become more capable of helpful response.

> Because I'm open with my kids, they're like two little adults. You know, I've shared my feelings with them, and I've shared my hurt with them. And they have seen me hurt. They have seen me cry. And they have said, "Gee, Mom, are you ever going to be happy again? Are you ever going to stop crying?" And I said, "Yes, some day, I suppose, I will."

As one consequence of this increased closeness, the single-parent family may develop a sense of common cause and of strong family boundaries not often seen in two-parent families. A widower with two small children described this feeling:

> My family is a very tight-knit group, a very closed shop. By closed shop I don't mean that it is forever closed, that it will not ever allow anybody else in, but for now it is closed. We're in there, the three of us, and we are terribly close.

The increased closeness between parent and children in the single-parent family is not necessarily the product of increased time spent in each other's presence. Rather it comes about as a result of a broader sector of interchange, as well as increased parental accessibility during those times when parent and children are together. Indeed, in households in which the parent is newly working or in which a separated parent has agreed that the children will live part time with the other parent, increased closeness between parent and children may actually be accompanied by a reduction in shared time.

In some single-parent families there is an increase in closeness in the parent's relationships with only one or two of the children. The older children, perhaps, become companions and confidants of the parent, while the younger children are treated as children are in two-parent families. Or one of the children maintains a position of withdrawal or antagonism that effectively confounds the parent's overtures:

> The kids don't have someone else to relay their problems to, so you hear the whole thing. They can't go to the other parent. But closeness—closeness depends on the type of relation you have with your kids. I have two daughters. With one of them I'm very close. With the oldest one I've never been able to get close. We're like fire and water. There is no way. I think it's the character. There are just certain characters that you cannot get along with.

Some parents and children are, for any of dozens of reasons, unwilling to be open with each other. Single parents and their children are not close in every case. Nor is the increased closeness found within most single-parent families incompatible with occasional tensions; on the contrary, the greater mutual responsiveness and increased mutual reliance of parent and child in the single-parent family makes it more likely that disappointments and disagreements will be painful and reactions sharp.

The ending of parental echelon

The one-parent family tends to be different from the two-parent family not only in the greater closeness of its members to each other but also in its structure and in the way it works.

Everyone understands how a two-parent family works, or at least how it ought to work. Mother and father are supposed to agree on how things should be done. The children need not be consulted; even adolescents may have little voice in deciding mealtimes and bedtimes and the chores that will be expected of them. Indeed, Blood and Wolfe, in their examination of household decision making in two-parent families, gave no role to the children.[1] The children may be permitted to organize and decorate their own rooms, but the parents jointly run the family.

Because the parents are jointly responsible for the family's direction, each feels pledged to support the other. Should there be no prior agreement on a particular issue, each parent is expected to respect any position assumed by the other, at least while the parents are in the presence of the children. In reality, one parent may countermand the other's directives or may collude with the children to frustrate the other's wishes, but behavior of this sort is understood as irresponsible and, perhaps, hostile in intent. In a well-functioning two-parent household, parents can count on each other.

An example may make the point clear. We will again draw on our interviews with Mrs. Sherman, the nonworking married mother whose day was described in the previous chapter. The Shermans had three daughters, the middle one Laura, aged five and a half. One afternoon Laura damaged some furniture and Mr. Sherman prescribed as her punishment a mealless evening. Mrs. Sherman did not agree but would not openly dispute her husband's decision:

> Laura hadn't had any lunch and I couldn't see a child going to bed without supper. I could see spanking her, but not starving her. Well, we all ate, and Laura never asked for supper. She can be just as stubborn as anybody. After we finished eating I said, "George, do you think we could give her a little bit of supper, because she has had no lunch?" And he said, "Do you think she deserves supper? And I said, "No, I don't think she deserves supper, but I think I ought to give her a little and make sure she eats it. What do you think?" And he said, "Okay."

As it happened, Mr. Sherman was scheduled to go out that evening. Our interviewer asked Mrs. Sherman why she had not waited until her husband left the house since then she could feed her daughter without opposition. Mrs. Sherman was shocked at the idea: that would have been going behind her husband's back.

Erving Goffman has given the name "echelon structure" to an authority structure in which an implicit partnership agreement exists among those on a superordinate level so that anyone on the higher level has authority in relation to anyone on the lower level.[2] The army maintains this sort of authority structure; so do hospitals; so do two-parent families. One-parent families do not. Without at least two members on the superordinate level, an echelon structure will not be formed; without the second parent in the home, the echelon system of the two-parent family collapses.

The absence of parental echelon permits, although it does not require, a parent's relationships to the children to undergo change. In particular, it permits the development of new relationships between parent and children in which the children are defined as having responsibilities and rights in the household not very different from the parent's own. Children now can be asked not only to perform additional chores—this would be possible within an echelon structure—but also to participate in deciding what is to be done.

The actual consequences of the collapse of the echelon structure of the two-parent household may vary with the level of demand for task performance to which the single parent must respond. If the parent is not employed, or has only one child and a job that is not especially pressing, the parent may not be forced to share task responsibilities. A working single parent, on the other hand—especially if there is more than one child—is likely to feel quite unable to do without the children's help. And since the absence of echelon makes it possible for the parent to redefine family roles and responsibilities, the parent is likely to decide that the children must not only perform a greater share of the family's tasks but must also accept responsibility for seeing to it that the tasks are performed. The parent wants to be able to rely on the children as fully participant in the functioning of the family.

Many parents report having called their children into a family council in which they announced to the children that now, with only one parent in the household, the family would have to be run in a new way, with every member of the family assuming a full share of responsibility. By earning the family's living the parents were doing their part; they would do more, of course, but the children would have to do their parts too. A substantial minority of the single parents we talked with indicated that a speech of this sort marked the beginning of the new structure of relationships within their households. The following report is from an interview with a mother of four children, ranging in age from about ten to about sixteen:

> As soon as I was on my own I sat down with the children—I always had a good rapport with the children—and I told them, "Now things are different. Instead of more or less being a family of mother and four children, we're all one family with all equal responsibility, and we all have a say, and we're all very important. And if it is going to work right, we all have to be able to cooperate with each other."

This is, in a way, a single parent's Inaugural Address. It establishes just how things will now be different. Here is another version, a speech made by a mother of three school-aged children just after she began work:

> I told them that I felt I was working full time and they had to help. And they weren't going to get paid for the jobs they did. It was just that everybody had to contribute. We were either going to sink or swim, and that was it. And everybody had to do their part.

Even if parents would like things to remain as they had been when they were married, they are likely to find that working full time forces them to require their children to share responsibility for home management. One woman, after separating from her husband, was left to care for five children, four boys aged nine to sixteen and a girl aged three. She did not work the first few months and during that interval asked rather little of her children. But after a few weeks of working she realized that her children would simply have to pitch in, and like other working single parents she insisted that responsibility would have to be shared:

> That first month I was working, I would walk in from work and they would all want this and that done, and I had left the house in a mess in the morning and I had to start getting supper. And I would be tired and I would get upset and might cry. And then the boys would say, "What's the matter?" Well, we had to sit down and talk about it. I said, "I'm tired. I'm doing more right now than I feel I can handle. You're going to have to help out. There are things you are going to have to do. You can set the table while I'm getting supper. You can help with the baby."

Once children accept the increased responsibility, it becomes natural for the single parent to consult the children regarding household decisions. If the family has to move, the children might be asked what they think of the new apartment; and if they are very much against it, the single parent might look further. The children almost certainly will be consulted about when meals should be scheduled and what should be served; it is so much easier to consult the children than to argue with them later. The children, in short, become junior partners in the management of the household. One woman, mother of two girls aged seven and five, said:

> We all make decisions together as far as . . . where we're going, what we're going to eat; or, if they go with me to the store, they help make decisions as far as things that I buy for the house. They make decisions on their own clothes, of course.

This parent later added, "Sometimes they dislike things I want them to get and I force it on them. But usually we agree." At least until the children become adolescent, single parents can become authoritative when they believe the issue demands it. Single parents generally try to get their children to behave properly by cajoling and nagging, but they can shift into firmness if necessary. As one mother put it, "My voice changes, and it's like, 'This is your *mother* talking!' " If the single parent has up until that point been treating the children as partners in the household enterprise, it may require something approaching desperation for the parent to become heavy-handed. Still, it is understood by all family members that the single parent is first among equals, the Chairman of the Board. It is to the single parent that the children direct their protests when they think the allocation of chores has been unfair, and it is the single parent who decides, ultimately, what the family will do. The single-parent family is hardly a perfect democracy. It is only more nearly one than the two-parent family. One mother said:

> I would have family conferences with the three kids and we would discuss whatever was coming up. I started that five years ago when we moved because we couldn't have this and we couldn't have that, and so we'd discuss what we *could* do. But my boy says to me that sometimes I didn't listen, that I always thought I was right.

A Different Kind of Parenting

The parent continues to carry ultimate responsibility for the family and to carry it alone. This may mean that the parent has to say that some issues are not family decisions—whether the parent should work, for example. But even when the parent makes the decision, the parent is likely to discuss the issue with the children and to do what is possible to reduce their objections. The mother of the two little girls, quoted above, described another incident that displayed the quality of parental leadership in joint decision making:

> Nellie is the older. During New Year's we decided to go visit my family, and we had this big discussion. Nellie wanted to ride in an airplane, but Helen was afraid. And so we sat down and we let Nellie use her calculator, and we figured out how much it would cost if we all took the airplane and how much it would cost if we took the bus. And Nellie said, "Well, it's cheaper if we take the bus." And I convinced her that if we did take the bus we would have more money to spend when we were there.

In most instances, single parents move quite far toward sharing responsibility for family management with their children. The allocation of chores ordinarily is decided by children and parent together. Here is how the allocation of chores was dealt with by one woman and her three children, a girl of fourteen, a boy of twelve, and a girl of ten:

> I said, "This is your house too. What do you want to do about the way it is run?" So we outlined the jobs that were reasonable for them to do and I said what I would do and then I left it to the three of them to carve up who did what. I let them do their own arranging.

To someone accustomed to the management style of two-parent households, single-parent households may appear extremely permissive. The parents give greater weight to the children's wishes than is customary in two-parent households, while the children, as befits junior partners, are less deferential towards their parents.

The parents are often unaware of how the structure of their household has changed. They may recognize that they are closer to their children and rely more on their children than they had when they were married, but they are less likely to recognize that their family is no longer hierarchical, and that they have shared with their children some of their decision-making responsibilities as well as responsibilities for specific chores. They may, therefore, be uncertain how to respond to others who say that they overindulge their children, that they are too permissive, that their children are not deferential enough. The criticism seems to them unfair, but they do not know how to combat it. Here, for example, is one mother's report:

> My sister told me that she thought I was too permissive with my children. I got very angry with her when she said this. Then I realized that

I am a lot more permissive with them when I'm alone with them than when there is another person in the house.

And yet the nonhierarchical single-parent family is very different from an overpermissive two-parent family. In an overpermissive two-parent family, the parents retain authority and responsibility while requiring little contribution to family functioning from the children. In the one-parent family, authority and responsibility are more nearly shared, and at the same time much is required of the children. Indeed, the indulgence of children's immaturtiy, which is one aspect of overpermissive two-parent families, is the very opposite of the insistence in single-parent families that the children assume genuine responsibility.

Not every single parent moves toward sharing decision-making responsibilities with the children. A few retain full authority, just as they would have had their marriages continued. To accomplish this, they must be able to maintain an image of what must be done without relying on anyone else in their families for support; it may help if they possess a certain rigidity of character. Here is a statement by a man who had been a strong family head before his wife left him and who remained firmly in charge of his home as a single parent. It might be noted that he, like other single parents, required his children to assume new responsibilities. He was distinctive in the extent to which he retained the right to say what should be done and who should do it.

As long as the children are here, they are going to go by my rules. And I'm a very hard man to get to change the rules. They have a little more responsibility now that their mother isn't here. I think that is a good thing, because they have to grow up some day and they might as well start learning a little responsibility now. But my children usually do what they are told.

Most single parents are not nearly so authoritative. They may have difficulty in defending to an outsider their practice of working things out with their children, but they have found that doing so is the only sensible way of managing their households.

Working parents and nonworking parents and the meaning of the children's tasks

Because working single parents realize that only if their children help can their households function, they are likely to have little guilt about expecting their children to assume responsibility.

A Different Kind of Parenting

> Now I am working a forty-hour week, and I come home in the afternoon and supper is on. I have the oldest doing it. And I find I don't feel any guilt at all making them do these things. I think it's great for them. They are a lot more responsible.

Whatever the children do is one less job for the parent. Even very young children can make significant contributions to the household. Children of only three can keep their toys in order. Children of four and five can make their own beds—although they may complain that the beds will only have to be unmade in the evening. Five-year-olds can help with the dishes. Eight-year-olds can vacuum floors and clean up a kitchen. Ten-year-olds can cook. A man with three daughters, aged four to nine, described how they helped during the breakfast rush:

> Each of the kids has a chore. Patsy makes her bed in the morning when she gets up. Shirley gets the cereal down if we are having cereal. Lenore clears the table and puts the dishes in the dishwasher. While one is in the bathroom the others have something to do. By the time we leave the house in the morning, the beds are made, the table is cleared, and the dishes are put away in the dishwasher.

One way in which a single parent may share responsibility with a child is by having that child care for younger children in the family. The following comment was made by a widow:

> My older son, even though he's only fourteen, realizes the difficulty, and he's very good in helping with the little one. He's a very conscientious, very sensitive kid and it helps. He does a lot with his younger brother. It doesn't take the place of his father, but it does help.

If the parent works full time, this delegation of parental responsibility may happen even though the older child is still quite young. Another widow said:

> Shirley was only seven when her father died. I went back to work right away. Then she was only nine when I first had to leave Glenn with her a couple of times on a Saturday, as much as I didn't want to. My mother would come down halfway through the day or something, but Shirley was forced into responsibility quicker than she might have been, sooner than I would have wanted her to be under ordinary circumstances.

Children appear to have mixed feelings about looking after younger siblings. Some resent giving up time they could otherwise use for their own affairs. A fifteen-year-old girl, the oldest of three children, noted with some resentment, "I feel as though I spent my childhood taking care of my younger brothers." And a thirteen-year-old boy is reported to have balked at babysitting for his younger brother because that task, if no other, was his mother's responsibility. But there are attractions in the role of quasi-parent to younger siblings. There is reassurance in being able to provide security for another, and increased self-esteem as a result of being the one in charge. There is also a temporary besting of sibling rivals. Indeed, sometimes single parents have to limit the prerogatives of an older sibling who is too inclined to be bossy.

Single parents who are *not* employed outside their homes are often willing to care for their children just as they would have had they remained married. Indeed, in the absence of anything else to fill their days, they may take on additional tasks around the house. One mother of two school-aged girls said:

> I think I do more of the things around the house now. I was the one that cut the grass this summer. My husband used to do it sometimes, or one of the girls would do it, but the girls were busy with school work and their friends, and I found I had the time, so why not do it? It wasn't that hard to do. So I did it.

Children in single-parent households very much prefer it if their parents remain home to care for them rather than go off to work. And yet, if parents share authority with their children—decide with the children, for example, when supper should be served—while retaining responsibility for performance of the task, the parents may risk feeling themselves to be the children's servants: the children decide what is to be done and the parents then set about doing it. The following story was told by another mother of school-aged children:

> They would complain about the laundry not being done or supper not perfect or whatever else kids complain about. Then one day Lillian put it in front of me. She came into the kitchen and asked me to do something. I said, "I don't have to drop what I'm doing to do it for you, and I'm not going to do it." I've forgotten what it was. It was something or other. She said, "Well, you should! That's your job! You're the housemaid!" She meant to say "housewife" because she saw the little housewife on TV and in her mind that's what I was supposed to do. She forgot the word. And I started laughing because of the word, "housemaid." Well, she was ready to pick a fight. She said, again, "You're the housemaid!" I said, "I'm not the housemaid."
>
> I went out and got a job. Now they understand that I am not the housemaid. I have another job and I have to earn a living so that we have food on the table and we have a roof over our heads.

Some single parents who are without paid employment, like many parents in two-parent households, assign tasks to their children not because they need the children's contributions but because they believe that the children will be benefited by responsibility. They want to foster in the children a sense of family citizenship together with a capacity for cooperative work. A child in any situation is likely now and again to slough off a task. When the parent has not truly been dependent on the child's contribution, the parent may be upset by the child's apparent indifference to responsibility but will not be dismayed because the task remains undone. The parent can always do it. Here, for example, is a report by a mother without paid employment of her reaction to a daughter's avoidance of a chore. The daughter was about seven.

> One thing I try to have the children do is make their beds, just to give them a taste of a little bit of responsibility. That hasn't worked out with Barbara because she forgets conveniently. There are days when she says, "Oh, I forgot to make my bed." And I know that she is full of malarkey, that she remembered, but she didn't want to be bothered. So I have told her that I will make a deal with her. She can have a nickel if she remembers to make her bed.

The mother here is skeptical but nevertheless patient and encouraging. Her reliance on bribery as a socialization technique might be questioned, but she clearly is as concerned with teaching her daughter work habits as with getting the bed made. One can easily imagine the mother deciding that it is too much trouble and letting the matter drop.

Single parents who have full-time jobs respond differently to situations in which children fail to help. Imagine a working single parent coming home after a tiring day, having stopped at a grocery so that there will be bread and milk for the morning's breakfast. The living room has not been picked up as she requested, but the real shock is the kitchen. The children have fixed themselves milk shakes and left the unwashed glasses on the kitchen table along with their school books and homework assignments. Some single parents would try to check their dismay and simply tell the children to get the kitchen clean. One mother at such times called her children together to contemplate her workworn hands. Many, perhaps most, parents would blow up. They would shout that the children must do what they have been asked to do, that the parent cannot do it all.

Sometimes these blowups are half-calculated displays intended to impress on the children that they must do their share. Sometimes the blowups are entirely genuine, quite uncontrolled releasings of accumulated tensions. In any event, the children learn, vividly, that they have been asked to help not in order to improve their characters but because their help is essential. The following report, though it described a response not so much to a responsibility unmet as to a new task created, suggests the potential intensity of parental reactions:

> With four kids it's not too easy to keep a house picked up. The kids do their share, but not overly so. They manage to keep things picked up, not like you would like it, but they have school work and social things and so forth, so I don't push. But I hate with a passion coming in to a dirty kitchen. It is just my thing. If a kitchen table isn't cleared, I loathe that. If I come in and the kitchen is a mess, I'll scream bloody murder. I'll raise Cain. I'll say, "Can't I at least come home to a clean kitchen? That's all I ask!"

If there is only one child in the household, a working single parent sometimes can forgo the child's help. Parents of only children may even discourage the children from helping out. They say that it is easier for them to do things themselves than to wait for the children to get around to doing them. This may be especially the case when the parent is the mother and the child a boy. Then by discouraging her son from contributing to the household's functioning, the mother can play a wifelike role, with her son a complementary figure from whom little household work is expected. This issue is considered further in the next chapter.

The children grow up a little faster

The ending of the parental echelon makes it possible for children to deal with their parent as a near-equal. Responsibility and authority may have been shared. The parent may occasionally have called on the children for companionship, understanding, support, or advice. In addition, if the parent is working full time, the children will have been on their own a good deal; the parent may have been available to them only evenings and weekends. Even children of nonworking parents occasionally will have been left in the care of sitters or relatives while the parents attended to family responsibilities or went out with friends.

The result is that children in single-parent households often become surprisingly self-reliant and adult in their manner. Single parents sometimes describe one of their children as "nine going on forty-nine." Their children are young, yes, but they appear mature. Adolescents, especially, may interact with adults almost as if they were themselves adult. One woman said, about her relationship with her fifteen-year-old daughter, "We talk on a very adult, one-to-one basis, because she *is* an adult. She is fifteen going on fifty." And another woman said:

> My son is thirteen, and, although I don't very often have adult conversations with him, there are times that we have conversations, about VD or something, that I would never, never have thought I would be able to have with a child.

Single parents sometimes say that their children have had to "grow up a little bit faster." Generally the parents think this a good thing: a kind of precocity deserving of respect. Indeed, the single parent may couple the expectation that the children will assume increased responsibility for the household with an expectation that the children will also become more self-reliant, more responsible for themselves. A mother of teenagers said:

> I think what happens to single parents is that they become more mature people, and they look at their children and they say, "Listen, you've got to do the same thing. You've got to grow up and you've got to be a mature person and learn to take care of yourself."

The absence of parental echelon permits the single parent to be more open with the children about the parent's uncertainties. And should the children's failure to understand the parent's concerns threaten to make matters worse, the parent may simply explain what the problems are. This is particularly true should the children want something for which there is no money.

> You're hit with these bills and who can you talk to about it but the kids? They're the only other people that you can really talk to. You have to have someone to share it with, and so you share it with the people that you're doing it for. And, every so often, if they're bugging me for something that costs too much money, that's out of proportion to what I can afford, I take the bills out and show them the bills, show them what we get in monthly, and say, "Now you make sense out of it. If you can do it and get that amount of dollars that you want, fine; do it!" And then they'll shut up for a while.

By the time the children reach adolescence they may be thoroughly familiar with their parents' worries about money. Sometimes the children become worried themselves. One adolescent girl spoke of checking the food pantry to reassure herself that starvation was not an immediate prospect; she was both chagrined and relieved to find the shelves well stocked. Where there is in reality too little money for the family's needs, children may contribute to their families' income, often paying for some of their own expenses from part-time, after-school work. Or they may join with their parents in economizing. The following story was told by the mother of a thirteen-year-old boy:

> A lot of times we live off what Danny makes on his paper route. After I pay the mortgage, the gas, the telephone, the food, buy the clothes, that's the money we have to live off. And Danny is really a super kid; he doesn't really mind.
>
> We had no money yesterday, absolutely zilch. I had twenty-three cents. Payday is Friday. And Danny wanted to go for an ice cream. I said, "Well, why don't we first go down to the store to buy some soap because I have a lot of wash to do." So we went down to the store for soap and we found the cheapest box of soap we could find. We got to the checkout; he had a dollar thirty and I had the twenty-three cents. And the soap came to a dollar fifty-three. I said, terrific, we have just enough. So then we went to another grocery down the way because I needed milk, and I had some food stamps so I was going to get the milk, and we found a box of soap that was cheaper. So I said, "Why don't we

return it? Danny, go get the soap, it's out in the car, and take it back."
So that's what he did. He got to buy a doughnut with the difference.

Children of separated and divorced parents often are aware of conflicts between their parents over money. Some children report that their fathers complain to them about their mothers' financial demands while their mothers complain to them of their fathers' unwillingness to help. The mothers may ask them to persuade the fathers to contribute more to their households or the fathers may ask them to tell their mothers to be more reasonable. One adolescent girl said, of the way things had been different in her growing up:

> You don't have—not necessarily the childhood—but you don't have the freedom of not worrying about things, of not worrying about money.

Yet adolescents seem to be pleased, on the whole, that their parents have acknowledged, even fostered, their capabilities for maturity. And they display enhanced self-esteem for having learned to manage by themselves—though they may regret having had to. The daily intervals of freedom from adult supervision they are likely to have had since they were nine or ten or eleven have allowed them to develop, along with a sort of responsible independence, feelings of self-sufficiency. Here is a comment by a sixteen-year-old girl:

> My mother works days, and I have to make sure that I get home when I say I will. And I do my share of the housework. Not as much as my mother would like, maybe, but enough. I have become very independent. I am an independent person. I'm a loner. So is my brother; we both are loners. I can probably get along by myself if I have to. Not completely, but if my mother died and I did not have to live with my father, I would probably go live with my aunt. And I'd be crying, but I could get along. I think it's because I already do a lot of things by myself. I suppose if I had both parents I wouldn't have to.

Contributing further to the self-esteem of adolescents, particularly girls, in single-parent families may be a sense of having developed skills not possessed by other children. In contrast to other children, they can cook, clean a house, care for themselves, and care for others. They may be slightly contemptuous of children who have not been required to meet the same challenges. Here is a comment by a nineteen-year-old girl:

> Where there is a father off working and a mother home taking care of the house, the kids never learn to do anything for themselves. It seems that they become very dependent on the mother to do everything. I think of my friends, like Bobbie. At least I've learned to cook a little bit and I've had to cook, like in high school, when mother wasn't here at night. But they've never had to do anything like that. And then when they have to do something like that, it's "Oh, my God, I don't know what I'm doing."

Indeed, some adolescent children of single parents see friends from two-parent families as having had an indulged and pampered life. Here is a comment by a sixteen-year-old girl:

> I get very angry at times, like, when I hear this girl. She said, "My mother yelled at me this morning because I didn't make my bed. And I am so upset today." And I just think, "You little twerp! I have to make my bed, my mother's bed; I have to clean the whole house; I have to cook the dinner; I have to take trash out!" And I was just so angry!

Even the most mature child is liable now and again to be childish. Single parents are sometimes surprised when children who have been functioning as young adults suddenly act their age. A widowed mother of three children, the oldest about fourteen, said:

> I tend to treat them as older. We'll sit down and we'll discuss something together or we'll talk together or something. Then they act like they should for their age and I have to get after them. And they're only doing what they should be doing.

Whether there is something lost to children in growing up faster is very difficult to say. Children who have had more to do than their contemporaries do sometimes regret the absence of a more nearly carefree childhood. And some children who have had to look after themselves from the time they were small may harbor unmet needs for nurturance. It may be that when these latter children become parents themselves they will be made uncomfortable by the dependence of their own children. But at least in the short run, as most single parents observe, there seems nothing wrong in growing up a little faster.[3] A mother of three children, the oldest not yet in his teens, described in this way the consequences for her children of living in a single-parent family:

> I have not seen any adverse effect. In fact, they have become a little more independent and more mature. Since I started working, they have had to pitch in a bit. Before that, I waited on them hand and foot, and that's not good for any child.

Role reversal and other role changes in the single-parent household

The changes in family functioning thus far described have involved modification in the roles of parents and children rather than fundamental change in those roles. The parents continue to be devoted to the care of

A Parent, Though Single: The Single Parent at Home

the children, although they may skimp on time spent with them; the children continue to rely on the parents as guarantors of their security, although they may be more on their own than are other children of their age; and the parents continue to be ultimately in charge of the household, despite sharing responsibility and authority with their children. But the single-parent family can also experience fundamental changes in the assumptions underlying the relationships of parents and children.

Single parents, when they feel unhappy or upset, often make their distress evident to their children. Sometimes they rely on the children for sympathy or support. And sometimes the children go beyond simply feeling sad because the parent is sad and feel that they must assume responsibility for helping the parent to recover. The children become care providers for their parents, supportive or nurturant or directing in the way that parents ordinarily are when trying to be helpful to children. This is role reversal.

Role reversal may be especially likely to occur during the troubled months immediately following the ending of a marriage, for it is then that single parents are most in need of comfort and reassurance and may also be most dependent on their children for companionship. One mother of two boys, aged four and six at the time of her divorce, said:

> At the time of my emotional instability I stayed with the kids and I really did draw from them a lot of strength. I'm not sure that was good for them or for me, but that was what I did.

Role reversals can be seen in parents' relationships with children as young as three and four. Here is an instance reported by a widower as having occurred a few months after the death of his wife. The child was four years old at the time.

> A lot of times in the beginning my son was like a father and I was like a son. One night we were sitting in the house watching television. I had kept him up late because I didn't want to be alone. And he said to me, "Daddy, let's play a game." And I said, "Okay." He said, "You be the Mommy and I'll be the God." I said, "Okay." And then he said, "Okay, you knock on my door." So I knocked on the door. He opens up the door and says, "Who is this at my door?" He's got the deep voice and everything. I said, "It's Mommy."
>
> And he brightened all up and he said, "Mommy, come in." And he pulled me in by the hand. And he says, "I've been waiting for you." And I said, "What is there for me to do here?" And he said, "Oh, we have baseball games, barbecues, picnics, birthday parties, and everything. And we're going to have a birthday party for you." So we had this imaginary cake and we had to blow out the candles and then at the end of it he just looked at me and he put his arms around me and he told me he loved me.

Role reversals may be encouraged by parents who are made anxious by the awareness that they are now solely responsible for the well-being of their families. One woman established a pattern of looking to her son for reassurance:

> If my fourteen-year-old sees me getting upset about something, he'll come over and say, "Now, Mom, calm down. I'll take care of it." And I really love that. When he does that I really feel good.

Sometimes children display concern for a troubled parent quite without the parent's encouragement. One mother had sent her two little girls to live with their father because she was so depressed. After the girls returned to live with her, the mother discovered that they had become alert to her moods and extremely solicitous. She told the following story:

> I picked the children up at day care and brought them home, and when we got home they immediately both went into the bathroom and I heard them saying, "She's in a bad mood." One is six and the other is five! Until I heard that I hadn't realized I was putting this trip on them. So I said to them, "I'm in a bad mood because I'm having troubles at work." And they proceeded to want to help me fix the troubles.

Occasionally a parent is disconcerted by a child's uninvited attempt at role reversal. This may especially be the case should the child try to take the role of admonitory adult. The boy in the following story was not quite ten.

> I called my house and Mark said, "When are you coming home?" And I said, "Pretty soon." And he said, "Ma, it's a quarter of eight. Now you had better get home here quick." And I said, "Okay, Mark. I'm just having drinks with a few friends." And he said, "Well, don't drink too much and be home soon." And I said, "All right, give me about an hour." And he said, "Are you sure?" And I said, "Yes, about an hour." And I got off the phone, and I said, "I did this with my mother when I was a kid! I'd call up and have to give these excuses! I'm still doing it and I'm twenty-nine years old!"

We do not know the effects on children of persisting role reversals. Children seem to take role reversals of brief duration entirely in stride. They seem to recognize that their parents will soon be back to normal and that it is just a matter of getting them through a temporary incapacity. There also is reassurance to a child in being able to take over the role of parent when the real parent appears to be lost in sorrow or paralyzed by anxiety; at least there is still a functioning parent somewhere.

More persistant than role reversals may be shifts from parent-child complementarity to a complementarity more appropriate in a husband-wife relationship. A change of this sort occurs when a single mother relies on her son to take on the responsibilities of man of the house—to care for the family car, to be in charge of household repairs, or to help in the care and management of the other children. Or it can happen when a single father relies on his daughter to act as woman of the house—to be in charge of housekeeping, to act as the hostess for his friends, or to help in the care and management of the other children. The shift is potentially more persistant because neither parent nor child may feel pressed to return to more usual parent-child understandings. Here is a widowed mother describing an instance of complementarity:

> I expect my seventeen-year-old son to understand that even if his friends don't explain to the plumber what happened, that in his particular situation he should do it, because a plumber will pay more attention to another male.

A child's playing a complementary role makes it possible for the parent to function within the role the parent may have become accustomed to in marriage. At the same time, it provides the child the gratification of earning the parent's respect, and the reassurance of being not only loved, but also indispensable. But because it can work so well for both parent and child for the child to play a complementary role, there are risks in the arrangement. One risk is that the child will be ambivalent about moving off into an independent adult life; the home situation can be too gratifying, and leaving it—and the parent—would make the child feel too guilty. And the parent may be reluctant to see the child leave. One boy who had long played the role of man of the house finally made his departure by joining the navy. His mother said:

> Bill was really the man of the house around here for years. Any kind of physical labor that I couldn't do, he would always just do it for me. When he went into the service I missed him more than I had missed my husband.

Another risk is that children with whom parents have established complementary relationships, or who themselves seek to establish such relationships, may impose themselves on their siblings in ways the siblings find unpleasant:

> My oldest son has taken on that role of being a parent, telling the others what they should do and what they shouldn't do and how he will send so-and-so to bed if so-and-so doesn't do this or that. He'll take on all kinds of responsibilities. I don't think it's good for him, because he's only eleven.

Quite intolerable for parents is a development in which their children act toward them as might a demanding spouse. At that point a parent is almost certain to say that complementarity has gone too far. The following story was told by the mother of four, the oldest a sixteen-year-old boy:

> Unconsciously I was asking my oldest, "Would you fix that for me?" Or, "What would you like for supper?" But then one time he was working after school and he said to me, "I expect my meals on the table when I come in from work." I said, "Who the hell do you think you are? You are my son and you will eat when I put it on the table!"

Instead of role complementarity, a child may display role competition and may attempt to displace the parent as the leader of the household. The parent is apt to feel threatened—and angry. A mother of three children, the oldest a thirteen-year-old boy, said:

> I find my oldest boy getting very bossy with the other kids and I have to stop this. I have told him that when he is the babysitter they have to listen to him, but other times, no. But when I am reprimanding one of the other kids he will come out of his room and butt in.

Sometimes it is hard for a single parent to distinguish between a child who only wants to be helpful and a child for wants to take over the parent's role. But generally a parent will limit the extent to which one child can act in a bossy fashion towards another, even if the parent isn't sure what is going on. A mother of three daughters, the oldest just entering her teens, said:

> In the beginning my oldest girl would get after the other kids and say, "Pick this up," "Do that." And when the baby would be outside, she'd say, "Get in here." And I would say, "Leave her alone. It's not your responsibility. I will handle it."

These developments in parent-child relationships—role reversal, complementarity, competition for familial leadership—are made possible by the structure of single-parent households. With no parental echelon to hold parents to their parental roles, with children becoming, in limited ways, both the parents' companions and their partners, there is no barrier to still further modifications of parent-child understandings. Some of these may be entirely acceptable to both parents and children as continuing arrangements; others are acceptable only briefly; still others are troublesome from the first.

Problems of management and control in the one-parent household

The structure and mode of functioning of the single-parent household make for distinct problems in management and control. Some single parents do say that their families are easier to manage just because there is no other parent with whom to argue about what the children are to do, and no opportunity for the children to play divide and manipulate. A divorced man who had custody of his two children, both school-aged, said:

Single parent means that there is only one person to discipline. They only have the one person to answer to, and that is me. They can't play me and Mommy against each other, because Mommy isn't here.

But this single parent was not nearly as authoritative as he presented himself as being. Like other single parents, he often found himself caught up in negotiations with the children. Since children in a one-parent household carry more responsibility than children in a two-parent household, they want to have more voice in family decisions. Indeed, decision making is likely already to be shared with them. And if the children have been used by the parent as confidants, if the parent has now and again turned to them for understanding and support, it will be doubly difficult for the parent suddenly to assume the voice of command.

Shared decision making seems to be an appropriate management style for single-parent homes; it provides parents with the assurance of children's understanding of what is to be done and their acceptance of arrangements; it facilitates cooperation within the household. But it does give rise to characteristic problems.

Single parents may have to insist that certain decisions are theirs to make or risk the children's taking over by force of numbers. If everyone has an equal vote on television programs, the set will always be tuned to the children's programs. Parents may have to insist that they can choose shows under some circumstances—or get two sets, one for themselves and one for the children. And parents may have to insist that their taste in home decoration will govern, except within the children's rooms:

Trying to redecorate a room with the kids is terrible, because if I do what I want and they don't like it, well, it's their home, too, and they have to live in it, so why shouldn't they get to pick the wallpaper?

Acknowledging children's equal rights in the household can sometimes result in the parent's relinquishing claims to common space. One mother was effectively moved out of her living room by her adolescent children. When her husband had lived with her, she and her husband would often sit together in the living room, chatting, reading, or listening to records. After her husband's departure, she felt she could not prohibit the children from playing their rock music on the living room stereo only so that she might be in the living room alone. So she regularly retired to her bedroom after dinner and left the living room to the children.

Children may question a parent's right to special privilege. If a parent intends to stay up late to watch a movie on television, the children may ask, "If you can do it, why can't we?" The children may expect that the parent will observe the same rules they observe, even though the rules were designed by the parent to govern the children's behavior.

We were having supper and the phone started ringing. Larry answers. He says, "I'm sorry, my mother can't talk. We're having supper." Because that was his rule, and he figured that the rule applied to me, too. It was my girlfriend, Linda, so I said, "Okay, Larry, tell Linda that we have a rule and it applies to me, too." But I would have talked if he hadn't answered the phone.

Or the children may ask why the parent isn't included in the distribution of chores. A mother of three daughters reported:

Marcia said, "One of us always has to do the garbage. Why don't you ever do the garbage?" And I started thinking, actually there isn't any reason why I shouldn't do garbage too and rotate my jobs with them.

The absence of a second parent not only produces a situation in which children feel justified in negotiating rules and chores but also, since the parent is without obligation to another parent to hold to a particular line, makes it possible for the parent to participate in the negotiating. Some children, recognizing this, seem determined to negotiate every request the parent makes, and parents are then left frustrated and helpless. A divorced mother said:

I can't handle discipline. I think that's probably why I have problems with my son. My daughter, who is eleven, doesn't give me that much of a problem. But my son, who is nine—it seems like no matter what I say, he's got to argue with me. And it just drives me crazy. I can't say one thing to him and have him accept it! He's got to come back and say, "Well, how about this, how about that, and the other thing?" And I'm just about ready to blow my mind!

Yet parents' dependence on their children as well as devotion to them makes the parents try to understand the children's point of view and to be accommodating if they can be. So, although the children may argue about chores, about when to come in at night, about baths and bedtimes and which pajamas to wear, the single parent may try to remain patient and reasonable. One mother of two boys aged eleven and eight said:

As a single parent you have to negotiate an awful lot with the kids. My mother was up this week taking care of the kids and she said I negotiate too much. "Don't talk. Just hit them." That's her cure for everything. Well, if there were two parents in my house I could make the guy the heavy. I'd tell him they've been bugging me, and maybe he'd give them a licking. I don't do it. Once in a while, when they really push me, I'll lay into them. But I negotiate more with my kids than I ever would with an adult. I always take the kids' feelings into consideration. And it's negotiation, negotiation, negotiation.

The absence of a second parent permits the single parent to accept children's proposals that, had a second parent been present, would have been dismissed out of hand. But now there is no one else to review the single parent's agreements, and so, sometimes against the single parent's better judgment, the child can gain the parent's assent to proposals of dubious merit:

> I was in the kitchen when I realized I had no cigarettes. I thought I would try to do without them. But after about fifteen minutes I couldn't anymore. I was just going out of my mind for a cigarette. Larry was there, doing his homework, and I said, "Larry, would you go to the store and buy me a package of cigarettes?" And he said, "Well, what's in it for me? Can I have a candy bar?" I said, "Yeah, if you want to rot out your teeth you can have a candy bar." "And a Coke?" He was trying to get the most for this run, right? He was working his way up to a car. I agreed to the candy bar and the Coke. I would have agreed to anything. I would have agreed to a car.

Single parents, like other parents, are likely to feel that parents are not supposed to be this way. Parents are not supposed to enter into negotiations with children as though the children were equals. They are supposed to be firm, though kindly; they are supposed to maintain clear standards of appropriate behavior, establish rules, and set limits, so that the children have the security of always knowing what is proper and of knowing, too, that the improper will not be permitted. As single parents observe themselves failing to behave as parents are supposed to behave, they feel guilty. They say, uncomfortably, "Sometimes I let them get away with too much. It's harder when you are by yourself. You give in to them."

But conflict with the children may impose a higher price on a single parent than the single parent is willing to pay. Here is a story of one woman's conflict with her nine-year-old son over the boy's refusal to do an assigned chore. The woman never did learn why her son would not take out the garbage on his return home from school. Perhaps he felt that because his age-mates didn't have to do this, it was unfair for him to have to. The woman tried punishment, and the turmoil that followed was more than she could tolerate. It was easier for her to take out the garbage herself.

> Matt is a hard person for me to motivate to do any chores. I don't know how to go about it. I guess I should be very severe and go through this spanking thing, but I don't. I don't like to yell and scream and have temper tantrums and go through all that with my kids. Sally, I ask her something once and she does it, and there's never really a whole lot of argument. Maybe sometimes there's some discussion, but it isn't a flare-up thing.
>
> But Matt, the first week I said, "You take out the garbage. You're supposed to take the garbage out after school." And he said, "I can't do that." And I said, "You can and will." And he said, "I won't." And I said, "Well, you get a spanking!" And then I spanked him, and then he had a temper tantrum because I spanked him. He goes upstairs and he slams his door, and I go running up the stairs and he locks his door,

and I say, "Don't you lock that bedroom door on me! I'm going to take off your lock!" And he refuses to open his door.

How long can you sit out there and stew? You can tear the door down, or when he comes down you can spank him again and stand over him and walk out with him to the garbage. But I can't. I'm not in the mood for that when I get home from work. I'm tired. It's easier for me to do it myself. I know it's a mistake. I really should be handling it differently. But I don't, and that's all.

When there is only the one parent, fights with the children can take so much of that parent's energy that it may seem to the parent preferable to avoid them. And the single parent may wonder whether punishing the children is really the right way to manage them; there is no other parent with whom to discuss the issue and come to some shared decision. Beyond this, punishing the children dissolves the sense of partnership with them that is so important for the single parent. It isolates the parent from the children. It means that for a time the single parent will have to act alone, without the children's support; the parent may, instead, have to cope with their resentment. The single parent, as a result, is likely to learn to overlook whatever can be overlooked. A mother of three school-aged children said:

There are a lot of things I overlook, because if I didn't, I'd be constantly disciplining them, constantly punishing them. So there aren't many things that get me uptight. When they are noisy or they do something foolish and it was an accident, what am I going to do? Take a baseball bat and beat them over the head with it? It's not a case of letting them get away with murder. It's just, what the hell am I going to do?

Women who were previously married sometimes say that since the ending of their marriages they have had problems disciplining their children. They may not recognize that the single-parent situation itself—in which the parent, without an adult ally, has become closer to the children and more dependent on their help—makes it more difficult for the parent to act authoritatively. Instead they may feel it is their gender that is to blame, that boys, in particular, just don't listen to their mothers as they might to their fathers. One divorced mother of two boys not yet adolescent said:

When Warner was there, the kids behaved better. I guess they feared him a little bit. They're not brats; they're not bad kids. I don't have any real problems with them. But if Warner said, "Shut up," they shut up. When I say, "Shut up," they say, "Oh, yeah? Make me!" There's a lot of things the kids do now that they couldn't do when Warner lived here, because they knew they couldn't get away with it, like giving me fresh answers.

Research as yet has little to say about whether women are right to feel that it is their gender that makes it difficult for them to command their children's respect. A recent study by Hetherington, Cox, and Cox suggests that mothers on their own have only limited success in gaining their children's acceptance of authoritative directives, but whether fathers on their own would have less difficulty remains an open question.[4] It may be significant that few of the men we spoke with in our various studies considered disciplining their children to be a very serious problem, and at least one felt that discipline was less of a problem for him than it had been when he was married.

It does appear that single mothers may have a somewhat more difficult time controlling some children, perhaps adolescent boys in particular, than single fathers would. But all single parents, fathers as well as mothers, may be less controlling—and less capable of being controlling if they wanted to be—than parents who are partnered. The single-parent situation inhibits parental authoritarianism.

On the other hand, many parents, both single and married, believe that physical punishment is appropriate with younger children to make them behave or "mind." But single parents (and married parents, under some circumstances), unable to call on another parent for relief and made desperate by a child's opposition, can find themselves suddenly frenzied, with the result that the punishment is oversevere or is accompanied by harsh verbal rejection. A mother of an only son, six years old, said:

> My son would do something bad and I would punish him, and he would pout or he would have temper tantrums. Or he would try to be loving, and I would not want him to be loving, so I would push him away. And then I would feel guilty. You know, I am rejecting him and he's going to feel it. Then I would get angrier and it would be just a vicious circle of anger and guilt. And after a while I would start screaming at him and saying awful things that I wouldn't say to anybody. You know, "I can't stand you. I don't want you near me. I don't like you. I don't want you." That's a horrible thing to say. But at the moment I mean it. At that moment I don't want to see his face. Later I realize I don't really mean it. I apologize and say I was tired or I didn't feel good. And I tell him that I was wrong. But it doesn't help. It has been said. He is still hurt.

The sequence of rage and remorse described here is one that could occur in almost any single-parent household in which the children are not yet adolescent. The children play so large a role in the parent's world that when things go badly, one or more of them tends to be identified as part of the cause, perhaps the only part within reach. Parents of small children may avoid punishing their children physically for fear they will lose control of themselves; parents of older children may forgo punishment entirely rather than risk rage and remorse. And when children are sharing responsibility for the household, meting out punishment to them may simply make no sense. But just as husbands and wives can turn on each other when a reason for misadventure must be found, so can single parents turn on their children.

A Different Kind of Parenting

If punishment is two-edged, hurting the parent along with the child, how can a single parent ensure that a child meets the responsibilities the child has been assigned? One approach is to nag. Here is the mother of an eleven-year-old only daughter:

> I find myself saying to her, "You've got to help me out. I have no one else who can help me." She's been given a lot more to do, and although she's accepted it a lot more, she's not fully accepted it. It really is a hassle if I have to nag her. And I have become a nag. She's been complaining that I pick on her.

Single parents may appeal to their children's consciences: "Look how much *I'm* doing for *you*." Or they may repeatedly remind their children that with one fewer adult in the household the children have to help. A father of four children, their ages stretching from primary school to nearly adult, described keeping his children aware of how badly needed their help was:

> Sometimes the kids can't understand why they should clean the garage or why they should clean the yard. One will say, "Well, he doesn't do it; I'm not going to do it." I say, "Hey, that's not the way the ballgame goes. Either we all work together or nothing gets done, because one person just can't do it all."

Many parents ask children who balk at a chore assignment what would happen if the parent decided not to do what he or she was supposed to do. Who would earn the living? Manage the household? Be there for the children?

One mother did go on strike. This woman's three daughters were all teenagers, but still she felt it took some courage to absent herself as fully as she did from managing her family.

> Laundry was piling up and the dishes hadn't been done and it was chaos. Rather than get mad, I put a sign up on the kitchen door that I was on strike until the following things were done. And I listed all the things that weren't done and had to be done. I said I wouldn't do any cooking and that they would have to clean up any messes they made in the kitchen and that I wouldn't listen to any bickering. I also said I would come off strike only if they got all the work done and didn't fight about it.
>
> At first they thought it was marvelous, cooking their own meals. But after three days somebody wanted to be driven to a birthday party and I said, "No deal." So then they got together somehow and they got the work done. It took three days. I did it a second time, but then they knew I was serious about it, so they did their jobs instantly.

Because single parents are so dependent on their children's cooperation, they have management problems different from those of parents in two-parent households. What are they to do when the children are less than helpful? Punishment can be disruptive, except when used in limited amounts. Parents can nag or cajole or point out to the children how much they themselves are doing. But perhaps most effective in gaining children's cooperation is the children's realization of how much their help is needed. (This means, incidentally, that children are most likely to be cooperative if the tasks clearly need doing.) The strength of the single-parent household lies in its shared recognition of interdependence.

CHAPTER 5

Different Children,
Different Issues

$\mathbf{A}$S ONE single parent noted, "What you do for one child turns out to be a perfect solution. When you do it for the next child, no." Children differ in many ways—age, sex, and temperament are only the beginning —and the experience of raising them differs accordingly. The number of children in the household and their relationships with each other make for further differences in parental experience.

We are accustomed to thinking of the development of children as progressing through phases: infant, toddler, preschool, school-aged, adolescent. We have no comparable terms for the phases of parenting. And yet, as any parent can attest, such phases exist. There is the phase of coping with a very small baby unable to communicate its needs except by whimpers or sobs. This is the phase in which parents are worried about feeding schedules, and about the baby's sleeping through the night so that they can sleep, too. Next comes the phase of taking the child for outings, of teaching the child use of the toilet, and of coping with the child's negativism. And this in turn is followed by the phase of supervising the child's play with friends and looking into nursery schools. And after this come the child's school years, each of them different, and then the high school years, each different again.

Rather than attempt to describe how the experience of parenting may change year by year, it seems useful to consider the phases of parenting in three broad groups: first, the phases during which children are not yet of school age and require the continuous availability of a parent or parent substitute; second, the phases beginning when children approach school age and continuing through their preadolescent years, when they move actively into peer-group society, develop social identities, and in these and other areas need parental guidance and support; and third, the set of phases initiated by the children's adolescence, when the children begin to move toward independence.

Phase one: Raising the preschool child

Very small children need adult attention much of the time. Three-year-olds can be permitted to go out and play, but only if the setting is safe and an adult can check frequently to make sure they are all right. Parents cannot permit them to wander off on their own. Nor are the children willing to be on their own too long. If there is no one else to look after them, children not yet of school age are likely to be single parents' constant companions. One mother of three children said about her youngest, a four-year-old:

> Edwin is my shadow. I can't even go to the bathroom without him. Wherever I go, he's along. If I go to the dentist, he goes to the dentist. He'll sit for three and a half hours. If he gets bored, he'll go to sleep. He would be in with me all day long if I let him. It drives me crazy when the other kids are at school.

Some single parents are lucky enough to live near other families who have children the ages of their children, so their children have playmates and the parents can, now and again, exchange surveillance chores with the other parents. Others live in settings where it is safe for children to play outside by themselves. They may be fortunate enough to have children who, despite the loss of one parent, are not driven to cling to the parent who remains. But under the best of circumstances a small child is a constant, inescapable responsibility, and the younger the child, the more this is the case. A woman with a one-year-old child said:

> Having a baby, the one thing I find is, it's a twenty-four-hour thing, seven days a week. There's no end to it. You know, you can go to sleep for the night, but she's right there, and you have to wake up during the night if she's crying or something.

The uninterrupted demand for attention and care that is presented by a small child can be extremely wearing when there is no second parent in the home to provide relief. Few parents can escape becoming dis-

Different Children, Different Issues

traught after days of taking the child everywhere the parent goes, evenings closeted with the child, and nights in which sleep is interrupted. A mother of two preschool children described the feeling of being constantly on call:

> You can't take a lunch hour and leave the kids at home, leave a two-year-old and a four-year-old in the house while you go to lunch for an hour. Being a mother is more than a full-time job. You don't quit at five o'clock. The kids go to bed, you still got to watch over them and worry about them. How many times do they wake at two in the morning with a stomach ache or sick?

When, in addition to requiring the parent's constant attention, the child is old enough to be negativistic or irritatingly demanding, but not yet old enough to recognize increasing parental tension and modify its behavior accordingly, the child may push the parent into sudden rages. Many single parents have experienced a kind of aggravation cycle in which their preschool children wore away at them by talkiness, testiness, and incessant claims on their attention, until the parents blew up, yelled, stormed, sometimes yanked or shook or slapped or hit the children. Afterwards the parents were remorseful and worried that they had inflicted permanent harm, if not on their children's bodies, then on their children's emotional development:

> Edwin can just irritate you. In little things. Most of the time I ignore him until I can't stand it any more, and then I put him in his room and shut the door. For a while there I did nothing but whack him real good.

Any single parent, no matter how loving under usual circumstances, may succumb to aggravation. One woman, for example, after she and her husband separated, devoted herself to the care of her two-and-a-half year old son to the exclusion of almost everything else. She said:

> Paul goes everywhere with me. I've never left him with anybody. I'm just concentrating on him right now. These first few years of his life seem to me to be more important than my own. I really feel that, maybe until he's three or four, he needs all that security and love.

But it is in the nature of two-year-olds that they are charmed to discover that they can define themselves by opposition, that they can control the state of the universe by using the magic word, "No." And so Paul's mother, devoted though she was, had gotten caught up in an aggravation cycle:

> At times I wanted to pull my hair out of my head. I've seen lots of kids, but he's got me baffled. He's a very difficult child. He's stubborn. And we seem to clash. He's just got me so buffaloed that nothing works. I have to restrict him in some things, but he gets away with quite a bit. And sometimes he just pushes me that far that I get so mad that I'm afraid I will hurt him. I never hit him on the bottom like they say you should. I just reach for him and I just smash him.

Some parents pledge to themselves that they will never hit their children, or that they will never hit them again. They may drop even thoroughly controlled physical punishment from their repertoire of sanctions. But until their children become old enough to learn when it is politic to stay out of their way, single parents remain vulnerable to rage, especially should they already feel overburdened at a time when their children become unaccountably irritating. Parents in two-parent situations have similar experiences, of course. But the uninterrupted responsibility, the absence of relief, makes the single parent especially vulnerable. Parents may barely be able to keep themselves from lashing out at their children even when the parents are entirely aware that they are displacing onto their children anger at their own situation, tension produced by having too much to do, irritation caused by events entirely unrelated to the children, and, in addition to everything else, resentment because they feel guilty for not giving their children the attention they need. Yet the parents want to be patient, understanding, supportive: all the things good parents are. And so they feel still guiltier, and still angrier. The following is from an interview with the mother of one child, a five-year-old boy:

> I come home and Sammy is at me. I'm trying to get supper and he's at me. "Mom, I'm hungry." "I have to cook it first." "But I'm hungry now, Mom." By the time I finish getting supper, feeding him, and getting the dishes done, and there is time for him, I could kill him. I don't want him near me. Don't walk into the room, don't say, "Hi," don't say anything at all, because I'll kill you if you do. And then I feel guilty because I know my son needs me. And then I get angry because I'm guilty. So I'm pretty furious at the poor kid.

A mother of two children not yet six spoke of displacing anger that should properly have been directed at her husband. Her self-control was not as good as that of the woman above:

> I really got furious at them and did physical acts to them. But it wasn't at them. I was mad at my former husband. It was displaced rage. I just took it out on the kids. It really didn't have anything to do with them.

Single parents who are especially beset may suppress so much rage that when their children exhibit willfulness blatant enough to justify the ending of parental restraint, the parents simply explode. It is as if the parents suddenly identified a child, or rather a willful, mean aspect of the child, as the enemy who must be defeated at all costs. The parents are carried away by rage. Afterwards, aware of how badly the child has been hurt, they may be almost frantic with remorse. A woman in her late twenties, with two boys three and five, said that her five-year-old was a torment, teasing his younger brother, dashing out of the apartment without her permission, running away from his grandmother when left in the grandmother's care. She went on to say:

> I'm not hitting him any more, because hitting doesn't work. And I don't like to hit him. I can't sleep nights if I hit him. I say the rosary and everything, just to get along with him. But I'll get mad and I'll hit him. And that's not the way to do it. I get awful bothered after he is in bed. Why couldn't I have talked to him like I should? There's a lot of reasons he's doing these things. But I don't think of that at the time. I just go wild.

One single parent, her children now grown, said that memories of having shouted at the children or, more rarely, hit them, continued to plague her. Her children seemed to be doing well, and yet certain incidents, recalled, made her shudder.

It is important to note that it is not every single parent, perhaps not even the majority of single parents, who experience rage and later remorse. And, certainly, parents in two-parent situations have similar experiences. Yet the single parent situation does seem to facilitate this development in the parent-child relationship.

A second problem, also shared with parents in two-parent situations but again more marked among single parents, is resentment of the restricted lives they must lead because of their responsibility for their children. Single parents who have no other adult in their lives to whom they can turn for understanding and support, for whom loneliness may be a chronic burden, are likely to become especially resentful. A mother of a three-year-old girl commented:

> I take her every place with me. I don't like the lack of freedom because I've never been tied down before. If the situation were different with her father and myself, I probably wouldn't mind it so much.

We noted earlier that single parents who, because they worked outside their homes, delegated responsibility for care of their children to relatives, neighbors, babysitters, or day-care centers might then worry that their children had been hurt by the separation from them. This is especially likely if the children when first left were very small. One woman whose only son had been cared for by her mother each working day and many evenings during the boy's first years expressed concern that she had damaged her son in ways that would display themselves only when the boy became older:

> At one point I think I completely abandoned Alex, except to feed him and take care of his basic needs. I was trying to handle my own self, and it wasn't easy. I used to feel guilty about that, very guilty. But now I say, hell, Alex's no worse for it. He was young enough that I got away with it. If he had been older, I really don't think I would have got away so easy. I could have had a lot of problems. And maybe I still will. I don't know.

A sense of being all-important for their small children leads some parents to worry that illness may make them unable to care for the children or that death may take them away forever. They see themselves, properly, as being of unique emotional importance for their children, in addition to being the only adults truly devoted to their children's welfare. Widows and widowers are especially prone to worry since they have witnessed how fragile is life. But the divorced, too, excepting those who have been able to maintain some confidence in their former spouses, are made uneasy by awareness of their importance for their children. A divorced mother of a four-year-old boy, her former husband a mental patient, said:

> I get a frightened feeling, "My God, what if something happens to me? When will he be old enough to take care of himself?"

Phase two: Raising school-age children

When children reach the age of six parents not only have the relief of having them in school weekdays but also can begin to feel less guilty for leaving the children alone or with a babysitter. The children begin to be able to use the telephone so the parent can be in touch with them even though away; they can take themselves to a neighbor's home if necessary; they can tell the parent if staying alone disturbs them or if a babysitter was disagreeable. They can begin to contribute to their own care. In addition, they can, increasingly, contribute to management of the household. And older children are often better attuned to a parent's emotional state and so are less likely inadvertently to push the parent into frenzy, although they are also more effective in opposing the parent should conflict develop. But if children's increased maturity diminishes one set of problems, their new engagement with activities and people outside their homes produces new ones.

A new problem for parents, as children begin acting in social roles as pupils, as Cub Scouts, as participants in Sunday Schools, and also begin to function as members of friendship networks in which there are birthday parties and sleep-overs, is that the parents may be asked to make arrangements for them, to attend some of their activities with them, to participate with other adults in directing the activities, and to drive them to meeting places or take them by public transportation. Also, because of the children's social participation, parents will repeatedly be called on to help the children decide what behavior is proper and, when necessary, to act in their interests.

It is not easy for children just becoming active participants in the wider social world to work out how they should behave. They are taught to avoid fights but to defend themselves, to be generous but not foolish, to be considerate of others but to maintain their self-respect. Sometimes the lines are hard to find. Parents, too, must find their way between requiring their children to observe social rules and restrictions and supporting their children's right to be themselves. Again and again the parent's own resources for dealing with conflict are under challenge, the parent's own understandings of social forms put to the test.

Here is a story of an ordinary neighborhood altercation. A single parent's child quarreled with a friend. Single parents, without allies other than their children, may be especially uncomfortable when dealing with such neighborhood clashes. In this instance the friend's parent was the first to enter the children's quarrel and the single parent was then required to respond. The single parent moved from cautioning her daughter to be respectful of her friend's mother to acting as an antagonist herself. The daughter in the story was nine years old.

> Katherine had this very good friend, Nancy, who lives a couple of doors down. Anyway, Katherine and Nancy got into an argument. The next thing I heard is that Nancy's mother is butting in, going to bat for Nancy. Her mother nails Katherine one day and says, "Why don't you stop picking on Nancy?" I said to Katherine, "Ignore her. Don't be rude. Stay away from Nancy if you want to, but don't be fresh to Mrs. Lindner." About a week later Katherine came in crying because Mrs. Lindner had said, "How come you are such a troublemaker?" So I called Mrs. Lindner and asked, "What's going on?" She said, "Oh, it is your Katherine." I said, "I think Katherine is acting more grown-up than some people around here."

Single parents sometimes feel they must oppose certain aspects of their children's character or modes of behavior. A woman who saw her son hit a younger child stormed out of her apartment to tell her son loudly and forcefully that he was never to do that again. Almost in a panic, a mother whose son had brought home a trinket he had pilfered hauled the boy to a nearby police station where a cooperative policeman lectured him on the punishments that await those who steal. As difficult for the parent as any other aspect of these incidents was that the parent had to act alone, without another parent's support—and, of course, without the child's support.

Insofar as single parents have become dependent on their children's support or are emotionally sustained by identification with their children, they can be sorely troubled if they must act in opposition to the children. The single parent who must oppose a child is relinquishing a valued ally. By the same token, when a parent can act on a child's behalf, and help the child manage what would otherwise be beyond the child's resources, the parent may be deeply gratified. Here is a story of this sort. The mother was about thirty and lived in a low-income district. Her boy was eight, the older of two boys. He had just been given a new bicycle.

> Pat was out on his bicycle. And these two kids pushed him off and took the bike. They are about thirteen or fourteen, but they are as big as I am. Pat knew who one of the boys was. I called the police and they were wonderful. They went right up to the boy's house. The boy wasn't home, but they told the mother about the bike and everything. That's all they could do. But I just couldn't let it go like that. So about nine o'clock—it was dark—I said, "Come on, Pat, let's go." I was going to that boy's house. And we were crossing the street by his house when I saw the two boys with the bike. So I said, "Pat, that looks like them." They threw the bike up against the wall and ran. Well, coming home, Pat, he didn't show anything. He just grabbed hold of my hand. That was his thanking me. And that was all he had to do.

Children's conflicts with institutional authority present parents with dilemmas. Suppose a school teacher criticizes a child for breaking school rules, or a shopkeeper tells a parent that a child is being unruly. The parent is pledged to the child's support and defense. Indeed, the parent is likely to be identified with the child to an even greater extent than would be a parent in a two-parent situation. But, on the other hand, the institutional authority may be right, and the child does have to learn to accept rules. And the parent, without a spouse, may feel unwilling to engage in conflict.

Some single parents choose to defend their children against authority partly because they *are* single parents and there is no one else on whom their children can rely. In one situation, a twelve-year-old boy was about to be suspended from school for smoking. His mother angrily criticized the principal, in the principal's office, for an arbitrary application of a frequently broken school rule (and then, against her will, she burst into tears). In another situation, a gym teacher, momentarily exasperated, had pushed a single parent's thirteen-year-old daughter. The mother told the teacher, again in a meeting held in the principal's office, that she would permit no corporal punishment of her daughter by anyone except herself. She threatened both a lawsuit and personal retaliation and was forceful enough to impress everyone who attended the meeting. We cannot know whether, in these instances, the school authorities had felt that the mothers' single-parent status gave them greater discretion in dealing with their children. But in each instance the parent suspected that this might be so and was determined that her child not be misused.

During the first part of this phase of parenting, roughly corresponding to the children's latency, parents continue to feel it necessary to arrange for a babysitter if they themselves must be away. Gradually, as children approach adolescence, parents are willing to experiment with leaving the children on their own. When children are about nine, parents begin to leave them alone now and again: after school, in the evening, for a

Different Children, Different Issues

few hours on the weekend. Parental policies differ. One mother of two children, the older aged nine, was uneasy if the children were alone during the day but was willing to leave them at night because at night they could not get into trouble. She said:

> I don't have a sitter at night. They are older and they don't need one. I don't worry at night, because they are in. I just hope they don't burn the house down.

This mother added that she tried to cut her evenings short so that her children would not be alone for too many hours.

Parents tend to be worried when they first leave their children alone lest the children be anxious or lonely. They worry, too, about what the children are up to; they especially fear the possibility of fire, and they caution the children not to play with matches and not to turn on the stove—unless, that is, they have begun to count on the children to do some of the cooking. If they are out in the evening, they tend to check at least once to make sure that everything is all right, and they try not to stay out too long. A mother of two children, the older a boy aged eleven, the younger a girl aged eight, had been leaving her children alone in the evening for some time. She still called them at least once when she was out and made it a rule not to stay out too long:

> I've been leaving them alone at night for the past two years. Not often, not once a week; I don't go out that often. And it is usually early evening. I'm not talking one, two, three in the morning. And I might call them to tell them that they aren't to watch any violent shows on television or stuff like that.

One mother's two boys, aged eleven and nine, frightened her by swimming in what she believed to be a dangerous place—a boy had drowned there the previous summer—and it was essential to her that she be reassured that the boys could be trusted not to repeat the adventure. Only then would she feel able to leave the boys on their own. It is noteworthy that she imposed no punishment. Instead, with the older boy, she did what she could to invoke his feelings of guilt and to elicit his cooperation. With the younger, she was as threatening as she could be:

> I went out for the afternoon, and my two boys didn't want to come with me. And I've trusted them on their own. When I came home, they came in the house and I was preparing supper, and the older one, Roger, said, "What would you do if you found out we were at the quarry?" And I said, "Swimming?" And he said, "No, just up there." I looked at his shorts, and they looked wet. And I looked at his hair, and it looked wet. And his eyes looked like he had been in water. And I said, "You were swimming at the quarry. Tell me the truth." And he said, "Yes, I was." And I jumped three feet. And I said, "Who were you out with?" And he said, "Gene," who is my nine-year-old, and two of the neighbors' children. And he told me they were hanging on to the edge of the

quarry. It's nice, clear, clean water and it's very tempting for boys eleven and nine, but there's no bottom to it.

So when we sat down to dinner, I said to Roger, "The only reason I'm not going to punish you is I'm very proud and I'm very pleased that you came and told me that you were swimming in the quarry, but I really don't want you up there swimming. It's too dangerous. You could drown." And he said, "I won't drown. I can swim." I said, "You're not that great a swimmer." But I got no response. And I thought about it and I worried about it, because being a single parent with all the job of maintaining a home, taking care of a family, working, my friends, my social life, I'm not home all the time. I'm in and I'm out. And I have to trust these boys on their own.

So the next day I said to them, "I didn't sleep all night, I was so worried and so nervous. All I kept thinking about was you two boys at the quarry. And every time I go out I think about the quarry." And Roger said, "Well, we won't go." And I said, "You know, certain things I can handle with you kids. You have a fall, need stitches, I can handle it. I take you in the car, take you to the hospital, have you stitched, and bring you home. But if something drastic happens to one of you children, I don't know if I can handle that. I feel as though things are going well with all of us and I just don't feel that you boys going up to the quarry would make me very happy." So Roger said he would never do it again. Gene was still. So I turned to Gene and I said, "And if you do go up, you will receive such a punishment you will never forget it. You will never get over it. Because it won't be for a week and it won't be for a month. And you know I don't threaten idly." So that was that.

As children move towards adolescence their parents must, increasingly, rely on their cooperativeness. They are still, largely, responsive to parents' directives. But the assertions of autonomy that will be an aspect of adolescence may already be foreshadowed. Increasingly, as adolescence approaches, parents will find themselves attempting to direct their children by appealing to the children's understanding and conscience.

Phase three: Raising adolescents

The coming of adolescence largely frees parents from dependence on babysitters. Now their children may be called on to act as babysitters for others. But, just as was true of latency, while adolescence marks the end of one set of concerns, it marks the beginning of another.

With adolescence both single parents and parents in two-parent families often feel that an external force has entered their children to make them suddenly unpredictable and unreachable. Issues of drugs and drink-

Different Children, Different Issues

ing may arise. Friends begin to have cars. New friends appear, engaging the children in interests and activities from which the parent is excluded, and taking the children away from the home. One mother said:

> The frightening thing is that when they are little you can lock the front door at night and turn out the lights, and you know they are safe and secure; you really don't have to worry about anything outside that is going to come in and be a threat to either you or them. But when they discover at the age of eleven or twelve that there is something outside, when they begin to have activities outside the home not only during the day but when they start going out at night, then you keep a vigil.

Adolescence can usher in a struggle over control. Children may have begun to challenge parents' ideas of appropriate behavior even before they were fully arrived at adolescence, but until they have moved beyond the early years of adolescence, they are comparatively easy to manage. Even single parents, despite their nonhierarchical homes and the absence of a second parent to help them withstand the opposition of their children, can hold a line. The following comment, made by a divorced father of an eleven-year-old girl, suggests what is possible with a child not yet adolescent:

> My daughter started junior high school and came home with a list of things that she was going to do now because she was a year older. She wanted to go out nights to the movies, things like that. I just told her she couldn't.

Adolescents are less likely to be acquiescent. Now the parent who has always been reasonable, if firm, can anticipate argument and the parent who lays down the law can anticipate rebellion. A mother of two adolescent girls, sixteen and fourteen, reported that while the girls had once accepted her rules about times they should be home by and parties they could attend, they now questioned the rules and the assumptions behind them:

> I have two teenagers and they've come to the point where they are questioning my decisions. It is a constant kind of battle between my moral judgment and their trying to set up their own moral code to go by.

It may be somewhat easier for widows or widowers to maintain a firm value position when dealing with adolescents' importunities. The widow or widower can, if necessary, invoke a parental echelon that no long exists in reality: can vote the absent parent's proxy. Here is a widow, almost incidentally drawing support for her rules from confidence that she would have her husband's backing were he alive:

> I like to know where they are, where they are going, and I expect them to be home when I tell them to. And if for some reason they can't, I expect them to call. I tell them, "It is not that I don't trust you, it is that I don't trust your age, because at your age you want to experiment." So I want to know where they are. And I'm sure my husband would, too.

A Parent, Though Single: The Single Parent at Home

Most divorced parents feel themselves to be entirely alone in dealing with their children. Even when two divorced parents have fashioned a reasonable working relationship in which each respects the other's parental status, only rarely can either speak as a representative of the couple. Much more often one divorced parent will fear that the other will find in his or her difficulties with the children a justification for criticism. For example, one mother reported that when she complained to her former husband (with whom she got on comparatively well) that the children were becoming ungovernable, her husband said, judiciously, "Well, the kids never give *me* trouble."

The usefulness, for a divorced parent, of being able to call on the other parent for backing may be suggested by the following story. It was reported by a woman who, while still angry with her husband, respected both his devotion to their child and his judgment in matters affecting the child:

> Our daughter was going through this girl-boy thing, and she's very young, only eleven. She wanted to go to a girl-boy party. My ex-husband and I sat down for about an hour one day and we made the decision that there were not going to be any girl-boy parties for a long time.

Children of single parents may be especially insistent that their parents respect their movement toward autonomy. After children have been treated for several years as junior partners in the management of the household, it can seem to them inconsistent, to say the least, for their parents to expect them to begin observing arbitrary rules as they become adolescent. One girl entering adolescence told her mother that it made little sense to her to be closely supervised at fourteen when she had been looking after herself and her younger brothers from the time she was nine. Another girl, fifteen, was irritated when her mother suddenly became untrusting of her:

> I get questioned about what I'm doing, and not only what I'm doing, things that I'm thinking and feeling and things that I don't want to deal with. I really resent my mother imposing on my freedom. I think it's because I was left to my own devices so early that I got used to handling things my way, and . . . maybe she saw too late that we were becoming too independent or something and now wants to have a finger in the pie to some extent. It is sort of impossible now.

It is more nearly consistent with their previous nonhierarchical relationship with their parents for adolescent children to be asked to join in establishing familial understandings regarding rules than for rules and restrictions now to be imposed on them. They can more easily accept parents' acting in an advisory role than in a directive or restrictive one. One mother, although she was very much against her thirteen-year-old daughter's having her ears pierced, found it politic to treat the matter lightly:

> Terry was bugging me and bugging me to have her ears pierced. Finally she called me at work and said, "I'm going to the doctor's. I've got my own $10." I said, "Look, Terry, do what you want. Don't let me influence you. But if you do it, of course I'll never speak to you again." So she didn't get her ears pierced.

In early adolescence, when children are only thirteen or fourteen, almost any parental approach has a reasonable chance of being effective. The children may protest, but they generally accept a parent's rules. At this point parents may be worried primarily about what they will do when the children become older. The following comment was made by the mother of a fourteen-year-old boy:

> I set fairly firm rules. If ten-thirty comes and he is not home, he knows darned well that he's grounded for however long he is late. If he is late five minutes, he's grounded for maybe one day. Grounding is about the hardest thing that I can put on him. And yet, I know that although right now my grounding him holds, there may come a time in the future when he's going to say, "Too bad, Mother, but I'm going out."

And, indeed, as children move further into adolescence, neither authoritarian insistence, unless the parent is very determined, nor negotiation appears very effective. At an earlier point than happens in other families, the single parent is likely to say, "I have taught my children what I believe; now it's up to them. They can talk to me if they want, but I can no longer direct them." Here, for example, is a comment made by a mother of two boys, one nineteen, the other seventeen:

> I've come to the conclusion that the children are responsible for their own actions. That is what I'm telling them. I brought them up in a certain way and have given them certain values. If they turn their backs on those values, then that's their business.

If the single parent is fortunate, the children's direction is a good one. But even if it is clearly a disaster course, there may be little the single parent can do:

> I have boys thirteen, fifteen, sixteen, and seventeen years old. The one that's seventeen, he's six feet already. And he weighs about 200 pounds. And when he comes in stoned, what am I going to do? He pats me on the head when he comes by. What do you do with him? My youngest says to me, "Why don't you do something with Phillip? He's stoned and so is the other one and you don't even know it!" I say, "I know it. What do you want me to do with him?" He says, "You don't do anything with him!" And I'm sitting there; "What do you want me to do?"

A request by an eighteen-year-old for parental permission is probably an expression of uncertainty more than anything else, since a child that age in most single-parent families need ask permission for very little.

> My daughter said to me, "I want to go away for the weekend with my boyfriend and another couple. Can I go?" Well, I can't give her that

permission. And yet, I can't stop her from going if she wants to. So I said to her, "I can't make that decision, because you're eighteen." I said, "I can't make that decision, because if I say 'No,' you're going to go anyway. And if I say 'Yes,' and you go and something happens, you're going to blame me. So I'm giving you back the decision. It is your decision to make."

As it happened the daughter in this story decided to stay home. But what is significant is the mother's appraisal that she could not control the behavior of an eighteen-year-old. This mother also had a fourteen-year-old son whose dating she felt perfectly capable of restricting.

Most single parents relinquish responsibility for their children's behavior toward the end of their children's high school years. Parents in two-parent situations can join with their spouses to attempt to direct their children's lives as long as the children live with them, whatever the children's ages. But single parents, for just the reasons they permit younger children a greater degree of independence, are more likely to accept the autonomy of older children.

Some parents discover that while they are becoming less invasive of their adolescent children's space and time, their children are becoming more invasive of theirs. Their children fill the living room with friends and high-decibel music, as a matter of course tune the television set to their programs, and appropriate the telephone. The children's tastes and activities begin to dominate the household. One mother of an adolescent boy said:

> I wish he'd bring his friends in more often because the stereo is soft when his friends are here. When they're not here you get blown out of the house. He brings a couple of friends in maybe once a month or something, to listen to records for a couple of hours. They go in the parlor and I'm either in the kitchen or in my room, which is right next to the parlor, reading a book. Except that I can't concentrate on my book because I hear them talking. So I go in the kitchen anyway.

No longer does the single parent have an hour or two of privacy after the children are in bed. Now the children stay up as late as the parent, or later:

> It was great when they were little. They would go to bed and that was the end. I would have my evenings just for me. Now they are not for me any more. I'm sharing with my son's friends or my daughter's friends or they are on the telephone or God knows what else.

The increased autonomy of older adolescent children often expresses itself in a sharp reduction in the frequency of family meals. The parent may prepare a family meal on the weekend and for the rest of the week permit the children to cook their own meals when they want them, insisting only that they clean up after themselves. But accompanying increased autonomy may be increased responsibility. A late adolescent may well be asked to take over cooking for the younger children or make house repairs or do the family food shopping. And many late adolescents are expected to earn money that can pay for their keep or be put away toward college tuition.

When the children were small they may sometimes have provided the parent with a measure of companionship, but hardly anything approaching the parent's needs. They may, on occasion, have been able to comment on a problem the parent was having with a neighbor or relative, or to respond to a room's rearrangement; but such moments of interchange would have been noteworthy interruptions of extended intervals during which the children were simply being cared for. Now, as the children move through adolescence, they become capable of serving as companions and sources of support. Their perceptions can be felt to be as valid as any adult's, their responses as useful. Here, for example, is the report of a mother of several children, the oldest a boy of seventeen:

> I will tell the older children things that I would not tell the younger ones because I don't think they can handle it yet. My oldest—I can sit down and talk to him and he will listen. If he thinks I'm wrong, he will tell me, and he will tell me why he thinks I'm wrong.

The children, too, may begin to see the parent as someone with whom they can share their problems, whose advice may be valuable. One mother described how her children were beginning to seek her out just as someone to talk to:

> I always wanted all the children to be able to talk to me. I've always told them if there's anything, you can talk to Mama. And they never have. They've come very slowly now to doing that. It's always been at the wrong time; you know, when I'm taking something out of the oven, when I'm concentrating on something. They've been doing that purposely. They'd like to talk to me, but they were kind of afraid, so they'd pick an inopportune time. But now that's going better, you know. They see me sitting with a cup of tea, just relaxing, they'll sit down and start talking. It doesn't have to be anything that is bothering them. Just talk, you know. I like that. It's good.

However, because dependence on the parent is reduced with adolescence, an adolescent child whose relationship with a parent is troubled, perhaps as a result of earlier quarrels, perhaps in response to a new figure in the parent's life whom the adolescent dislikes, can choose to move from home. Trouble in the relationship of parent and child can now justify their separation. If there is a second parent whose home is open to the child, the child may first threaten to move, then act on the threat.

Or it may happen that it is the parent who decides, perhaps after a particularly searing encounter, that an adolescent must live elsewhere and sends the child to boarding school or pays for the child to live with another family or, in a development that might have been unthinkable earlier, delivers the child's custody to the other parent. A woman who suffered from recurrent tachycardia told the following story. Her daughter was fourteen at the time.

> I never thought the day would ever come that I would be happy to see my daughter walk out of the house and go stay with her father. But I couldn't hack her any more. She was really being rude and I finally ended up picking her up by her ponytail and was about to drag her around. And then she whacked me, and that was it. I thought I was going to go bananas.
>
> I don't even remember what happened, except that my husband called and I told him, "You've got to do something with her. I just can't handle her. I don't know what I'm going to do with her!" I said, "I'm sick, and I'm not supposed to be doing dumb things like dragging this ninety-pound kid around by the ponytail!" And he said, "I'll come down tonight and get her." I almost passed out, him being so nice to me. And I was so happy to have her go! I was finally going to get some peace and quiet. I didn't feel bad or guilty or anything at all. I was happy!

On the other hand, the departure from the home of a child who has become a valued companion can constitute a new loss for the single parent. While the child is still at home the parent may subtly or directly communicate a reluctance to see the child go and may search for rationalizations for the child's attending a nearby college rather than going to a school farther away, and for the child's continuing to live at home rather than taking an apartment with friends or marrying. Although the child's prospective departure from home signifies, finally, an end of responsibility for that child, yet when the child is ready to leave he or she may have become more a source of support than a burden.

There are other reasons for regret, too, when a last child is ready to leave home. For some single parents losing a last child from home means the end of the parent's occupational role. This is particularly the case for a woman who has had no other work. Now the task to which much of her adult life has been devoted, the task of raising the children, is done. Suddenly everything henceforward appears anticlimactic. One mother said, after her children had left home:

> If I have a chance to go out, I go out. I can relax. But I don't want the freedom. I'm not a girl for freedom, probably. Maybe, like my friend said the other night to my daughter, "Your mother needs to be home with kids around." And that's probably what it is. I hadn't realized it, but the more I see my daughter's baby, the more I don't want to give her the baby back!

Different Children, Different Issues

Another woman had daydreamed through her children's growing-up years of the trips she would take when they were on their own. But when they did leave she discovered that she had lost the relationships that had anchored her identity. She felt herself without direction. She had no interest in travel; only in, somehow, reestablishing meaning in her life.

Just one child or more than one

The only child

If the single-parent experience is different for parents of children of different ages, it is different again for the parent of an only child and the parent of more than one.

The previous chapter noted the heightened importance of the relationship with children for the parent whose marriage has ended. When there is just one child in the household, that child becomes the sole recipient of this heightened parental investment. A mother of a four-year-old boy, in describing the nature of her relationship with her son, suggested how intensely focused on the one child the hopes and concerns of a single parent can be:

> I carry the responsibility for Danny financially, but he's helped me a lot emotionally. I don't know where I would be without him. He's made me grow up. He's helped me mature a lot. Because of him I think my goals for the future are more definite. He's helped me realize what responsibility really means and what it means to have a child and to know that he is dependent on you. And you have got to make sure that this kid's going to be all right, not just financially but emotionally, that he's going to grow up strong and healthy in all respects. I think when you're a little bit younger you really don't know what you want to do, and you figure, "Oh, well, I'm going to have a good time while I'm young." But I don't feel that way any more. My main concern is him and our life together.

The single parent of just one child concentrates on that child all the devotion that might otherwise be shared among several children. The only child can easily be seen as all the single parent has. It is also easier for the single parent to identify with an only child, to perceive the child as an extension of the parent's self, than would be the case if there were another child to demand the parent's attention and to produce children's quarrels from which the parent would have to remain disengaged. But the only child can also be seen as solely responsible for the parent's constricted life, the one reason the parent cannot travel, go out, take courses, have money, meet someone. The only child is the sole recipient of the single parent's resentment as well as concern.

We have seen that the absence of a second adult in the one-parent household leads to a diminution of the hierarchical character of two-parent families. The absence of a second child virtually erases its hierarchical character. Now not only is there no second adult with whom the single parent can establish a distinct parental level, but there is no sibling with whom the only child might have established a child level. Where there are several children in a family, the children sometimes act as subordinates do in echelon systems, despite the absence of a parental echelon. They exchange information among themselves—especially, if their parents are separated or divorced, information about the non-custodial parent—protect each other from a potentially admonitory parent, and tend to develop a sense of shared situation. With only one child, there is no vestige of echelon; the relationship of parent and child is the entire structure of the household. Parent and child can be as close as they wish, with neither required to consider a competing commitment to another household member. And, with no other child in the household, it becomes easy for the mother to interpret her relationship with her child as based on affection rather than kinship.

> Danny and I get along great. He crawls in bed with me at night and we fool around. I take him places. We fly kites together. I try to do the things that maybe a guy would do with him. . . . And we have a good relationship. We have a lot of fun. We bake cakes together. He loves to help me. He makes his own room up—does a terrible job—but he does it. And we have a lot of fun. We really do.

Because within the household the only child relates solely to an adult, and because the only child is likely to be treated as a near-equal by that adult, the maturity that is so often characteristic of children in single-parent situations may be especially marked among only children. For the same reasons, the sensitivity towards their parents that children in single-parent situations develop may be especially acute among only children. Indeed, because only children have no allies in coping with their parents' moods and because they are the only targets for their parents' discomforts, only children sometimes become hyperalert to their parents' emotional states. One mother of a seven-year-old commented on this:

> Sometimes I'm strict with Alex and sometimes I'm not. When I get too strict I realize what I'm doing and I get lenient. I get too lenient and I say, "Wait a minute. He's walking on me." And I come back very heavy. So Alex never knows if I'm going to be hard or soft. But he knows he can get around me either way. And he's sensitive. He's a con artist at seven years old.

In a similar way, the single parent may become highly responsive to the only child. The single parent learns to empathize strongly with the child's feelings. Separation from the child can become more difficult because the parent is so aware of its meaning to the child. A mother of a nine-year-old boy said:

> I think there is more work, really, if you have only one child, because you have to spend a lot of time entertaining him. When I leave my son alone now, although he is old enough to be alone, he is really all alone. Even adults sometimes don't want to be left alone. If I had another child his age, or even one two years younger, I might not feel so bad about leaving him.

The mother and only son

The relationship of single mother and only son easily develops aspects of the role complementarity of a marital relationship. Even though the mother may be working and supporting the home, she can relate to her son as to a well-meaning but not very helpful partner in the household, just as she might have related to one sort of husband. Her role as mother is little different from what would have been her role as wife: woman of the house, making a home for a male.

As is true of a marital partnership, the relationship of mother and son can be sustaining for each or nearly disabling, or now one and now the other. Nor is the mother entirely responsible for the course the relationship takes. Even a very young son is an independent actor, and often boys find it necessary to combat their mothers in order to foster their sense of masculinity. And relationships develop trajectories of their own, as participants respond not only to the present but also to what has gone before.

Mothers seem to bring to relationships with only sons the style they would bring to any relationship with a male. If in her relationship with a suitor or a husband, a mother would be giving, or helpless, or flirtatious, or moody, or competitive, or supportive, she is likely to display these elements in her relationship with her son and to sponsor the complementary style in him. But to lessen the discomfort that could be created by the son's responding to her as a mature male might, the mother may emphasize the still childlike and helpless characteristics of the son. She may discourage her son from displays of competence and minimize, by treating them as charming or cute, those behaviors in which the son attempts to assert himself.

Because the mother of an only son may discourage the son from full participation in the household does not mean that the mother is happy to do everything herself. Instead she is apt to be ambivalent, not only finding a sense of continued worth in the role of housewife to her son but also feeling resentful because she receives no help from him. And so the mother may simultaneously encourage her son to be uncooperative, perhaps half-recognizing that this is what she is doing, and feel annoyed at the result:

> Things that he could do for himself, I rush in to do. For example, cleaning up his toys. I can do it faster, so I get very impatient. I say, "Alex, clean up." He says, "Okay, Mom." And in the meantime he's got to finish setting his toys up before he can clean them up. Then I get aggravated and I go in and I clean it up, instead of telling him to do it. Now it is to the point that he expects me to clean up. He'll fool around and fool around until I go in there and clean up. I shouldn't do it. I should just get after him to clean up.

Or the mother may be inconsistent in her treatment of a son's capabilities. She may at times treat him as essentially mature, discussing problems with him and seeking his advice, and at other times infantilize him. One mother asked her fourteen-year-old son to advise her about insurance policies and then insisted that he not try to fix a window shade since he was all thumbs and she would rather do it herself. A mother of an eight-year-old son said:

> I baby him to an extent and then again I expect too much of him. I expect him to understand things that he really can't understand because he's too young.

As the only son approaches adolescence, the sexual overtones often present in the relationship may threaten to become evident to the mother despite her insistence that the son is, after all, only a child. The resulting anxiety may cause the mother to withdraw from the boy or become angry with him. A mother of an eleven-year-old boy said, "Sometimes he wants to cuddle, and I push him away." One mother we talked with recognized that she treated her adolescent son as younger than he was because she was made anxious by the sexual overtones in their relationship; but we found such awareness to be unusual.

Because the mother is so intensely invested in the one child who carries all her hopes, without whom she would be entirely bereft, she may become overly restrictive and overly protective. The following story was told by a mother of a nine-year-old boy. The mother's panic when the boy did not appear home at the time he was expected is not, perhaps, out of the ordinary. Her very restrictive reaction, however, is.

> One night he had been at a friend's. I had told him he could stay there until nine o'clock. He was to call me when he left the house and immediately come home. And he called me when he left the house, but he just didn't show up. His friend lives just five minutes away. So after it had been half an hour I called up, panic-stricken. I could just see, "Kidnapped child!" "Molested child!" "Frozen child!" You know, something terrible had happened. What actually happened was that he had told me he would stay out of the street because of the cars, and therefore he waded home through four-foot snowdrifts. And that's what took him so long. Except he also took the long way home.

> I felt he was testing me. And he really was very severely punished. And he realized I wasn't fooling around. Now he's not allowed out after school, period.

Following this incident the boy was required to remain alone at home from the time he returned from school until the time his mother arrived from work, an interval of not quite three hours. The boy did as his mother wanted. But because, as another aspect of his relationship with his mother, he was encouraged to display a premature maturity, he was not always deferential to her; onlookers were said by the mother to be shocked by his assertiveness with her.

The mother and only daughter

Relationships of mothers and only daughters develop differently. The mother can more easily identify with the daughter. The daughter is, like her, a female making do without a male: perhaps bereft, perhaps disappointed, perhaps disdainful of men, in any event required to forgo a male presence within the household. Even when a divorced and rarely seen former husband is frequently visited by the daughter, the daughter can be felt by the mother to be an emissary rather than a successful rival.

This is not to say that mothers and only daughters do not have quarrels. In one instance described to us, a mother's relationship with her ten-year-old only daughter appeared quite hectic. Yet, even here, the mother could identify with her daughter enough to see her daughter's point of view:

> I don't get along with Shelley and then all of a sudden I'll turn around and I'll realize, she's really quite a precocious person. She really wants her rights. She'll say, "Well, Abraham Lincoln freed the slaves, but who is going to free the children?" And I'll sit there and I'll just chuckle. The kid's got something there.

When only daughters become adolescent, issues of competition are likely to emerge. The adolescent daughter may want to stay up as late or later than the mother does, may be determined to win her point in debates with the mother, may measure her success with boys against her mother's with men. A mother of a twelve-year-old girl said:

> Recently my daughter and I have been having a lot of hassles. She's been battling me on everything. You know, real battles all the time. I ask her to do something and it's grumping and groaning. I've really blown up at her. And what she has finally admitted was she's trying to prove that she's bigger than me. She's hit this age—she's only twelve— but she's sort of challenging me. She doesn't want to take orders from me and she doesn't want to do things and she wants to prove that she's the big person in the house. But still the closet doors have to be closed in her room, and we go through this full rigamorole at night, with me

tucking her into bed. And at the same time she's going through this challenging and battling.

But it is not only daughters who feel competitive. Mothers may see in adolescent daughters youthfulness the mothers no longer possess. The mother quoted above went on to say:

> Jennifer and I went to a department store to get her a dress. Well, there were all these people in the dressing room trying on shorts and slacks and bikinis and tops. Me, I hate trying on clothes. I look terrible in all of them. And Jennifer looks gorgeous in this little dress. And all I wanted to do is kill her. It wasn't her fault that she looked adorable. So I get angry at myself and angry with her and angry with the world and angry with all these people who look good in shorts.

The mother of an only daughter, perhaps even more than the mother of an only son, is likely to have learned to count on her child for companionship. The competition that may then arise between them when the daughter reaches adolescence can make the mother doubly uncomfortable.

> Quite often the way I feel depends on the way Jennifer has been. If Jennifer and I have had a lousy time, I'm depressed, because I have nowhere else to express my feelings.

Given a mother who is likely to be lonely and, to an extent, dependent on the companionship of her daughter, it would not be surprising if she was perturbed by her daughter's increasing success in attracting male attention. The daughter's dating can highlight the mother's failure at the same time that it represents the loss to the mother of the daughter's company. The mother of a sixteen-year-old daughter told the following story:

> She'd been going out with this young man for almost a year. And I resented it. I was aware I was thinking, "Gee, how the hell did she get this kid?" I was thinking like a woman to a woman. I was able to say to her, "I know what is wrong with me. I'm angry at you because you've got a steady boyfriend, and you're going out and there's nobody to ask me out." And she said, "I don't know why you're so upset. You had your chance." And I thought, "You little bitch!" But she was able to say this to me because I allowed her to.

Although tension between identification and competition would seem to be a recurrent issue in the relationships of mothers and only daughters, resolutions differ. Some mothers do seem able to maintain proud identifications with their daughters, suppressing all feelings of envy. And we were told of one relationship of mother and only daughter in which, although competition was present, it took a rather different turn from that described above. The mother, a rather glamorous woman in her early forties, had many suitors. Her daughter, whom she described as plain, envied her mother's success with men. The mother worried about how she might help her daughter surmount her shyness.

More than one child

It isn't quite the case that two children are twice the work of one, four twice the work of two, and so on. With more children there is more housework, shopping, and cooking, but not that much more. And as the children become older they are increasingly able to help. But each child does need a certain measure of surveillance, of nurturance and caring, of attention. Each child needs a certain amount of parental energy, irrespective of the amount being given to the other children or the total amount available. And since children's needs are felt by their parents to constitute bases for legitimate claims, the parents try to respond to them. This is the primary way in which additional children make additional work. But also there will be each child's schedule to coordinate with the others' and each child's rights to protect when in conflict with the others'. When there are several children in the single-parent home, there is always something going on.

One divorced woman said that she would have felt comfortable asking a friend to look after her children if she had had only one child. But she had two, a girl aged twelve and a boy aged ten, and they would be, she thought, just too much work:

> I feel there's a great difference in having one child and having two children. I think that if I had one child everything would have been much easier right from the beginning, because it would have been much easier to find a friend who would say, "Yes, I'd be happy to take care of 'him' or 'her' as opposed to 'them.' " Two might as well be twelve. There's a big difference. Myself, if I were to volunteer, I'd rather take one than two. If there's two kids, you have to have four eyeballs. And it's constant work.

An interviewer in one of our studies recorded a few minutes of evening interaction in a well-functioning household of mother and four children. The mother was about thirty-five and had been on her own about two years. Her children were Mary Jean, thirteen; Katherine, twelve; Ralph, seven; and Doreen, five. It was past bedtime for Ralph and Doreen, and approaching bedtime for the others. Within the brief interval of our interviewer's recording the mother entered into a series of encounters with her children during which she took the roles of rule setter, disciplinarian, arbiter, and prize:

> KATHERINE: Doreen is playing with my checker game. Will you make sure she puts it away?
> MOTHER: I'll take care of it. It's getting to be your bedtime. Are you going to bed?
> KATHERINE: I'm finishing my homework.
> MOTHER: Then finish it, go brush your teeth, and get into bed. All right?
> KATHERINE: I have a lot of homework.
> MOTHER: All right, but make sure you get to bed by nine o'clock. Now what is Doreen crying about?
> KATHERINE: Mary Jean took her shoes.
> MOTHER: What?
> KATHERINE: She always does.
> MOTHER: Go tell Mary Jean to stop teasing her. Go ahead. Go ahead now, before I start screaming.
> DOREEN: My program was on television and Mary Jean wouldn't let me watch it.
> MOTHER (*calling out*): Mary Jean, I am getting aggravated with you.
> MARY JEAN: Why?
> MOTHER: You know why. And give Doreen back her shoes.
> MARY JEAN: How come? She said I could have them.
> MOTHER: You are going to get a licking. (*A few moments of quiet.*)
> MOTHER (*to Doreen*): Going to say goodnight?
> DOREEN: Goodnight.
> MOTHER: Goodnight. Throw me a kiss. Goodnight. See you in the morning.
> MOTHER (*to Ralph*): I asked you to go to bed.
> RALPH: I know.
> MOTHER: You are going to get punished if you don't. Get your fingers out of your mouth. Did you brush your teeth?
> RALPH: No.
> MOTHER: Well, go brush them! What happens when you don't brush your teeth is you get cavities, and I am not going to have any more dentists' bills.
> KATHERINE: Ma, can I have an orange?
> MOTHER: If there are any.

The children constantly challenge the mother's alertness. Should the mother permit a child to bend a rule? Should she intervene when one child teases another? If there is a quarrel, should she ally herself with one of the children? Nor do the children offer the mother much support. When the youngest child toddles off to bed the mother asks for a kiss, and perhaps for a moment feels valuable because this child clearly values her. But the mother had to ask for the kiss.

A common feature of families with more than one child is competition among the children for the parent's attention. Sibling rivalry, is, of course, a commonplace in family life whether there are two parents or one. But where sibling rivalry was already established in a two-parent

Different Children, Different Issues

family, it seems to become more intense with one parent no longer present. The stock of parental investment has been reduced and so the children fight all the harder to get what remains. One mother of two boys said, with some awe, "They did have fights while we were together, but nothing like after the separation; nothing like it."

The intensified rivalry in the one-parent home springs from the children's need for reassurance that they can count on the one parent still in the household. The children want to be reassured that no other child, not even a brother or sister, has a prior claim on the parent's commitment. The concern was made unusually clear in a family of mother and two boys, one aged eleven, the other aged seven. Mark was the eleven-year-old.

> Mark has brought this up two or three times. He says, "If an army invaded this country and a foreign soldier came up and he said, 'One of your kids has to die," which one would you give up?" I say, "Mark, I can't answer that." "I want an answer, Mom. What would you do?" I say, "Mark, I suppose what I would do is I'd let him kill me, or I'd try to make a run for it with you two kids, or I'd try to distract him. There is no way I could possibly answer that question. There is no way that I could make that decision."

> Then I'll tell him how jealous I was of my brother growing up, that all I ever looked at was what my parents did for him; I never looked at what they were doing for me. I was so busy watching the piece of cake that he got I never looked at the piece of cake that I got. And that seems to calm Mark down for a while. But then when it is really bothering him again, we'll go through the whole invasion-of-an-army routine all over again.

Generally when a rivalrous child is alone with the parent, the child is fine. It is when other children are present and receiving some of the parent's attention that the child feels the stirrings of anxiety. The child appears to feel a partial abandonment when the parent is attending to another child. The child may then react against the other child or, with anger, against the parent.

> If Maxine is in school and I have Nancy, Nancy is a beautiful child. If Nancy is asleep, Maxine is a beautiful child. I can relate to either of my children alone and they become like a friend, like a peer almost. But together, they are competing for my attention, and something blows up.

One mother of five children reported that for some time the quarrelling of her two adolescent boys upset her greatly. Finally, convinced that nothing she could do would end their fighting, she disengaged herself from the battle. She stopped trying to interrupt the fighting, avoided saying to either that he or the other or both were in the wrong, and simply withdrew. The struggle between the two boys almost immediately ended:

> For a while when they were fighting, I just got into the middle and tried to separate them, and that would make it worse. Recently I just made believe I didn't know they were fighting. They came right into my room and I just continued to read my book. A ruler or something went flying, and I just kept reading my book. And they said, "She doesn't even care!" And they went out, slammed a door, and that was that.

Despite the intense rivalry between siblings for the parent's commitment, siblings in single-parent families often rely on one another for support. Without a second parent in the home, siblings become more important to one another as potential allies. Single parents sometimes comment on the confusing phenomenon of siblings who appear to hate each other when they are inside the home becoming fiercely loyal to each other outside the home. Adults we have spoken with who were themselves raised in single-parent homes have said that siblings who regularly acted to blight their lives were also trusted confidants to whom they could turn when there was no one else.

In some multichild families the impulses that might otherwise be expressed in sibling rivalry follow another course. An older child, instead of trying to become the parent's favored child, may act as a kind of second parent to the other children. This can be as sustaining of the younger children as uninterrupted competitiveness can be damaging. Sometimes the same sibling will act both as parent and as rival, at times caring for the younger children and defending them from parents and outsiders, at other times attempting to disparage or intimidate them. The variations in expression between siblings of commitment and competition are many.

Nor is it always the oldest who is the sibling of greatest power. In one family the oldest of three, a boy about fourteen, had failed repeatedly in school, and in consequence was slighted within the family. The second child, a bright and active boy of about twelve, became the spokesman for the children and incidentally a defender and protector of the older brother. The second boy was clearly favored by his mother, with whom the children lived, and also by his father, a frequent visitor. With his place as favored son assured, his affection for his older brother, and perhaps his guilt toward him as well, resulted in solicitude rather than rivalry.

One compensation for the increased work represented by two or more children, in addition to the children themselves, is the recognition that bonds of affection have developed among the children and that each is stronger because of the presence of the others. The following comment was made by the mother of two children, a girl of twelve and a boy of nine:

> They have each other for moral support, and so far they have a fantastic relationship with each other. They are a great moral support for each other. And there is a lot of genuine love.

Different Children, Different Issues

The woman then congratulated herself for having had the foresight to have a second child before leaving her husband.

With more than one child a parent need not be concerned that a child will be lonely without the parent's presence. The parent may do without babysitters earlier than would seem advisable if there were only one child, alone. Nor is it necessary for the parent to talk with the child or play games with the child to provide the child with companionship. Having more than one child can be freeing of parental energies in some ways even as it is more demanding of parental energies in others.

There are still other compensations in having more than one child. Parents with more than a single child are able to recognize how different children are one from another, and so are able to feel less responsible for the development of each child. It is easier for them to see their children as separate beings rather than as externalizations of themselves. All their hopes need not be concentrated in just one child.

Sometimes parents identify with one child and not with another, feel close to one child and not to another. Why their relationships with their children should develop differently may be a mystery to the parents. Or, on the contrary, the parents may have worked out a variety of explanations. One child reminds the parent of the other parent—looks like the other parent or has the other parent's personality or mannerisms—and, as a result, inherits the parent's feelings about the other parent. Or different children are thought to have taken after different sides of the family, to have been different from birth, or to have been born at different stages of the parents' lives. One mother blamed overidentification for her ambivalance towards her elder daughter. The mother had been divorced about four years; her daughters, at the time we talked with her, were aged seventeen and fifteen.

> As I was growing up there were many things that I wanted to be able to do. I was a very plain child and I remember being very unhappy about it. So when I got my first child and she was a girl, in my mind she was gorgeous, and every part of my life that I did not fulfill, I wanted her to fulfill it. As time went on, she didn't fulfill any of the things that I missed. I wasn't too popular with boys; she wasn't either. All those things I wanted to do as I was growing up, when she started to go through it, it hurt me double, like a double pain, because I felt through her everything would come out beautiful and it didn't. So it was like a double failure for me. I failed once and I was going through the same trauma all over again.
>
> Now my younger one—when I got divorced, she was only eleven. And through the years I've talked with her. And she and I are very close.

The division of labor in the single-parent home is, of course, different when there is more than one child. With only one child, the parent may encourage that child to a role complementary or parallel to the parent's own. With more than one child the tasks of the household are apt to be parcelled out on the basis of who can do what. Sometimes chores are distributed to the children according to the children's ages and sex. The older children may be asked to look after the younger. The boys may be asked to do the work that is traditionally male: shoveling the walk in the winter, mowing the lawn in the summer. The girls may be asked to cook and clean and make the beds.

Where boys are the only children or the older children, they may have to accept responsibility for the chores that need doing, irrespective of their apparent gender-appropriateness. In one instance an older boy objected to making beds and running a vacuum cleaner, and his mother responded that traditional ideas of man's work and woman's work are really not suitable to the single-parent family. The boy was fourteen; there were two younger children, a boy of eleven and a girl of six.

> George doesn't mind at all cutting the grass and doing a man's work. All his friends do yard work and things like that. But he has to wash dishes; he has to hang clothes and bring them in. And he doesn't really want to do that. I've just said to him, "Well, by your estimation I'm out doing the man's job. I'm out working and supporting the family. So if you don't want to do 'woman's work,' then I shouldn't do 'man's work.' But if I stay home we're going to get awful hungry. And if you want a clean house and clean clothes, this is how it is." Well, he really has no comeback to that. And I said, "Besides, some day you may be on your own and you'll be able to take care of yourself, and, if you're married, you will be able to help."

When there are both boys and girls, and chores are distributed by gender, the girls may object that the distribution is unfair, that the walk needs to be shoveled only a few times in the winter, while the beds need to be made every day. And then the single parent may have to sit down with the children and work out something more equitable.

Despite its demands on the parent's energies, and its potential for rivalries and resentments, the family of parent and two or more children can, at its best, be a setting of warmth, closeness, and mutual support. And in their mutual interdependence, and their understanding that each is equal to the others in standing and responsibility (although the parent is clearly the leader), the members of the single-parent family can find affirmation of their individual importance and worth.

Different Children, Different Issues

Dealing with opposite-sex children

Mothers of boys and fathers of girls often regret that they are so little adept in the culture of the young of the other sex. Some make valiant efforts to develop interests or awarenesses they previously lacked. One mother commented:

> I had to learn the whole National Football League so I could at least talk to him. He asked me about Larry Csonka's score. I said, "Larry Csonka, who's he?" I had to start reading the sports page to keep up with him.

Even when a mother is able to share her son's interests, she may feel that her son is deprived because of the absence of a man who could share his activities, who could teach him to pitch a baseball or shoot a basketball, who would go with him on walks or take him fishing. Mothers of very young boys seem less concerned that their sons do not "have a man around," but once boys reach an age at which their interests are distinctly masculine, mothers seem to feel their own insufficiency.

> There are a lot of things now with Bobby that he needs a father for. He's nine years old and that's an age where he could really be a good friend to a father and do a lot of things with a father. And he just doesn't have that.

Mothers sometimes feel that their sons are handicapped in competitive activities because they lack a father's sponsorship and instruction. A divorced mother of two boys said:

> My oldest joined a basketball team. It was an evening thing. My feeling was that it was just a thing where the children went down and nobody can play, but what the heck, they would have a good time. Well, it wasn't that way. They all can play. And my son is at a disadvantage because he's never played. I can't teach him how to play basketball.

Fathers of sons seem to be expected to sponsor their sons' social activities in a way that seems much less true for mothers or, for that matter, for fathers of daughters. Fathers, for example, are expected to support their sons' efforts in Cub Scouts, Little League, and soap box derbies. Often these activities assume that fathers will be as involved as their sons. A divorced mother of an eight-year-old boy said:

> Jimmy is in Cub Scouts. It's a little hard that he doesn't have a father. He does have a father, but his father won't go to the Cub Scout meetings with him. He has to do a project on designing cars. One of my girlfriends' husbands helped him with it.

Mothers raising boys by themselves may exaggerate the extent to which boys in two-parent families can count on their fathers to be supportive of their enterprises. Some fathers are heavily invested in their sons; others much less so. The mothers are likely to contrast their sons' situation not with that of sons in the usual two-parent household but rather with that of sons in an idealized two-parent household. Quite possibly sons in mother-headed families are not, comparatively, as badly off as some of their mothers fear.

Fathers caring for daughters seem to be less concerned than mothers caring for sons that the absence of a same-sex parent will impede their children's development. But fathers of daughters as well as mothers of sons often appear diffident when called on to instruct their children in specifically sexual matters. Indeed, fathers of daughters may have the greater difficulty. Mothers can choose to be inattentive to their sons' sexual development. They can assume that prepubescent boys have no urgent need for sexual information and that adolescent boys have already learned what they need to know from their friends (although one mother of a precocious fifteen-year-old boy asked a male friend to assure her son that he could buy contraceptives from a drugstore despite his age). Fathers of maturing daughters, no matter how reluctant they are to discuss sexual matters with their children, are sooner or later confronted by the onset of menstruation. One man, a high school biology teacher, reported:

> The day-to-day running of life when my two girls were little was fine, until it came to the facts of life. Perhaps I'm a little bit better prepared than some men because I teach science, but I had problems when my girls were approaching the age when they were going to get their period. What I did was, I went to a friend of mine, a woman who was a doctor, and I explained the situation. I said I could tell the girls all about biology, but I couldn't show them how to use any of the pads or whatever. She came out to the house one night and took the older one aside.

Mothers as well as fathers feel uncomfortable in the role of sexual educator to children of the other sex. There is, to begin with, recognition that the topic of sexual behavior is nearly taboo between a parent and a child of the other sex. It may have been this recognition that led one mother to anticipate that any discussion with her son would end with both of them giggling nervously. But there is a second problem in trying to instruct a child of the other sex in sexual matters. Even though the facts of physiological development and sexual functioning may be communicated accurately—and this is asking a lot—how can a man tell a girl how to behave in a dating situation, or a woman tell a boy? Parents often recognize that instruction in sexual matters includes instruction regarding comportment and values and social expectations. And many parents are concerned that they may not understand precisely the culture of the other sex.

Different Children, Different Issues

The following comment, though not concerned with strictly sexual matters, may suggest the perplexity of a parent of opposite-sex adolescent children. How can a mother advise and direct sons, this woman wonders. A woman is simply not the figure sons want to consult about masculine behavior:

> I worry about the two boys now that they are teenagers. There's the drinking and the problems of dope and all that. It's harder for a mother bringing up boys, I think. You can't cope with all their problems. There are problems that they could sit down and speak to a father about.

But would a father in the household really make so much difference? Let us again refer to materials from our interviews with two-parent families.

The Millers have three children, the second a son, Joshua, aged sixteen. Joshua had made two friends about whom Mr. Miller was skeptical. One evening Mr. Miller asked one of the friends whether his parents knew where he was, and the boy said that they did. But later that evening the boy's mother called to ask whether her son was with Joshua, since she did not know where he was. Mr. Miller was disturbed by the boy's lying and asked Joshua to see less of the boy and also of his other new friend.

> From what we hear, those two kids are starting to get themselves into trouble. They sneak out of school. They tell their parents that they are going to be in one place and they're someplace else. And I said to Joshua, "If you hang around with somebody you're going to do pretty much what they're doing." The last time I brought it up he said, "Dad, we've already been over that ground before. You don't have to raise it again. You make me think that you don't trust me by raising it again." I said, "It isn't a question of not trusting you. I do trust you." But what I tried to get across to him is that if he's with a couple of kids who are doing something wrong, maybe selling drugs, if they are picked up, he's part of it. I explained this to him, and he understood. And I think the problem is resolving itself because he has pretty much disassociated himself from them.

The Millers both felt that had their admonishment come from the boy's mother it might have been discounted by the boy as unwarranted anxiety. Coming from the boy's father or, presumably, from any male emotionally important to the boy, the admonishment could stand as a reminder of the value of good judgment and trustworthiness. It would be an exaggeration to say that it is essential that a boy's sense of social responsibility be fostered by a man, and it is certainly not the case that boys necessarily resist their mothers' directives. But it does seem to be helpful to some boys of latency age or older if conscience is supported by a masculine voice. The mother of a ten-year old boy said:

He misses a male figure. He knows that I love him and his brothers and sisters love him, but he has always craved this male image. He had a problem of not taking a bath and not brushing his teeth, but my brother stayed with us for a while and—it was fantastic—it stopped.

Troubled children, troubled parents

Children in single-parent households often differ from other children not only in that they are members of a different family form, but also in that both they and their parents have experienced intense familial crises ending in loss. Those children whose parents never married are unique among children in single-parent households in having been spared both crisis and loss.

The child whose father or mother died will have lived through a time when one parent was hospitalized and the other preoccupied, when life seemed to be almost entirely absorbed by the parent's fatal illness. Or, if the parent's death occurred without forewarning, the child will have experienced sudden, inexplicable disruption of what had appeared to be a home as reliable as any other. In either event the child and the remaining parent will have been grief-stricken, and the child's development will have been affected by the further course of both the child's and the parent's grieving.

The child whose parents separated and divorced is likely to have been exposed to a series of events associated with the parents' dissolving marriage, including quarrels, tensions, and the increasing absence of one parent from the home. Many children remember times when their parents shouted at each other or were morose or wept. A few children remember violent scenes. One girl with whom we spoke witnessed a brutal attack by her father on her mother. As it happened, a friend was visiting her at the time, and so shame was added to horror.

Some children were taken by surprise by their parents' separation, despite having recognized the parents' unhappiness. Other children anticipated what was to happen only by putting together overheard snatches of parental discussion. Few children were able to grasp the full meaning of parental separation at the time the separation took place. All children, prepared and unprepared, younger and older, were deeply upset when the parental separation brought with it the loss of a loved parent.

For some children the loss of a parent, whether by death or parental separation, was followed by a move to a new house or apartment in a new school district and brought with it the need to form new friendships. For many children there was a changed financial situation, as a result of which their plans for their own futures may have had to be modified. When a mother who had previously been at home went to work, the children may have had to cope with her daily absence as well as with the more nearly complete loss of the father.

During the first year or so after the disruption of the parents' marriage, the parent who remained with the children will have been uncharacteristically preoccupied and is likely to have exhibited sudden shifts in mood. Eventually the parent may have become involved with new people and the children will have witnessed their mother going out with strange men or their father with strange women.

In addition to these quite special experiences, children whose parents separated or divorced are also likely to have had to learn to maintain relationships with parents who are mutually antagonistic. Children feel intensely uncomfortable when their parents seek to involve them in their quarrels. They dislike being lobbied by one parent to ally themselves with that parent. They also dislike being used as messengers who are told by one parent what to ask or tell the other. Some older children report, as minor compensation for having parents who have separated, that they can treat their noncustodial parents' homes as refuges to which they can escape should their own homes become intolerable. But often the value of noncustodial homes is reduced by the presence there of second marriages, perhaps augmented by second families.

Given these experiences, it may be surprising that children in single-parent situations manage as well as they do. Yet interviews with single parents, interviews and observations of children in single-parent homes, and the findings of an extensive research literature all suggest that some children in single-parent families do well and some do badly, just as is true of children in two-parent homes. Much may depend on the native resilience of the children and on the ability of their parents to invest energy in the furtherance of their well-being. And much may depend on just what happened to the child, at what time in the child's development it happened, and what resources were then available to the child. The parent who was lost may never have been a fully participant member of the family; the loss may have been cushioned by a caring older sibling; despite parental separation both parents may have remained fully accessible to the child. In these ways and others, the impact of loss may have been reduced.

However, some children in single-parent households do seem to have problems of a sort unlikely to be encountered in two-parent households. They may be fearful of further loss. If still young, they may cling to the parent who remains to them, not let that parent out of their sight, even to go to the bathroom, and attempt to tug the parent away from the telephone. They may appear depressed or anxious or in still other ways show that reaction to loss has become a leading aspect of their personalities.[1]

Among small children depression only occasionally assumes the easily recognizable form of sadness, pining, and withdrawal. More often, especially in boys, depression is masked by hyperactivity. The child may seem constantly in motion: squirming, darting, running where another child would walk. The usefulness of this syndrome as a defense against distress was suggested by one boy whose parents had separated: "Mommy," he said, "if I didn't run so much I would cry."

An overactive child can get into trouble anywhere. His teachers are likely to describe him as impulse-ridden. His attention seems always to be wandering. His playmates, with whom he is likely to be as impulsive as he is with adults, may fight with him, and older boys annoyed by him may react by bullying. At home he may find it difficult to tolerate the parent's attention being directed elsewhere and so he may interrupt his parent's telephone conversations and disrupt his parent's meetings with friends. He can totally absorb his parent's energies.

One of our respondents had been married to an outgoing, jovial man who had spent a great deal of time with their only child, Donald. When Donald was four, the father died. At age seven, Donald was overactive, aggressive with other children, and ceaselessly demanding of his mother:

> Once Donald gets home from school there is no time for anything else. He keeps me hopping from the time he gets home till the time he goes to bed. Either he is fighting with the kids outside or he's watching TV and saying to me, "Come look at this television commercial," or, "I want that for Christmas," or, "Mommy, can I have some of this?" Or, "Can I have some of that?" When he goes to bed I say, "Amen."
>
> He told me the other day that I was a mean mother. He said, "Your voice sounds mean." Well, I was hollering at him, and my voice did sound mean.

When Donald was with her, his mother had little peace. At one point his mother thought he was developing a cold and so kept him home from school:

> It was bitter cold Monday and I couldn't see sending him out. But it was a terrible day. He was racing around all day. He kept buzzing in my ear, "Mommy, let's do this," "Mommy, let's do that." We colored and we played *Password* and we played *Candyland*. And I was ready to hang him up by his thumbs. He just wouldn't be still. If I told him to go upstairs and lie down on his bed he would say, "No, you come with me." Or he would lie down on the couch and five minutes later it would be, "Let's do something." And if I got on the phone he was buzzing in my ear.

Different Children, Different Issues

The price of caring for a child who has this capacity to create disturbance often is a restricted social life. Here, for example, is a comment made by a woman whose younger son, also aged seven, was overactive in the same way:

> My brother's wife invited me for moussaka. She is Greek and she knows how much I like that food. And she meant for me to bring the two kids. But I wouldn't go if I had to take Leon, because he'd ruin her house. What he does here is one thing, but what he does in somebody else's house is different. So I thought I wouldn't go. But then I got my older brother to watch Leon and I went with the older boy.

In an older child, overactivity may be replaced by a kind of action-seeking. A mother of a ten-year-old boy said:

> He got into a little trouble about a month ago, breaking windows at a used-car place up here. He ended up at the police station. I tried punishing him and he jumped out his bedroom window and took off. It has gotten to the point that he'll run out the door if I try to keep him in for punishment. You know, you chase a ten-year-old, and he takes off, and you just can't keep up with him.

Single parents who have girls may have problems that parallel those just described. Girls, too, may react to parental loss by behavioral change. But overactivity seems less often to be a development among girls— although some do become rebellious. More often noted, among those whose father is the departed parent, is a tendency for the girls to attempt to ingratiate themselves with potential parent substitutes. Here is a mother of two girls talking about the older, now fifteen, but only six when the mother sent the father away:

> Edith used to follow any man that came in the house. It was like she was looking for a substitute for her father or something. There was this guy I knew that was divorced, who used to drop in to visit. And Edith would be all over him, sitting on his lap and making up to him and stuff like that. She doesn't do it any more. Whether she worked it out in her own mind or not, I don't really know.

Sometimes, when their parents have separated or divorced, girls as well as boys exhibit loyalty to the parent with whom they are not living by representing that parent within their household. They find fault with the parent who is caring for them or quarrel with that parent in the way the absent parent would have. A single parent whose emotional resources are already stretched may be little inclined to respond to internal opposition of this sort with tolerant understanding.

It is easy to see how a troubled child can exasperate and enrage a single parent. Not only does the troubled child absorb the parent's energy, isolate the parent, and at times wound the parent morally if not physically, but in addition the troubled child is evidence that the parent has once again failed. Here, again, is a situation in which the parent's self-control may be tested. One woman, mother of a thirteen-year-old boy, said that her son was unrelenting in his opposition to her. The following incident led her to obtain psychiatric help for herself and her son:

> One time we were in the cellar and I got so upset that I grabbed him and I pinned him down on the floor. He is a strong boy, but he still is a little bit smaller than I am. I put him on the floor and I just held him there and all I could think of was, "My God, I'm going to hurt him." I was afraid that I would seriously hurt my own son.

These situations, in which a child in difficulty produces tension and chaos like that of a strife-filled marriage, occur in only a small minority of single-parent homes. But just as a troubled parent makes for a troubled child, so a troubled child can make for a troubled parent.

CHAPTER 6

The Other Parent

I F WE EXCEPT those who became parents through formal or informal adoption, all single parents were once partnered. The partnerships of widows and widowers will have been ended by the deaths of the husbands or wives and the partnerships of unmarried mothers will have been informal and, in some instances, brief. But what of the partnerships of the separated and divorced? Does having had five or ten years of shared commitment to raising children together ensure a continued sense of partnership after the marriage ends?

In general, it does not. There is continued linkage, at least insofar as the parent without custody continues to see the children and to provide in some measure for their support. But only rarely is there partnership in the sense of integration of effort toward the achievement of a shared goal. Indeed, among the afflictions of those single parents who are separated or divorced is that they must tolerate the continued presence in their children's lives, and therefore in their own, of parents who are no longer partners.

From partner to children's visitor

When a couple are married, even unhappily, though they may dispute with each other or withdraw from each other in hurt silence, they are understood by themselves and others to be partnered. They live in the same home; they subsist on the same income; they are jointly responsible for debts, relationships with neighbors, and the upbringing of their children. They must inform each other if something has happened or will happen to change the character of their lives or of their children's lives. Whether they get along or not, they are co-directors of a shared enterprise.

When a household breaks up, the foundations of the marital partnership are lost. Now husband and wife live in different homes, have separate incomes, maintain relationships with the children from which the other is excluded, and have routines that intermesh only when the parent without custody visits the children. In addition, husband or wife or both may want every aspect of the relationship, including its partnership aspect, brought as near to an end as possible. It is enough if only one member of the couple feels this way:

> He picks the children up outside. We tried it with him coming in the house and he wouldn't leave. He might go through the house and question this and that or look into this or that, and there would be a commotion, an argument. I think he felt that this was his home, his wife, his children.

Some couples, despite separation, do maintain some vestige of partnership. For example, the parent caring for the children may be able to ask the other parent to help out by taking the children temporarily. And so a father who does not have custody of the children may take them for a weekend or a week to give his former wife a breather, to permit her to go on vacation, to paint and furnish an apartment, or to recover from illness. One woman, divorced two years, said:

> My ex-husband usually has a chunk of four days off at Thanksgiving, so I'm seriously considering saying, "If you're going to take them for four days like you did this year, how about arranging for an extra three days with a babysitter? Can you take them for the seven days while I go off on a trip?" We have a type of relationship where I feel I can ask this sort of thing. I'm asking a favor.

After a marital separation, to ask for help from the former spouse is to ask a favor. Before the marriage ended, the father would have been responsible for helping make the family work. If this required that he look after the children for a time, that too would have been his responsibility. After the end of the marriage he can, if he wishes, say that he would rather not. The same holds true for fixing a leaky faucet when he comes to see the children or offering an opinion on a balky car: he need not accede to the request. The marital partnership is over. A woman separated about a month said:

> I've asked him to help me with little petty things and it's just a waste of time. Like the kid's bike broke, and I'm not a mechanic. So I called

him up and I said, "Henry's pedal broke. I don't know if it's the threads are worn or what." So he says, "What do you want me to do about it?" And I said, "I just thought maybe you knew something about it. You're an engineer. Aren't you supposed to know about things like that?" And then I said, "The hell with you! I'll get a goddamned book out of the library and do it myself."

Parents who are no longer married to each other sometimes agree to maintain the appearance of partnership for special occasions. They suppress their antagonism when together with the children or present themselves as a couple when attending a child's graduation. A separated father was requested by his nineteen-year-old daughter to attend the daughter's wedding and the mother, though irritated, was forced to join with the father in the role of parents of the bride. But either parent may disclaim the image of continued partnership the other may hope to project.

Ross came to see Maureen when she was sick and in the hospital. I was there, and I wanted to make his visit nice for Maureen. I wasn't trying to pretend to be a family or anything, but I was just saying to him, "This went on today with her, and this is how she felt." And her older brothers were there. And Ross said in front of everybody in the room, "I didn't come to talk to you. I came to visit Maureen."

Some couples engage in a kind of contest to establish which was the more burdened in the marriage by demonstrating which can now better manage life without the partnership. Their encounters can be occasions for the ex-husband to announce that his business is going especially well or to display his contentment with his new life, or for the ex-wife to talk about the beginnings of a promising career, or about being truly respected by the man she is seeing, or about having, through functioning as a single parent, developed the self-esteem that had been denied her in the marriage. Each may want to demonstrate an ability to manage without any need of the partnership:

A couple of months ago I sold the house we were living in and we moved to another. My husband had said, "When you get your mortgage, if you need someone to cosign, let me know." He called about ten days later and said, "You didn't call. I thought you needed a cosigner." And I said, "Oh, no. I'm doing it all on my own through the bank." And in a way he was very relieved, but in another way it hurt his pride. And he was absolutely flabbergasted that I was coping.

The single parent's sexual relationship with the other parent may end before separation or may persist for weeks and months after separation. One woman spoke of celebrating her divorce by going with her husband to a motel room—"He was a lousy husband but a marvelous lover"— and it is not unusual for single partners to report that in the mixed-up time following separation they and their former partners sought comfort and respite in bed with each other. But as single partners teach themselves to see their former partners as strangers, such occasions become less likely, although, for some, never entirely impossible.

To an extent after separation, and without question after divorce, the right to jealousy can no longer be claimed. Now if a woman becomes upset on hearing that her former husband is seeing another woman, it is herself she must be angry at for having the feelings. A single parent after divorce may be quite willing to display to the former partner a new relationship and may even find gratification in the demonstration of an attractiveness the spouse could not see.

> I was walking into this restaurant with this fellow. I was wearing a very expensive white summer skirt and top, and it looked gorgeous. And as I'm walking in, my ex—he's only just my ex, by the way—is walking out with this girl. And if you could have seen the look on his face! He looked at me from top to bottom. The next day he called up and he said, "You must realize that it was a bit of a shock to see you out on the arm of some man who obviously cares for you." I thought it was marvelous.

Because the single parent's person is understood as no longer pledged to the former spouse, not only is the single parent no longer sexually accessible to the former spouse as a matter of course, but the single parent is also no longer accessible to the kind of physical misuse that sometimes accompanies marital quarrels. Yet, if a husband had, during marriage, grown accustomed to emphasizing his arguments with blows, he may not immediately accept that separation and divorce make matters different:

> This was four, five months after the divorce. I had a fever and I was really sick. I had the girl upstairs doing my washing for me, so I had left the door unlocked. And I heard it open and I called out, "The wash is in the kitchen, thanks very much." And then I heard his voice. I went out in the living room and I said, "Look, even though you have permission to see the kids, you should call first. And under the circumstances I would have said, 'No,' because I'm too sick to stand up." And he said, "That's not why I'm here. I'm here to make a deal with you." The deal was that he was going to buy me a house. And it was implicit that he would have access to the house any time he wanted. I said, "No. Right now I get welfare and it isn't much, but it's regular and I don't have to do anything I don't want to do to get it." And then he got mad and he started hitting me. And I said, "Hey, I'm not even married to you! What are you doing hitting me?"

The woman's neighbors heard noise in her apartment and asked through the door if she was all right. She told them to call the police. When the police came, they escorted her former husband to the street. Later that day she filed an assault charge against him. He did not again attack her.

Other women report having discouraged threatening and potentially brutal ex-husbands in various ways: in one instance, by having a detective call on the man; in another, by becoming involved with another man who then served as a protector; and in still another, by getting an adequately impressive dog. In the last instance the woman had bought a German shepherd to keep guard on her apartment without any thought of the dog's possible effect on her husband.

> I had the usual amount of harrassments from my ex-husband coming around and thinking he was going to bully me. At first I lived in fear of him. He'd call and if things didn't go his way he'd get rambunctious. And I was afraid to call the police because he threatened me, what he'd do to me if I did. The thing that finally ended it was, he rang the bell and I walked to the top of the stairs, and I had the dog beside me. He was a big dog. And my ex-husband looked up and he said, "Oh, Jesus, you've got a dog." And at first he wouldn't come up. But I convinced him that I had full control of the dog—and also, that if I gave the command, the dog would attack.

Though much changes in the relationships of single parents and their former spouses, much persists as well. Styles of relating tend to continue; the woman who was a domineering wife remains a domineering ex-wife; the woman who was self-abnegating during marriage finds it difficult to be demanding afterwards; the man who begrudged the money he had to give to his wife or gambled or drank it away turns out to be the same bad bet as a source of support after the marriage ends, while the man who was a model husband except that he maintained a mistress remains a considerate ex-husband even after the mistress has become his second wife.

In the period immediately after separation conflicts over property division, support, visitation, and custody are almost inescapable and produce new reasons for anger and new justifications for retaliation. The other parent is easily understood as responsible for all that has gone wrong with life. Indeed, the more the single parent feels frustrated by reverses and helpless to get life moving again, the angrier he or she is likely to be at having been abandoned—no matter who was responsible for the marriage's end. And the single parent will encounter these same reactions in the other parent. Here, for example, is a statement by a noncustodial parent. The man had been separated about six months when he was made an invalid by back pain.

> When I had that slipped disc and I had to stay in bed all day, I would just lie in bed and hate my wife. I would just hate her. I would say, "Goddamn it, she has the kids and she has the house and she has her health, while I lie here and I can't get up. I just hate her." Then I would say, "She can't help it that I'm here. Why am I hating her?" And I would really hate her.

At the same time that they feel hurt and angry, many among the separated harbor the hope that reconciliation may yet prove possible.

They find life alone to be bleak and uncomfortable, and they continue to feel attached to their former spouse. One woman, not quite two years beyond separation, and divorced about six months, was just in the process of relinquishing her hope of reconciliation:

> Through the separation I would be seeing my husband and making believe things had changed, because I really did want to go back with him. But they hadn't, and I don't want to go back with him the way he is. I'm going through a hard time right now, missing him something terrible, wanting to invite him over. But I don't dare because I just don't want to fall into the same trap. I've done it too many times already.

As the former husband and wife accept their separation as a part of their lives, they are likely to try to routinize their relationship with each other, to reduce its emotional intensity and its unpredictability. They may strive to establish with each other a tone of distant friendliness. Yet strong feelings are likely to persist indefinitely, and almost any interchange will carry some risk of eliciting them.

> It's been a year and a half. I was talking to my ex-husband because some camp forms came that he's going to fill out, because he's paying my son's camp. And I have all the medical records for his shots and everything. It was a very reasonable conversation. No acrimony. I mean, we agree on things. There's no acrimony. And when I hung up that phone after this pleasant conversation, I was just shaking. Why?

Despite parents' desire for cool, controlled, reasonably amicable relationships with their former husbands and wives, they seem regularly vulnerable to what one woman characterized as "flashbacks." A conversation with the spouse leads to the recall of past intimacy. A gesture, a turn of phrase, or a suddenly displayed liked or disliked trait provokes memories and, with them, yearning or compassion or apprehension or anger.

One woman, despite four years of divorce and despite her former husband's having become involved with another woman, still had to cope with continued attachment to him.

> We're still emotionally dependent on each other. We still have this emotional thing. About two and a half weeks ago when he came down we sat and we talked for about five hours. We talked about everything. And then we went to bed with each other. You know, you're not supposed to go to bed with your ex-husband. That, right there, kind of proves to me I still have feelings for him. I'm really too confused about what the feelings are, whether it is just my inability to let go completely or whether it's just that I have to accept the fact that I'm always going to have feelings for him. Maybe the intensity is going to die or something.

And another woman, divorced about two years, described how, to her embarrassment, she had been overcome by uncontrollable rage on encountering her ex-husband in her home:

> I came home from work about five o'clock or a little after and I was tired. And my husband was here in the house. I said, "What are you doing here?" I didn't say it nastily, I just said, "What are you doing here?" He had just come back from a business trip. He had been away for three weeks, and he had come to my house from the airport. I said to him, "Why didn't you go to your own apartment? Why did you come here?" And I told my daughter, "Your father is not allowed in this house." And then it started getting out of control and there was a scene. He slammed a cup on the table and broke it and I was yelling, "Get out! Get out! Get out!" So, from then, he has not been here. I really don't want him in my house. He stirs up a lot of anger in me, and I don't want to be angry.

Compassion, too, can be elicited, and it, too, can produce discomfort. One woman described talking by telephone to her ex-husband, from whom she had been divorced for five years:

> I talked to my husband Tuesday and he kept asking me to repeat what I was saying. And I said, "What's the matter?" And he said, "Well, I'm going deaf. And I don't have the money for an operation." Well, dumb me, I started to cry. Because that old feeling came back, that he's really a good guy. And then I thought, what is the matter with me? And I said, "I don't want to hear your problems. We both have problems."

It can be unsettling, even years after a marriage has ended, to learn that the other parent is remarrying. The single parent may then be made aware of how strong an attachment to the former spouse remains and may again experience a sense of loss.

> I heard from the kids. The kids told me, "Daddy's getting married next month." And what made it hard was I knew he still had strong feelings for me. He came over the night before he got married, with my two older kids. They were getting stuff ready for the wedding. I saw him, and we talked. And it was bad for both of us.

Anniversaries can also be distressing insofar as they elicit feelings that had been pushed out of awareness. One woman had been separated about three years, during the last two of which she had hardly seen her husband:

> A few weeks ago I called my ex-husband because he was supposed to come up and I was verifying the date. And he asked me how I was doing and I said that for some reason that day I didn't feel that terrific. For some reason I was feeling very down. I didn't realize until after the call that it was my anniversary. I even mentioned the date to him. And I was saying that for some reason I was feeling I had to call him. And then, after the telephone conversation, I realized that it was my anniversary, and that was probably what I was feeling.

The early phase of the single parent's relationship with the other parent is often marked by dispute, in many instances becoming quite bad until the zero-sum issues of property division and support are resolved and some pattern of visitation is arrived at. Then the relationship may, at least for a time, improve. The formerly brutal husband may play the good father and grudgingly be granted access to the home. The bitter wife may appear pleasant for the sake of the children. But always, in the relationships of single parents and their former husbands or wives, there are new events producing further change. A parent may move to a new area, making visitation awkward and expensive; remarriage of one or both parents many introduce new figures, complicating their earlier understandings. And, always, the children are growing older and changing; the daughter who, at the time the parents divorced, was too young to manage public transportation by herself becomes old enough to call her father and arrange to visit him without first consulting her mother, or to decide that she feels uncomfortable going alone with her father to a restaurant and would prefer not to visit her father unless she can bring a friend along. Or the son who, when younger, was quietly angry may become so rebellious that his mother, exhausted, startles them both by saying, "It might be better if you lived with your father." All these changes change the relationships of the parents.

Rarely do separated and divorced parents talk with each other more frequently than a few times a month; the talks are too often upsetting, however friendly their manifest tone. Only as a result of much effort, it seems, can single parents achieve the relatively uncomplicated co-operative relationship toward which they often strive, a relationship in which each can acknowledge the other's place in the lives of their children, and in which conversations and visits are unencumbered by memories or emotion. And even with effort, it would seem almost necessary that both parents be relatively content with their lives as they are; this, in turn, often means that each has formed acceptable new attachments. Then, when both parents feel secure and content in their new lives, and have accepted their shared past and unshared present, relationships like the following seem possible:

> Last Saturday my husband came over to get the kids and spend the whole day. He was coming over to take the boys bike riding. But he was running late, and it was a quarter after ten, and he hadn't even had breakfast yet. And we were just finishing breakfast. So he sat down to have coffee. Then he and the kids went off on their bikes. And then he came back and the man I see, Tommy, was there. So my husband, Tommy, I, and the kids all had lunch together. We really had a nice time.
>
> Tommy had a big table that he was going to get rid of, because it doesn't fit into his new apartment, and he asked my husband if he wanted it. So my husband gave it to his girlfriend. And Tommy and I are moving some of Tommy's furniture this weekend, and we're using my husband's station wagon. And that's how it goes.

This relationship, too, had its vicissitudes, its occasions of mutual irritation, its brief misunderstandings, as when the ex-husband had been expected to accompany the children to a community fair and failed to show up. But basically the relationship remained friendly. And it permitted the kind of half-serious sharing of responsibility suggested by the following:

> About a week ago the ski place near where we live had dollar day. So I took my kids over to the slope. My kids are nine and twelve. There were two teenagers from our street with them, and I left my phone number and went to work. When I got into work, I called my husband. I said, "Our children are out skiing. I want you to know so you can worry like me. Now you can worry like I will for the rest of the day."

But even when the noncustodial parent is friendly and cooperative, the custodial parent is ultimately responsible for the children. And because this is the case, the noncustodial parent, no matter how cooperative, no matter how useful as a consultant and advisor, is not really a partner.* Here is a comment by a mother of an only daughter, aged twelve:

> I have a trusting relationship with my ex-husband. If there is a problem, I can discuss it with him. But I feel that for the most part it is my values that my daughter is subject to, even though we both have influence over her. As far as taking responsibility, it seems to me that I have the responsibility. I have the final decision. My daughter has as good a relationship with her father as I think any child could have in a situation like ours, but I still think that ultimately I end up being the one who is bringing her up.

The other parent as troubling figure

The ways the other parent can be useful to the single parent are limited. The other parent can be available as a consultant, can help financially, can provide a respite from child care, and can be as good a fellow parent for the children as is possible, given different households and separate lives. But the ways in which the other parent can be troublesome are many. The very contributions the other makes offer opportunity for mischief. The other parent may insist on being consulted, although the consultation is not wanted and will not be respected; financial support may be given grudgingly; the other parent may be so attentive to the children when with them that the parent at home is shamed. If a noncustodial parent who feigns helpfulness can nevertheless be troublesome,

* We did not have any parents in our sample who legally shared custody.

still more troublesome can be a noncustodial parent who is bent on retaliating for real or imaginary hurt. Then the noncustodial parent may shrug off the parent's rules and encourage the children also to shrug them off; checks may be held up or not sent at all, or they may be sent through the children or to the children; appointments to see the children may be forgotten; the children may be returned from a visit long past the time they were expected; and visits may be occasions for quarrels or hostile silences.

It should not be surprising that most custodial parents find noncustodial parents more nearly a burden than a resource. The noncustodial parent is someone to worry about, an obligation that limits what can be done on a weekend, a source of distraction and disturbance to the children. Occasional freedom from child care isn't worth it: the interval without the children isn't long enough; the other parent isn't reliable enough, neither about the time the children are to be picked up nor about the time the children will be returned; and absence of control makes the situation maddening. When the children are with the other parent, the single parent may worry about not being with them, and so not being able to care for them. The single parent has given over responsibility for the children, not to a babysitter who can be told what to do, but to a fellow parent who cannot. And there are so many ways in which visitation can be misused. The other parent may seduce the children into accepting a version of what went wrong with the marriage that turns the children against the parent with whom they live. The other parent may require the children to accept second place to a date and the date's children. The other parent may indulge the children's desire for junk food. The single parent can request sensible parental behavior, but beyond this the single parent is almost helpless.

The single parent must stand ready to fill the breach if in any way there is a failure of coordination. A mother of four children, three of them teenaged, said:

> My ex-husband is supposed to pick the children up Wednesdays and give them dinner. Well, I come home from work, no dinner ready, and he's on the phone, "I can't see them." He says his car broke down. But he didn't call or anything. So I said to him, "Why didn't you just pick up the phone and let me know? You know where I work." I was angry because my kids were sitting there at the door, waiting to go out, and their father isn't showing up.

The single parent may have made plans for the children, have arranged for them to visit playmates or attend a school event, when the other parent decides to see them. Should the single parent accept the embarrassment and bother of changing plans? Or disappoint the children who might want to see the other parent? Would it be fair to ask the children to decide? A mother of two girls, aged eight and ten, said:

The Other Parent

> Last week I made plans to be part of the adult participation in the Sunday School Halloween party. At ten o'clock I said, "All right, children, get ready. We're going to the Halloween party." And the phone rings and one of the children runs to it and says, "It's Daddy. He will come to pick us up in two hours." Do I stay home from the party and not fulfill my part in it? Do I go off and leave them until their father shows up? Which might be all right to do if it was just half an hour, but I might come home four hours later and find them still waiting. Or do I go and take them with me?

There was, as it happened, another possibility. The woman called her ex-husband and asked him to come for the children on their return from Sunday School. The mother's dilemma developed because her ex-husband, like many other noncustodial parents, wanted an independent relationship to the children. He tried to achieve this by making arrangements directly with the children and refusing to clear them with his former wife. The aim of noncustodial parents who adopt this practice is to establish that the parent inside the home is not a gatekeeper to the children. But for the parent at home the issue is not one of power, but of being able to plan. Another woman with the same problem said:

> I asked their father to call me and deal with me on situations around visitation. "Don't call them, because they then have to tell me, and I don't know what the story is, and they are just put in the middle."

Another form of coordinative failure, often also motivated by the noncustodial parent's desire for an independent relationship to the children, may occur in relation to gift giving. The parent with whom the children live knows what the children want and need. But the other parent may be unwilling to simply follow directions, no matter how tactfully they are phrased. And, again, the parent with whom the children live must compensate for the other parent's failures. The following story was reported by a mother of an eight-year-old only daughter:

> I asked Eleanor what she wanted for her birthday and she said she wanted a bike. My husband talked with her and she said, "Mom is getting me a bike for my birthday." He said, "No, I'll get the bike for you." And I said, "No, I'm getting the bike. She also wants a fish tank." He said, "Well, you get the fish tank. I'll get the bike." And we went back and forth over this. Finally, I gave up. "Okay, you get the bike. I'll get the fish tank."

> Three weeks before her birthday I had already gotten the tank and had it in the house. And he was supposed to show up before her birthday with the bike. Her birthday came and went: no bike. I explained to her, in children's language, that he is inconsistent, and also that you don't always get what you are promised. But it was unfair. So I went out and got the bike, too.

Extremely difficult to deal with, for the parent who is living with the children, is the other parent who, for whatever reason, is rejecting of the children. Both mothers and fathers who are custodial parents complain bitterly of noncustodial parents who visit the children infrequently and, by their apparent indifference, sadden the children and cause them to feel unloved. Susan Anderson-Khlief, in an examination of patterns of support and visitation in mother-headed single-parent families, divided the noncustodial fathers into three groups: those who maintained regular visiting patterns, generally once a week or once every two weeks; those who saw their children only infrequently or sporadically; and those who saw their children not at all.[1] In Dr. Anderson-Khlief's study it was fathers in the latter two groups toward whom the children's mothers were most embittered.

Often the mothers of children whose fathers appeared rejecting found it difficult to know whether it would be better for the children if the children's images of their fathers were protected or if, instead, the children were helped to recognize their fathers' failings. To what extent, a mother might wonder, is it fair to children to share with them the mother's condemnation of the father? On the other hand, to what extent can a mother be expected to say nothing while her children are being hurt?

> My daughter has had to do all the contacting with her father from the time she was four years old. And we went through all the problems of his picking her up and bringing her back and his being upset because she was upset. We went through that for a long period of time. But he did come pretty consistently. Then we went through a time when she would call him and he wouldn't be there, so she would leave messages on his answering machine and for a couple of days in a row she would leave messages. And sometimes she would get him and he'd say, "I don't feel too good right now. Call me back in an hour." And then she'd call back again, and she would be very nice to him on the phone, and she would hang up and cry.

> For the longest time I was making excuses for him. "He doesn't feel well. He's busy." I finally said, I'm not going to do that any more. I wouldn't have cared if the contact were to have to come from her *once*, but to have the kid call two or three or four times in a row and leave messages on his tape and for me to listen to that brave little voice talking on the phone and then have her hang up and fall to pieces—no more. I sat down with her and I said, "Look, your father is having a hard time seeing you, and it is senseless for you to be calling him up and asking him over and over again to see you and then getting disappointed. I'm not going to let you call him any more. Your father is going to have to call. I am not going to watch you do this any more."

When the other parent sees the children infrequently or irregularly, the children may regret having to relinquish the other parent in order to return home. But it is the parent with whom they live who must deal with their distress. A mother of a seven-year-old only son said:

> I picked him up from the airport and he was very quiet. I asked what was wrong, and he said, "Well, you know how you feel when you leave

somebody." He said he was just feeling sad. I said that Daddy loved him, and that he had had such a good time down there that it was all right to feel sad. And he said he didn't want to talk about it in the car. So I said that if he wanted to, we could talk about it when we got home. But when we got home he just said that he didn't think he wanted to talk about it at all.

The parent with whom the children live may discover that the children take a few days to settle down again after returning from a visit to the other parent. Until they do, the children are overactive, hard to manage, and easily upset, just as in a version of the defense against depression noted in the previous chapter. A woman with two preadolescent children described her children's behavior in this way:

> It seems that every time they are with him, they come back in a very bad mood. The whole week will go fine and they will see him on a weekend, and they'll be fighting with each other. All week long they are no trouble, and then for about two of three days, after they come back, it just seems it's a constant battle.

The children may blame the parent who cares for them for the other parent's loss. Whether they hold the parent at home solely at fault or not, it is that parent who is there to hear their protests. A woman with two children, a boy of fourteen and a girl of thirteen, said:

> They come home, and they're very upset, and they start to fight with each other, and then they fight with me and they say, "You kicked him out! You kicked Daddy out!" The younger one, she'll cry and want us to be back together. And when she does that I feel like crying myself. She will say to me, "When are you going to go back?" And I just tell her it can't be. I say that Daddy and I can't live with each other; we just fight too much. And I don't want any more of that. And she'll say to me, "He won't fight any more. Bring him back and he won't fight. If you let Daddy back, things will be better."

If their noncustodial parents are easily accessible and regularly available so that the children know they can contact them whenever they want, the children appear less upset by the parental separation.[2] Of course, the custodial parent must accept that the other parent will influence the children's values and behavior. If the other parent's values are respected, all well and good; if they are not, then again the custodial parent has something to deal with. One mother whose former husband insisted on introducing her not-yet-adolescent children to marijuana finally refused to permit visitation (she relented when the children were older). Another mother regretted that her six-year-old only son was developing the same enthusiasm for hunting that her husband had. She did what she could to reduce it:

> My husband is into hunting, and at times he is very sadistic in his talk. He'll say, "I went hunting today and I blew the head off this squirrel."

He will say this in front of my son. So my son talks about going hunting when he gets bigger. But I want my son to realize the value of life, whether it is animal or human. I took him to see *Bambi* to try to counteract my husband's influence. And I sat there and impressed on him how Bambi's mother got shot by a hunter.

In the other parent's home the children may be permitted to stay up late, watch television programs ordinarily forbidden to them, be cheeky to adults, decide the food they will eat, be messy, and quarrel. The permissiveness of the other parent's home may become an argument against the single parent's rules. Now a child can bring to negotiations with the single parent an ally out of the single parent's reach: "Daddy lets me do it." A mother of three children reported:

They don't bring it up a lot, but you can see it's there: "When I'm with Daddy, he lets me do whatever I want." He knows how I raise the kids, but he doesn't follow through when he takes them. He lets them stay up until ten, eleven, twelve o'clock at night, which the kids aren't used to. They are used to getting a certain amount of sleep. And they'll come back from being with him completely exhausted. He lets them eat everything that I wouldn't let them eat here. And they can show any amount of disrespect to their grandmother or to their aunts and he won't correct them. It's hard for the kids, coming home, knowing Mom's here, and all this baloney is over with. When they're there, they can do whatever they want, whenever they want to do it. And when they come home, Mom has a set of rules that we have to go by.

Some mothers anticipate that an extended visit with the father means a week or so of conflict after the child returns. Here is a mother of an only son, about nine:

He's a very independent kid anyway, very obstinate. And he'll question why he has to go to bed at such and such a time when he was allowed staying up late at his father's. He'll tell me that he didn't have to go to bed at Daddy's until ten o'clock, something like that. Then I explain that school is tomorrow and that when he is on vacation it's allowed for him to stay up late. And after a while he gets back into the routine. It doesn't bother me. Maybe I do a little bit more screaming for the first week than I normally do.

Sometimes the noncustodial parent is critical of the approach to child-raising adopted by the parent with whom the children live. One working mother had arranged with an older woman who was her nine-year-old son's babysitter for the woman to remain with her son while she went off on a much-needed vacation. A few hours after she left, her former husband called unexpectedly, discovered that their son was, as he put it, "being left alone with a babysitter for a week," and insisted that the boy come to stay with him. When the mother returned from her vacation she was furious that the boy's father could so arrogantly override her arrangements. Another woman described an incident in which her former husband seemed to be collecting evidence for a neglect charge against her. She was sure he did not actually want to take their children from her, and she tried not to be disturbed by his invasiveness:

> The kids were maybe seven and five. I went out one night and left them alone. I didn't leave until ten-thirty and I went out for a pizza. And my husband called, and they were alone. So he went to the police station and went in the house with the police to verify the fact that the children were alone. I was gone maybe two hours, that's all. So, one-thirty in the morning, he called to check to see if I was home. I said, "Hello," and nobody's there. So I said, "I know it's you. Are you going to get the kids on Saturday?" And he said, "It's on record at the police station that you left the kids alone."

Parents who are themselves antagonistic are always potential competitors for their children's affiliation. This can be true even without an open battle over custody. The parent with whom the children live may be always aware of the threat of their loss:

> One of the fears I have—especially, I think, because I have boys—is that the kids will say, "Gee, he looks great." Because here this man comes in, a very romantic character from out of their past, from California, this very romantic state, Hollywood, Disneyland, and I'm afraid they'll say, "Hey, we'd like to go live with him." Which makes the twelve years that I have put in so far pretty useless. It wouldn't be like you'd raised your kids from beginning to end and then they'd gone off on their own. It would be a sudden, "I'm going to live with him." And oh, it would crush me!

Most appalling of all relationships between separated and divorced parents are those in which the parents are actively contesting possession of the children. An open battle for custody in which each parent engages a lawyer to threaten the other with loss of the children comes as close to a holy war as is likely to be experienced in the modern world. Each parent may be convinced that the children's welfare depends on that parent's winning the battle. Each parent may feel the other parent to be totally misguided, utterly unreachable, implacably hostile. It is a battle motivated by parental love, against an unyielding enemy, where loss would mean loss of the children. Each parent can feel justified in using any tactic whatsover to win the judge's decision. Custody fights, understandably, give rise to intense fear and hatred.

Occasionally the parent outside the home threatens to kidnap the children. Then the single parent may live almost in a state of siege:

> The last time my ex-husband was down here he threatened me that he will put Andy on a plane and take off with him. I told him, "You know, if you take that kid, that's all I've really got." And he says to me, "Gee, that's too bad." I went to a lawyer and asked about it; "What happens if he does this?" Well, I can take no legal action if he takes him out of the state. So I keep constant watch on Andy. The people at

the school know not to let him see him. Or, if he does come to his school, to notify me immediately and not to allow him to take Andy from the school.

It's always in the back of my head, even when I let Andy play out in the street. I have constantly got my eyes on him. Most of the time I'm at the window watching him, even with him five years old, to make sure somebody doesn't just drive up. And I've had to tell him that no matter who drives up, not to get in that car with them. I didn't say, "Even if it is your Dad." I just said, "No matter, I don't care *who* it is, don't get in the car with *anybody* without asking Mommy's permission first."

Kidnapping of children does occur, with devastating impact on the parent from whom the child is taken. In one instance a father convinced a fourteen-year-old daughter to go with him to his home in another country. The daughter may not quite have been kidnapped, but the mother could not make out from the one letter the daughter sent just why she had left. Although there were other children at home, the absence of her daughter was constantly in the mother's mind. In another instance, in the course of a hectic and quarrelsome separation, a father packed up the two younger of his five children and, without a word to the mother, left for another state. The police would do nothing. The private investigator the mother hired could not locate the father and the children. For two awful months the mother could think of nothing else. Then the father returned to begin divorce proceedings. He was in no way penalized.

Feelings toward the other parent

Single parents' emotions about those to whom they had been married tend to be persistent, deepseated, and mixed. Some single parents feel only animosity, some only solicitude, but most feel both at once—both anger and concern, both distrust and connection. The other parent was, once, the closest person in the world, the person with whom the single parent exchanged vows of eternal loyalty, the person who became the single parent's next of kin, with whom the single parent established a home and produced children. These ties persist. But the disappointments and betrayals that led to the marital separation may still be recalled; so, too, may be the injuries associated with the separation itself. And the subsequent difficulties of acting as fellow parents who are no longer partnered are likely to have led to further feelings of injury and anger.

The Other Parent

Let us consider first some of the ways in which persisting positive feelings toward the other parent may display themselves and then consider the negative feelings that very often outweigh them.

Persistent positive feelings

If a single parent has not found someone new, sometimes even if the single parent has, the former spouse may continue to be seen as family: estranged family, to be sure—a family member with whom there has been a falling out, with whom there now is tension rather than affiliation —but, still, family. A woman who had been divorced about ten years, with two adolescent children, said:

> I was sick about a month ago, and I had to go to the emergency room of the hospital. They asked me who to notify. Well, I'm an only child and I didn't know. And I said, "Well, you better put my ex-husband down." I hadn't felt that way before. But the children are his. And if something happens to me, I have reached the feeling that he would be good enough, that he would be pretty good with them.

The sense of familial connection may be based not only on having once been married, but also on recognition that shared parenthood of children establishes both a sense of kinship and the blood bond of common descendents. Because of shared investment in the children, the parent outside the home has some right to be informed of family matters affecting the children: changes in the children's lives and changes in the life situation of the other parent that will affect the children. The kinds of issues the other parent has a right to be informed of are the same issues any family member would want to know about: job change, illness, relocation, remarriage.

There may be an affective tie to the other parent as well as a lingering bond of kinship. It is the experience of many parents that they and those to whom they had been married continue for some time to elicit in each other special feelings, not always pleasant, of attachment.[3] If they both attend the same party, try as they will they cannot block out an excessive, unjustifiable awareness of each other. And, if there has not been too much anger, and the circumstances are just right, then long after the separation they can find themselves again drawn to each other. Here is a comment made by a woman who had been divorced from her former husband for about five years. Her former husband had, since their divorce, married and separated from another woman:

> He can get me to talk nice to him. Maybe we'll laugh over things we might talk about, like maybe little episodes in the past. Maybe he'll talk about when we were single and some of the things that we used to do. Or maybe some of the fights we had. He'll always say he wasn't all wrong. . . . He can still soften me, maybe because we knew each other for years. Most of the time I say, "I don't want to be bothered with

you." And then he'll try to weaken me as far as sex. Once in a while I have gone with him to a motel.

Finally, there persists a latent concern for the other parent, not only because the other parent is to an extent seen as an estranged family member, but also because of feelings of continued obligation to someone to whom the single parent was once married, for whom the single parent once cared. This latent concern emerges as compassion when the former spouse encounters a series of reverses, or becomes ill, or fails in work. So much once was shared with this person; how can one not now try to help? An illustrative story was told by a woman whose former husband was a compulsive gambler:

> I've never been able to get money from him. Sorry to say, I've given him money, which I shouldn't have. This was right after we separated. He was in terrible shape. He needed a shave, he was down in the dumps, and I just happened to meet him. I gave him some money.

All these positive feelings can be quite hidden beneath anger and bitterness. One divorced woman whose husband died said that she still could not explain her grief on losing from her life a man she had thought she hated.

Negative feelings: Mothers with custody

The intense hurt and bitterness that are by-products of separation seem to fade more quickly than feelings of connection. A certain wariness of the other parent does seem to persist; but, often, not much more. It is as if humans came equipped with a highly developed capacity to form persisting pair bonds, but with a less well developed capacity for maintaining aversions. But replacing the feelings of hurt and anger that were near to overwhelming when the husband and wife were voicing their condemnations of each other may be new negative feelings stemming from conflicts over support payments and visitation and each parent's disapproval of the other's relationships with the children.

Separated and divorced mothers feel that their former husbands have two obligations to them and the children. First, they are obligated still to be "good fathers." This requires that they see their children regularly, that they be loving and attentive without being overindulgent, and that they provide their children—especially their sons—with a model of adulthood worthy of emulation. The second obligation mothers believe their former husbands have is to provide for their children's support and, insofar as the mothers' own earnings are limited by the mother's parental responsibilities, for their support as well.

It is entirely understandable that mothers would resent fathers who seem indifferent to their children. They want their children to have the same sort of attentive fathers that other children have.

The Other Parent

I don't think my ex-husband's lack of interest in my children is right. I don't see how a father can do that. I know it's done all the time, but I just don't see how they can do it. I know guys that travel two hundred miles a week just to see their kids. There is a guy at work, his ex-wife and their three kids live a couple hundred miles from him, and he's there every single weekend. This I can understand. I can't understand a man who doesn't do it, that supposedly wanted children and that just pretends they don't exist.

One woman decided that her older son, aged eleven, had taken to fighting with other children partly because he missed his father. His father had been close to him before the parents' separation, and for several months afterwards. But his father had become depressed and reduced his visits. It was then that the boy's behavior became worrisome. The mother called her husband and arranged to meet him at a restaurant:

I said I was really upset, that Billy has been fighting in school with kids. And I said, "Wally, look, can you try and put your feelings aside and let's just think of the kids? Let's just be parents right now. We have two kids. They didn't ask for this. They didn't ask to even be brought into this world. Let's not screw them up the way we've screwed ourselves up, or our parents screwed us up."

He was very cold. And, Jesus, there was nobody that was a better father than Wally. So I said, "What happened to this father, Wally? You don't even call the kids up. They call you up; you could care less." I said, "You're rejecting them." I said, "What happened to this father?" And he said, "He died." I looked at him and all of a sudden I'd like to give him a kick in the ass. I said, "He what? You *died*?" I said, "You fucking bastard. What do I owe you for the coffee?" And I got out of that place so fast. I had no sympathy whatsoever. He was drowning in self-pity.

He called me up in half an hour and he said, " I'm sorry." I said, "I don't talk to dead people," and I hung up.

But even when an ex-husband is thought by her to be good enough as a father, the children's mother can find reason for resentment. The father's not being in the home to help raise the children is reason in itself. Having to observe a child sorrow because of a father's absence can impress on the mother how unsatisfactory—indeed, unnatural—is the situation in which she and the child are living. The following story was told by a mother of an eleven-year-old only daughter:

Sometimes I wish my ex-husband was not such a good father. He was a very good father when we were married and he has continued to be a very good father. He has seen my daughter every single weekend. But he and his new wife went to Canada for three weeks and the night he left all hell broke loose. My daughter had nightmares, couldn't get to sleep, got sick. A couple of days later she got a sprained ankle. It was unbelievable, the three weeks I went through. When he came back, all of a sudden she seemed to be able to function again. I think she thought he really wasn't coming back.

A Parent, Though Single: The Single Parent at Home

The father in the above story went off with his new wife, leaving behind, with his former wife, an anxious child. Before the parents' separation the father had occasionally been required to leave the child to go on a business trip. But then the mother's caring for the child was a partnership responsibility, a matter of one member of the marital partnership dealing with things while the other member was away. Now no marital partnership existed, and, without it, having to comfort a bereft daughter because of her father's absence was an imposition. And, undoubtedly, had there been no parental separation, the daughter would not have been so upset by the father's temporary inaccessibility.

In a similar fashion, fathers who fail in their obligation to provide support obviously incur resentment, but some fathers who provide an inadequate level of support, though it may be as much as they can manage, also incur resentment. The provision of support for the children, even at the cost of hardship to the father, is understood as a father's responsibility. One woman, the mother of three children, had been left by her husband for another woman. At the time we spoke with her they had been apart over two years, and the husband had begun to complain that he could not increase his support payment and meet his own bills:

> We had this argument about money, where my husband said, "Well, I have to live." And I said, "You get as much a month as I do. And you're single. You have no responsibilities. Your girlfriend cooks for you. She does your wash. Stop spending so much money taking her out! Then you will be able to give it to me for the kids, so they can eat!" So he said, "Go get food stamps." So I said, "What about their medical expenses?" And he said, "Go get medicaid." And I said, "No. That's still your responsibility."

Failure by the children's father to provide adequate support is a genuine injury to the family. But beyond this, it demonstrates an absence of concern for the children. In its own way, it constitutes rejection of the children. A woman who had forced her alcoholic husband to move out of their home said that she did not feel it right to ask for support for herself but that she resented her husband's failure to support their children:

> I did want him out. I have accepted that I am raising the kids. If I thought I could get money from him easily, I'd like it. And I think the kids deserve it. I feel a little resentful that he doesn't do that for his kids. I don't feel resentful that he's not doing it for me. I don't feel he owes me anything at all, really: not me, personally. But I feel bad that the kids are going to grow up and they are going to say, "My father didn't care enough to support us all those years." That kind of disturbs me.

The Other Parent

In addition, failing to support the children provides the children with a thoroughly undesirable model of adult behavior. And this, too, can be seen as expressive of indifference towards the children. A woman with older children reported:

> When we first were separated I had to apply for welfare because he was in arrears with his check. Then he was paying again and I went off welfare. Then he was in arrears again, and I had to go back to court. And going into court, he said, "Look what you are doing! You are taking me to court! What a wonderful inheritance you are giving your children!" And I said, "Well, you're showing your boys that they can get married, have children, leave them, go their merry way. That's the inheritance *you're* giving your sons. And your daughters, you are showing them that when they get married their husbands can walk out, and the hell with the kids."

Yet providing a generous level of support and providing it reliably still does not protect the former husband from the mother's resentment. To be sure, rarely is support felt to be adequate, whatever its level. But, apart from this, what has writing a check to do with raising childen? A woman who was receiving about $20,000 a year as child support for an only son said:

> I'm getting a certain fee a month for raising Elliott. It is not enough, compared with what I think he is making. I don't think it is adequate for all the things I would like to do for Elliott. And I feel like he has none of the responsibilities of taking care of Elliott twenty-four hours a day, taking him to the hospital every time he needs stitches, which is often, taking him to the doctor's, getting him shoes, all of these things. He's bringing Elliott up by check. He pays the check and I do all the work. And I don't think that's fair.

The resentment felt by the separated and divorced mother toward her former husband, though it may be justified in terms of visitation failures or inadequate support, seems often to be based rather on a sense of having been betrayed by him. For the mother on her own is apt to feel that she and her husband conceived their children together, but she has been left to raise them alone. Because she believed in the marital partnership she relinquished her ability to work without worrying about who would care for the children, her freedom to go where she pleased in the evening, and her chance to find another man with whom she might share a family. She gave all this up on the assumption that she could rely on the husband. She had children with him because she believed in their union. And, no matter how it happened—whether the man left her for another woman or proved impossible to live with because he gave all his energies to his work or was insensitive or gross or became alcoholic— the woman's trust that the man would be a partner in maintaining their home and raising their children was betrayed. The marriage has ended with the mother marooned with the children, while her former husband sails freely on.

> Sometimes I get very frustrated and very angry about it because I just don't think it's fair. You know, he's off scot free. I have all the responsibilities of the children, the home, and worrying about the bills and when the kids are sick. And he doesn't have to do anything. He's just off, having fun.

And should the father have initiated the separation, then, though he may be extraordinarily dutiful, and the mother grateful to him for his considerateness and availability, the mother can be resentful simply because he left her behind. There is no way the father can compensate for that.

> I'm glad that my ex-husband is still very much a part of my life. It has made things a lot easier. But even though he's good with the support check, and he's a good father and everything like that, there is still the basic fact that I think he treated me like shit, the fact that he was the guy that I thought I could trust with my life and he took advantage of it.

Mothers who were not married to the fathers of their children appear less likely to harbor feelings of betrayal, whatever other feelings they may have. One woman had had a son with a man to whom she had not been married, and then a second son with a man she married and later divorced. The father of her older son had kept in touch with her and had sent what money he could to help support their child. The woman was pleased that he continued to be concerned. She felt that whatever he did for their son was a kind of gift, an expression of his continued caring. She never felt any threat that he might take their son from her; it apparently never occurred to either of them that he might want custody. Nor has she ever felt that the father was inconsiderate of her or of their son by seeing the boy only irregularly. In dramatic contrast to the friendliness this woman feels toward the father of her first child is the bitterness and anger she feels toward her former husband. She had counted on her former husband and he let her down. In addition, her former husband had threatened at the time of the separation that he would contest the custody of their child. He did not make good on the threat, but she can still remember how terrified she was. And although her former husband has provided support fairly regularly, there have been occasional quarrels, and she feels he is a stingy and essentially ungiving father.

In general, where there was no marriage, mothers appear to have few expectations of their children's fathers. And, because the unmarried father is understood to have no clear obligation, whatever he does is felt to express an admirable commitment to the child. Also, because the unmarried father is understood to have no legal rights and few moral rights to custody of the child, he represents no threat.

The Other Parent

Negative feelings: Fathers with custody

Men who have custody of their children sometimes complain about their former wives in terms that are indistinguishable from those used by mothers with custody when complaining about their former husbands. For example, if gender references were changed, the following comment made by a custodial father would not be very different from comments made by many custodial mothers. Perhaps most mothers would give less emphasis to the child's need for the other parent. But in the main, the complaints are the same as those made by custodial mothers, except with gender reversed:

> The difficult thing for me now is to try to make my son aware that his mother still loves him, because it appears that she doesn't. She will go for weeks on end without even a phone call. One time she wasn't heard from for four months. And she has refused to contribute financially in spite of the fact that I took her to court and won an order. And the reason I find it all difficult is that I am aware of my son's continued need for his mother, and I feel angry that she is so callous about seeing him.

There may be a somewhat greater tendency for custodial fathers to describe themselves as having been failed by their former wives rather than as having been betrayed by them. Custodial fathers seem more likely than custodial mothers to describe the other parent as irresponsible, flighty, or unpredictable, whereas custodial mothers seem more likely to describe the other parent as self-centered. And so, whereas custodial mothers tend to communicate an image of husbands who escaped their obligations, custodial fathers seem more likely to describe wives who were not up to theirs because something was wrong in the wives' characters or motivations. A father of two small children said:

> I felt the responsibility for the children was mine. Their mother had abandoned them. She didn't want the responsibility. And I didn't feel I had any choice except to go to court and get custody so that she wouldn't come back in a week and pick up one of the children or both of them and say, "I'm going elsewhere."

To the extent that men define their wives as having failed them not out of calculation but rather out of incapacity, it can be easier for men to suspend their resentment. In addition, it may be more nearly in the masculine style to think of oneself as rational, in control of one's emotions, and to want others, too, to have this image of oneself. The ideal of constructive realism implicit in the following story would seem more likely to be met among custodial fathers than among custodial mothers.

> The kid's mother has been going with this guy and I figure she's going to move in with him. I was terribly bitter and I tried in my own way to poison the kids against her because she did this and she did that. And then I realized I was just making a fool of myself and it was completely

> unnecessary. I didn't want to be that kind of a person. And she wasn't going to make me that kind of a person. I called her and I told her, "Listen, this isn't what I want. I don't want this bitterness."

It is still an unusual development for a man to assume custody of his children. Because of this, noncustodial wives are more easily characterized as odd, whatever their actual psychic state. And this, in turn, may reduce the resentment of custodial fathers for the situation in which they find themselves: their wives could not help behaving as they did. There may be still another reason for custodial fathers expressing less resentment than is often seen among custodial mothers. Our societal understanding of the nature of men and women discourages custodial fathers from believing they were duped into accepting the obligations of parenthood and then abandoned.

For the sake of the children

Sometimes, when mothers act to foster their children's relationships with the children's fathers, the mothers feel that their own lives are bettered by the fathers' continued presence. These are the fortunate, and unusual, mothers who have fashioned effective working relationships with their former husbands despite separation or divorce. Most mothers, however, who act to foster their children's relationships with their former husbands do so at what they feel to be cost to themselves: their emotions are upset, their schedules complicated, their children unsettled—and all with no direct benefit to them. They do it for the sake of the children. If it were not for the children, they would allow their former husbands to play only the most peripheral roles in their lives.

One woman who had been married to an unstable and rather brutal man toward whom she still felt intense animosity wondered at her inability to say no when her former husband wanted to come to see the children. Just hearing from him upset her. She fervently wanted him out of her life. And yet she permitted him to visit almost whenever he wanted to:

> I was wondering, why do I put up with this? Is there something wrong with me? Is there something that I want, that I do this? I eliminated the possibility of still being attracted to him. I don't think that is it. I see his flaws more clearly than I did when I was married to him. And he's not the type of person that I like. So I was left with, "Is there something wrong with me? Am I masochistic?" And I then thought, no, it comes

back to the kids. He has me over a barrel because of the kids. If I didn't care about the kids, I could just say to him, "Drop dead."

Indeed, as they see it, separated and divorced mothers do not simply tolerate their former husbands' relationships with their children; they actively promote them. From the very first the mothers may have cautioned their children not to become involved in the parents' dispute, since that might endanger the children's relationships with their fathers:

> Right from the start I told the children that any time they wanted to see their father, there is the phone. They can call him up, he can come any time he wants. I said to the kids, "This trouble is between Daddy and me and it has nothing to do with you."

Mothers protect their children's relationships with the children's fathers even when they are dubious after the fathers' characters and worried about the fathers as parents. There are limits to this: a father who, in the mother's opinion, endangered the children might be prevented from taking the children unless the mother was also present. But a mother often will tolerate a good deal of anxiety rather than interrupt her children's relationships with the father. A mother of three school-aged children said:

> I don't say anything bad about him, although I let the children know that I do have bad feelings. But I worry when they go with him. He has no common sense. And his values are screwed up. He is very intelligent, very practical, but he drinks. And I worry. But the children do love him and do want to see him, and I couldn't interfere with that.

Mothers recognize that their children are identified with their fathers as well as with them. They fear that even if they did nothing to limit the extent to which their children could see the fathers, but only talked against the fathers, they would damage the children. One mother said:

> If I destroyed Larry to the children, then I destroyed 50 percent of *them*, because he is their father. They are half him and half me.

Sometimes mothers withhold from the children information about their father that would discredit him. They may be irritated by the extent to which the children idealize the father; yet they will say nothing. A mother of two children, a girl of nine and a boy of six, said:

> To the children, their father is God. There is nothing he can do that is wrong. He is the smartest person on earth. He can solve all their problems. I find it hard not to be bitter because I know he's a different person from what they think. Yet I won't destroy his image in their eyes. I won't say anything bad about him. When they say, "I want to go over and see Daddy," or, "I want to call Daddy," I won't say, "Your father won't pay the bills; your father doesn't worry about you; he doesn't wonder if you are fed or clothed, or where you get your clothing from."

If the children's father refuses to see the children, despite the mother's willingness to cooperate with his visiting, the mother can at least say, "I've done what I could." She may have new reason for bitterness as she witnesses her children's sadness, but she need not blame herself:

> The kids don't say much about not seeing their father. But Evey, particularly, is hurt, because she is the oldest and she remembers him better. She will say something like, "I wonder if Daddy is doing this?" or "if Dad is doing that?" And once in a great while they'll wonder aloud why they don't see him. All I can say to them is that he knows he can see them whenever he wants to and that it is up to him. There is nothing I can do about it.

Should children display reluctance to see the father, some mothers— far from all—will argue, cajole, do whatever they can to make the children maintain the relationship. A mother of two children, the younger a ten-year-old boy, said:

> Leonard was supposed to go away with his father last weekend. No way was he going to go with him. I told him that I thought he should go, that it would be a good experience; it would be camping. And I thought it would be a good idea for him to have a vacation from Mommy and from his older sister. Well, he still wasn't sure, because he wanted to go to this double feature on Saturday. The next morning he got up and said, "I think I might go, but I'm really not sure." And I said, "Well, if I had my druthers, I'd rather you would go." "Okay, fine." So I packed his bags fast and he went.

So long as a mother knows she did her best to encourage her otherwise reluctant children to see their father, she need not feel that she deprived her children of a relationship they needed. Though she may regret that the children feel as they do, the matter is out of her hands. A mother of four children whose three older children simply refused to see their father spoke of trying to get her ten-year-old to continue to see him. The father had left the family and moved in with another woman and her children. The ten-year-old insisted on joining his older siblings in their rejection of the father. Afterwards the mother could reassure herself that she had done what she could, and, if the children's relationships with the father were to end, at least it was not her fault.

> He'd say, "Do I have to go? Why do I have to go? I'm not going." And I said, "He is still your father. He supports you and he loves you." "No. He doesn't love us. If he loved us, he wouldn't have done what he did. He walked out and left us." What do you say to a ten-year-old boy that says that? I said, "Frank, he still loves you, even though he has his own life." But, finally, I just stopped fighting. I said, "If you want to go, go. If you don't, don't. It's your father; it's your privilege."

Noncustodial parents frequently suspect that their relationships with their children have been systematically undermined by the custodial parents. And, given the closeness of parent and child in many single-parent households, it is likely that the parents do let their children know how angry or hurt or resentful they are, and possible that the children become more nearly allied with them than with the parents outside the home. But most single parents do what they can to foster their children's relationships with their noncustodial parents. They do so despite their own feelings, because they believe it important for the children.

Custodial parents are undoubtedly correct in this belief. A study of ninety-two South African children whose parents had separated found 60 percent of them wanting unrestricted contact with their noncustodial parents. Desire for easy access to the noncustodial parent held true whether the noncustodial parent was the father or the mother.[4] Repeatedly, those children of separated and divorced parents who were able to see their noncustodial parents whenever they wished, said that only this made it possible for them to manage the separation of their parents without severe distress.

Wallerstein and Kelly, in their Marin County study, found that the usual visiting arrangement in which the noncustodial parent takes the children every other weekend appeared to the children to be woefully inadequate. Reporting on younger children, they said: "The only children reasonably content with the visiting situation were those seven- and eight-year-olds visiting two or three times per week, most often by pedaling to their father's apartment on a bicycle."[5] Older children, too, wanted easy access and frequent contact with the noncustodial parents, although adolescents appeared accepting of more widely spaced visits.

What is good for the children is not necessarily good for the mother. Even if the mother gets on well with her former husband—and certainly if she does not—the mother needs to feel that her husband cannot intrude into her life without her permission. She wants a situation in which the father has only the most restricted access to her family. But this produces a conflict of interest between the mother and the children, for the children want contact with the father to be as little restrained as possible.

When conflicts of interest exist within families they can be managed by avoidance, by quarreling, or by compromise and adaptation. All these devices are used in single-parent families. Often it becomes understood that the mother and children simply will not talk about the father, because their feelings about the father are so different. The children learn to be secretive when they return from a visit to the father. And despite the closeness of mother and children, there develops an emotionally important area they cannot discuss.

Perhaps the best resolution is that parent and children recognize that their interests in this area diverge and try to devise an arrangement that is not too unsatisfactory to anyone. The children's visits with the father can be routinized, so that the mother need not constantly be involved in making arrangements. The mother, on her part, can accept calls to the children from her ex-husband with good grace, so long as they are not too frequent, and permit some flexibility in the ex-husband's visiting. And she can keep in mind that a certain amount of discomfort may be worth putting up with, for the sake of the children.

Most fortunate are those unusual single parents who are able to feel friendly towards their former partners and to find continued contact with them valuable. They are fortunate not only because they are able to call on their former partners for favors now and again or to share with their former partners the responsibilities of child care. More than this, they are fortunate because they are spared an enduring conflict of interest within their households.

The father's new woman

Some single mothers report that their children, on returning home from a visit to the father, have said something like, "Daddy introduced us to a nice lady." Or that the father mentioned, when he came to pick up the children, that he had a friend of his, a woman, in the car. In this way the mother learned that the children's visit with the father was also a visit with the father's girlfriend.

> He said, "By the way, I have my girlfriend with me." And I made a wisecrack, something like, "Oh, you brought one of the legion." Well, this was a new girlfriend; who knows what kind of a person she is? But I was not particularly concerned with what kind of person she was, in terms of my kids' being exposed to her. What I was concerned about was that the younger one, John, does not handle a new situation well. I know my kids. I live with my kids. I know what they're like. John has a hard time handling anything the first time through, and he is just not that secure with my ex-husband. I said, "I really think you should have prepared me for this so that I could have prepared John."

Under some special circumstances the mother at home may feel injured or outraged by her ex-husband's including a girlfriend as part of a visit with the children. The point of the visit is to foster the father's relationships with the children. That is hardly likely to happen if the father is giving his attention to a girlfriend. And if the father's new girlfriend is believed by the mother to have been responsible for the ending of the marriage, then the mother may feel that she has already lost a husband to the new woman and is unwilling to risk loss of her children as well. Some women develop imageries of the other woman as unclean, and are in a panic lest their children be defiled by the other woman's touch: "I don't want her hands on you!"

Very occasionally an ex-husband, in an exuberance of tactlessness, will bring the new woman into the mother's home. The violation may seem to the mother so massive as to be bewildering:

> I just sat here and thought, "How can he expect me to handle things when he brings her in here?" He came in and he says to her, "Would you like a drink or something?" He was setting up a racing car set in my son's bedroom. I went in to see what he is doing, and she was, like, watching me. And I just felt it was really just too much to handle. You know, stay outside, give me a beep and I'll bring my son out to the car, but don't bring her into my house. It just cracked my brain. I mean he offered *her* a drink in *my* house! That really cracked my brain.

A few mothers are outraged by their children's being exposed to an unsanctioned sexual relationship. Although they may phrase their concern in terms of protection of their children, the most serious affront appears to be to themselves.

> My husband took the kids on a Thursday to where he is living now. Quentin, who is just thirteen, came back very upset. I asked him what was the matter and he said that his father had his girlfriend and her children up there. He said, "He even slept with her." I immediately called my ex-husband and told him that he was never, never to take those children up there again and to do that while they were there. I didn't even want her up there with them. I told him that they were not going to grow up with his moral standards! I said, "You have set a very poor example for these children. I don't want it to happen again."

For the most part, mothers on their own insist that they are indifferent to their ex-husband's dating life. Indeed, they may say, they are on the whole pleased if their ex-husbands are happy. They don't really wish their ex-husbands ill, and, if their ex-husbands are happy, it may in marginal ways be better for the children and for them. Their sole concern in relation to an ex-husband's new woman is the effect her presence may have on the children. And yet, despite their wish that they might feel differently, many mothers feel a bit chagrined on learning that the ex-husband has found someone new. The woman may appear to them to occupy a place that the mother would have liked to remain vacant a little while longer. And it can be galling if the husband displays an attentiveness in the new relationship that he failed to display in his marriage. But insofar as the woman is a figure in the children's lives, it is not possible to shut her out entirely:

> I have never met my husband's girl, and I don't intend to meet her. But I did tell my daughter that I'm perfectly willing to listen to her talk

about the girl when it concerns *her*. If it has to do with my daughter, I will listen. Only I don't want to know about all the good things that are happening in their life. And I don't want to know about her suits and blouses or her books.

Sometimes the mother will try to serve as the children's representative in matters involving the new woman. She may suggest that the father see the children alone part of the time, or that the father be more sympathetic to the children if they display some competitiveness toward the woman's children. In one instance a mother suggested that her ex-husband *not* keep his new women entirely hidden from the children:

My husband told me he had a girl, and I asked him if the kids had met her, and he said, "No, she hasn't said she would like to meet them." And I said, "You know, I think they *should* meet her, even if you just do something for Sunday afternoon, because they like to know who you are with and what you are doing."

Very occasionally a mother and her husband's girlfriend have reason for contacting each other. One mother, on learning that her ex-husband's new girlfriend was cool to her children, invited the new girlfriend to her home:

I called his girlfriend and I said, "I'd like to have coffee with you." She didn't want to see me, but I said I would appreciate it. So I had the two of them come to my home, my ex-husband and his girlfriend. We sat down and we talked. And she admitted that she could not have my kids in her house. They drove her crazy, because from the minute they came in they were trying to get Daddy's attention, and she didn't want to share my ex-husband's attention. I said, "It's only natural that they are going to try to get their Daddy's attention."

Another woman joined with her separated husband's girlfriend to try to rescue the husband from a self-destructive episode. The husband had called the woman to tell her he was ending it all, and the woman called the girlfriend to ask her to do something. The girlfriend first went to the husband's office, where she saw that his car was parked outside. The door was locked and there was no response to the bell. The girlfriend thereupon called the police. The police broke down the door and discovered the man in an alcoholic stupor: not dead or dying, merely very drunk. But it could have been worse and, since the man had access to poisons, might yet have become worse had he not been interrupted.

Instances in which a mother and the husband's new woman become friendly are rare. The discomforts on the mother's side and, perhaps, on the side of the other woman, appear too great. Here, however, is an instance in which mutual sympathy developed:

My ex-husband is living with a really nice girl. I like her very much. And I really feel bad for her. She has taken my place and she is going through the same thing that I did. She can handle it better than I can, because she has lasted four years so far and I only lasted two years. But she's not that happy. Sometimes she talks to me about it. I'm not sure how comfortable she is in talking to me about it, but she knows that I went through the same thing and it's easy to talk to me because I did. Sometimes I find myself getting angry at him because of her. I see her hurt in the same ways I was.

Usually the new figure in the other parent's life is understood as a successful rival, a usurper of the single parent's place, whom the children, unavoidably, will get to know and who may have occasional responsibility for them. Now and again there may be a basis for cautious collaboration with this new figure. But in general, single parents feel more comfortable if they have little to do with the new figure and so avoid what might be still another source of perplexity in the already perplexing relationship with the other parent.

PART THREE

*Single, as Well as
a Parent: The Single
Parent's Relationships
with Other Adults*

CHAPTER 7

Establishing
a Community

SINGLE ADULTS, more than the married, need ties outside their homes, for they are without that fellow adult within the household who can provide the married with assistance and companionship. But the single parent's need for ties outside the home is greater even than that of other single adults because the single parent, as head of a family, is more likely to need the help of others. All the forms of assistance—advice, relief, availability in emergencies—that a married parent could expect of a spouse, must be sought by a single parent from relationships outside the home.

Without a partner in the home, every emergency carries a double challenge: to deal with the emergency itself, and to arrange for the children's care. An incident in which a mother unexpectedly needed medical attention, although unusual both in the urgency of the mother's need and in the degree of her isolation, suggests the importance to single parents of people who can be called upon:

> This happened shortly after I had moved into this house, and the only people I knew at all in the neighborhood were across the street. I had had a D&C, and it was about two weeks afterwards, and I hemorrhaged. It was bad and I was scared. My folks lived far away and there was nobody around. It was a Sunday night, on a holiday weekend. My best friend, Martha—I couldn't get her for about two hours. I hated to call casual friends. And I don't think it even occurred to me to call my neighbors. I didn't want the kids to know, because I was afraid they would be frightened. Well, I did get Martha, after about two hours, and

she got another friend and the two of them came tearing over, and Martha took me to the hospital and Molly, the other friend, stayed with the kids.

Friends, relatives, and friendly neighbors are needed to provide the kind of backing for the single parent that a married parent would obtain from the spouse. Relationships outside the home are also the only source, for the single parent, of the companionship, the opportunity to talk over issues, and the support that is provided by the other parent in a two-parent home. Although the children may be closer to the single parent than they would be if another parent were in the household, they cannot take the place of other adults:

> I always remember a remark my ex-husband made, "How can you be alone if you have the kids?" Well, you talk to the kids and they are good company, but it's not the same. Even if the kids are older, you still have to keep a line up that you are the parent, so it's still a parent-child relationship and not a friend relationship. Although you can be friends with your children, you still can't confide in them the way you could in a good friend. You can tell them about your day, but you can't tell them about your inner emotions or your inner feelings.

While children in single-parent households may be more mature in their understandings of the adult world than their peers in two-parent households, they remain children, however precocious. Their concerns are those of children of their age. Some topics are beyond them: career issues, for example. Other topics, like money or their parents' relationships, may make them anxious. Both parents and children are likely to be reluctant to discuss sexual matters; indeed, the language parents and children use with each other is likely to be a scrubbed language, without off-color words or allusions.

Some single parents try to limit their use of the children as companions. They worry that the role of companion to a parent may direct the children's attention from the issues truly important to them: their relations with peers, for one. And they may anticipate that it will not work out that well for themselves; that if they learn to rely on their children for comfort and support they will have mixed feelings when their children, in adolescence, begin moving toward independence. One woman, a mother of three, the oldest a ten-year-old boy, said:

> I think you would be doing a kid a great favor if you could announce to him once a week, "Look, I've been with you all day long and now it is going to be my turn to be with my friends. I'm not going to go out and play hockey with you, and you can't come to the movies with me and my friends. We are grownups, and we deserve a certain amount of time to ourselves."

Establishing a Community

The children, no matter how helpful, are not enough. Single parents find life difficult and barren without ties outside their homes. Such ties can be formed with kin, with friends, or with neighbors. Each is a tie of distinct character; each has its own strengths and its own limitations.

Relatives

Relatives do what they can to help. Although the single parent's own parents may be reluctant again to devote their energies to child care, and the single parent's siblings may let it be known that they have their own families and their own lives to worry about, relatives can usually be counted on to provide a home in which children can stay during after-school hours, advice when a child is ill, a small loan if money runs short. Some relatives, particularly the single parent's own parents, may be willing to do more than this; some might prefer to do less. One woman, a mother of four children, lived not far from her parents and her mother's sister. She said:

> You can call them and they're there. They are very helpful people. My mother and my aunt do a lot of babysitting for me. They would rather I use them than hire a babysitter because they know I'm the sole supporter.

On the other hand, relatives—particularly the single parent's own parents—may prove to be limited as providers of understanding. They are likely to have difficulty in putting themselves in the single parent's shoes. Their goals for the single parent may conflict with the single parent's own goals; they may, for example, be more concerned that the parent be attentive to the children than that the parent establish an independent and gratifying life. And they may feel some obligation to ensure the parent's respectability. A mother of four said:

> My father is very "no"-minded in really almost ridiculous ways. I play tennis, and he says, "Why do you have to do that?" He hasn't any tolerance for people who take time to do something that is going to please them. And my mother—the first thing she said to me when she found out I was going to lunch with a married man was, "What are people going to say?" I said, "We're just going to lunch. No big deal."

Another woman said:

> My parents have helped me when I need money. If I ask them for money, they help me. My parents have been really good. But they can't

understand what I've done. My mother's phrase is, "Well, I have been married to your father for twenty-eight years, and it hasn't been easy." I have learned to accept the fact that my mother will never understand what I've gone through and what I'm all about. So I try to make it, like, I accept what she says, I respect her feelings, but she has to respect the way I feel, and I have to do what I think is right.

Single parents who have turned to their own parents for comfort or support may be disappointed by their parents' inability to understand how they have been affected by the dissolution of their marriages and what now concerns them. The parents' lives often have been too different from their children's to provide a basis for understanding. When the parents, in addition, want to limit their involvement with the single parent's problems, the single parent may feel rejected by them despite their helpfulness.

I don't think my family can cope with me now, because I need emotional support, and they are incapable of giving emotional support. To them, money is the answer to everything. You know, they buy me presents and they buy the kids presents, and whoopee, I should be ecstatic. They can't understand that love is more important than all the presents in the world they could buy.

Single parents sometimes find more to object to in their parents' attitudes than obtuseness. Their parents may be subtly disparaging of them for having failed in their marriages, or intrusive, patronizing, or oversolicitous. A woman who had not been married to her daughter's father said about her mother, "Sometimes she tries to help too much and gets in the way."

Sometimes, too, the parents, because they feel responsible but do not fully understand, offer criticism or advice that is neither wanted nor useful. They may criticize the single parent for being too permissive, when the single parent feels that only by the children's having autonomy can the family function. They may criticize the single parent for demanding too much of the children, not recognizing how dependent the single parent is on the children's contributions. They may advise the single parent to be less protective of the children or more attentive to them, to go out less or go out more, and by their advice add to the single parent's already substantial uncertainty that what he or she is doing is right.

Most single parents, and not only those whose parents appear willing to be intrusive or disparaging if given the chance, try to restrict their parents' presence in their lives. They try to do so even while remaining on good enough terms with their parents to keep them as helpful figures. They do this by maintaining a certain distance, both emotional and residential:

My father doesn't pass judgment on my dating. If I were living in his house, and he could see me coming and going and staying out late, then he would say something.

Establishing a Community

Brothers and sisters, like parents, may have some commitment to be of help, but their commitment may be more limited and less reliable, both because they have families and careers of their own and because early rivalries may have produced partial estrangements. Whether there is mutual sympathy may be important in deciding if a sibling will be called on at all. A sibling who is close and whose life situation makes helpfulness possible may be heavily relied on:

> I've always been close to my sister. She's got a good outlook on life and is able to accept things a lot easier than I can, because I have too high expectations of myself. When I was going through that difficult period when my marriage was ending, I guess I must have talked to her almost every day on the phone.

On the other hand, a sibling who is without sympathy or whose own life is already overly demanding may be of little help. A divorced woman with two small children said:

> I have one sister who is single, and I really don't see her too often. She lives in another town, and she has a boyfriend, so she is usually busy. And then there's my baby sister, who is twenty-two. She's my son's godmother, but she's not really much of a help. She just really can't understand it. I have found that they are too wrapped up in their own lives to give help to you.

Should there be the requisite sympathy, however, brothers and sisters can be counted on not only to help in practical ways but also to display greater understanding than do the parents. Siblings are less likely than parents to feel personally implicated by the question of whether the single parent is living a creditable life. In addition, because they are more nearly peers, siblings have a better sense of the single parent's needs and aims; they can more easily see themselves in the single parent's situation. And while siblings' investment in the single parent's children may be weaker than that of the children's grandparents, siblings usually feel obligated enough to the children, as well as to the single parent, for them to take the children now and again and give the parent a break. One mother of three said:

> When I need help I say to my two sisters, "Gee, these are your only nieces and nephew." I really let it out. I said to my oldest sister, "When they were cute and little you were around all the time, you couldn't get enough of them, and now that they are big, it is such a big deal to get you to come over and see them for a couple of hours." So then she took my younger daughter for the whole day.

Single parents often value the added security that comes with having family around, quite apart from the help they actually obtain. They feel that it is desirable for their children, too, to have the security of an extended family. Many single parents foster their children's relationships with the families of the children's other parent. It may be the widowed, especially, who do this, but it is common among the separated and divorced as well, and, to a lesser extent, among those who were not married to the children's other parent. There can be tensions on both sides, however the single parent came to that status; the family of the other parent may be cool or critical, or the single parent defensive or bitter. But single parents believe their children need family, and if they are without family themselves or if their families are far away, they may cultivate their in-laws for the children's sake. One divorced woman said:

> In my head it is good for Kenneth to see his father, his uncle, his Nana. In my head, where my own mother is gone, and my father is pretty far away, and my sisters are all scattered, I think it is good for Kenneth to have that family. And I get along good with my mother-in-law, over all. If we don't mention Kenneth's dad, everything is fine.

Kin can provide single parents with assurance that their children would not be without care if the single parents were themselves to be incapacitated or to die. Except for the minority of separated or divorced single parents who have confidence in their ex-husbands or ex-wives as parents, single parents worry about who would care for their children if they could not. In this respect, kin may be irreplaceable. Rarely is the bond of friendship strong enough to sustain so weighty a responsibility. Here is the experience of a woman without siblings whose parents were very old:

> I went on a trip one time when the children were small. And I thought, what if something happens to me? I have a real good friend who happens to be a godparent to one of the children, and I asked her, "Would you take care of the kids if something happened to me?" And she talked to her husband and said, "Sure." When I got back they called me up and said, "We're awfully glad you're home."

The single parent's kin already have some obligation to the single parent's children and some feeling of connection to them. The children's grandparents can function as back-up parents if they are not too old. Often, they are: one woman said, "My dad, who is seventy-six, says to me he'll take the kids if I'm not around." And then she laughed. But sisters and brothers, if they are not already dealing with as much as they can, might be ideal. Another woman said:

> My brother volunteered to be the children's guardian in case something should happen to me. So it's beautiful. My parents would take over with no problem, but I figure they already raised their family.

Everything considered, contact with relatives appears highly desirable for single parents. Indeed, single parents who feel their resources to be inadequate to their needs because their incomes are small or precarious or their social world barren, or because they are themselves depressed or upset, may move to be near to parents or siblings. One single parent who had for a year or so been closer to her mother than to any other adult felt that the relationship provided her with the companionship and support she needed. She said at that time:

> I depend on my mother for a lot of things. Little things, like if you run out of something, you know you've got somebody to run to and get it. Say you ran out of milk after the stores are closed. I might go to a neighbor, but I don't like to. You know, you borrow from neighbors and they are no longer friends; you borrow from your mother, and she is still your mother. If I need money in a hurry for the kids, for a pair of shoes, or for a cab or something, I know I can go there and get it immediately, no questions asked.
>
> I spend a lot of time with my mother. Sometimes my mother comes over at night and we sit and talk, maybe play a couple of hands of cards. Or she calls me, eleven o'clock. And if she doesn't call me, I call her.

But even those single parents who have large and sympathetic families living nearby are apt to need other relationships as well. A life organized around relationships with kin, although it may appear relatively untroubled, may well be without support for diversion or adventure or development. When the woman quoted above became involved with a man, her mother disapproved. She and her mother thereupon became estranged. The woman's affair ended, after two months, and her mother wanted to reinstate their former closeness. But now the woman was unwilling to accept so restricted a life:

> I know I can't go back to the way that my life was before. I have enjoyed living a little bit. Now the old way of living isn't enough. My mother . . . doesn't understand this. After you have been out of the world of the living for several years, and you get back into it, you are not going to go back into . . . seclusion and living for your kids, and that's it.

Engagement with issues beyond those of home and family ordinarily requires the single parent to have, in addition to ties to kin, friendships that are maintained because they enrich the single parent's life.

Friends

The change in social role from wife or husband to single person brings with it too many changes in concerns and routines for friendships to remain unaffected. Only a minority among the widowed, and a still smaller proportion among the separated and divorced, continue to construct their social worlds from the friendships of their married lives. This is not to say that the friendships of married days are entirely lost; rather, they fade in importance. There is less sense of closeness in them, more sense of lives that have taken diverging paths. One man, divorced, observed:

> I've got some married friends and we see each other occasionally, but I don't think we can be that close. You are not friendly on the same terms. You don't talk about the same things. You're doing things that are very different from married people.

The single parents' changed situation separates them from married friends, despite their desire that the friendships remain. A divorced woman said:

> I have one very good friend, and we were talking on the phone, and she said to me, "I think we are getting miles away. You are living in a different world now. Here I am, my husband comes home at half past five every night; I can always count on that. I feed the kids before he gets home, and he and I eat together." I said, "I know. I'm not married any more." I talk about different things and I'm doing different things.

The single parent may maintain an active friendship with the same-sex spouse of one or two of the couples who were friends, perhaps with both members of another couple. These now become the single parent's married friends. But, almost always, the community of the married is lost. The single parent no longer fits in. There are fewer invitations to mixed gatherings, more to same-sex lunches. The man newly a single father, when with couples, may feel marginal. Some of his concerns— arranging children's activities, for example—are closer to those of the women in the group than to those of the men. But he hardly can enter into their discussions, a single man among women. With the men he is conscious of how different his situation is from theirs, and again he feels marginal. The newly single woman, though she can share childraising concerns with the married women, has other concerns that she cannot share: establishing an adequate dating life, for one. A comment on this was made by one woman who had maintained an active social life before her divorce:

> When I moved to this area I joined organizations, and I was really anxious to get to know everybody. Then everything fell apart at the seams and I was on my own. I found out that my life was so different from the rest of the girls. They were all very well looked after. Some did work, but there again, it was a lot of sitting in an ivory tower. They weren't single and on their own. They weren't coping with the problems I was. And all of a sudden I was in the minority in everything we were discussing.

The newly single woman may feel she is seen as a threat by both the wives and the husbands. The wives appear to her to be alert lest she attract the husbands' attention; the husbands appear a bit worried that she will inspire their wives to become more independent themselves:

> I have stayed close with a few of the friends I had when I was married. Others, all of a sudden you just don't fit into the picture any more. You can't associate with them as a single woman. I think the women don't want you there because they feel as if you might be after their husband. And I think the men don't want you going out with their wives because they feel as if you're going to lead them off the straight and narrow path and give them some ideas. They are scared you will lead the wife astray.

Single parents usually are made aware of their having become marginal to their communities only by a reduction in invitations. But one single parent was bluntly informed by a former friend that she no longer fit in:

> My friend said, "Lenore, you are not going to be invited to our annual Christmas party, not because I don't want you, but because you will feel uncomfortable." I told her, "Don't do me any favors. I don't want to be there." You just drift away from these people—you have to start a whole new life.

Those widows who continue to see primarily the friends they had had when they were married are likely to feel less comfortable with them than they once did. Although they may be grateful for their friends' solicitude, they no longer are in the same situation as the friends. And they can hardly avoid being reminded of this when they are with them. One widow said:

> Friends have been very, very good to me, and they've included me in a lot of their functions and things, but always the fact that I am alone comes to mind. I find it very hard still when I'm out in a group of couples because it brings my oneness into perspective more than ever. There was a group that we were always very friendly with, and they invited me to some things, and I refused, and I think if you refuse too many times then they're not going to ask you again. But I still have some wonderful, wonderful friends, and if it wasn't for them I don't think I could have survived.

Yet it can be distressing to have become marginal to one's community. Another widow said:

> We had a multitude of friends. We were constantly on the go. Now, Saturday night after Saturday night, I'm alone. The friends that we had before, I'm still friends with. And, naturally, their life goes on and they go out and they still do things. I find they don't discuss what they've done with me as much as they might have before. They only do this so that it doesn't bring to mind that I might have done it, too. But sometimes it is worse this way, when you know they are avoiding it purposely.

Women who were single at the time they became mothers experienced a different sort of change. They had been without responsibility for others, free to set their own routines, their only constraint the time they were due at work and the need to remain on their jobs for eight hours or so. Their friends tended to be other single women with similar freedoms. When they became mothers their freedoms ended. Now they are much less able to go places with their friends. In addition, they have new interests and new concerns. As a result, their friendships change in character:

> I used to go out with my girlfriends and so forth. I don't really do that now. I used to go to work, come home from work, take a nap, wake up around eight or something like that. It was totally different from now.

> I really don't have the time or the energy to want to go buzzing around doing things at night or doing this activity or that activity. I still like to get out and get breaks, get a sitter and go out. But I have had to accept that it's a different life. I have a few friends. Most of them are telephone friends. I guess you get that way. You spend hours on the phone at night. One friend I call kind of frequently, maybe two or three times a week. We talk about everything.

No matter how single parenting came about, it brings with it the need to make new friends, as well as to modify, while retaining, at least some former friendships. Until a community of this sort is established, the single parent is likely to feel isolated, marginal to earlier friendship networks, not yet a member of new ones. The isolation produces a sense of empty, boring days. One woman described the feeling in this way:

> It's sort of an emptiness, sort of nonfulfilling time. You sort of feel like one day goes into the next. You just kind of feel as if it's an existence and not really living.

A never-married mother of a one-year-old daughter commented on the feeling that somewhere things were happening that were fun and enlivening from which she, as a single parent, was left out:

> I've felt lonely. Well, I don't know if it's feeling lonely so much—I feel left out, maybe—maybe just feeling left out. Your role changes. You just can't up and go out of the house if your mood takes you, and you're itchy that night, and you just want to get out or feel you've just got to get out or do something. You just can't up and go or do something. I mean, it's a case of being left out of things. So you just turn on the TV. You feel a little sorry for yourself, that's all.

When experiencing social isolation of this sort, a single parent may wonder if the isolation is not in part a consequence of others' rejection. The single parent may become sensitive to subtle slights, to subtle indications in the tone or timing of invitations that the single parent's standing with others has changed. Without anyone with whom to discuss the matter, isolated and aware of the isolation, alert to minimal cues in others' behavior, the single parent can begin to feel intentionally neglected by others. The parent's thinking takes on a paranoid quality. One man, a part-time single parent, quite isolated, provided an example:

> When you find yourself in a different family situation, you are kind of separated from the rest of society. People don't know how to talk to you. They just invite you over almost as a last resort.

Without the support of either a spouse or an existent community, it can be doubly difficult for single parents to begin constructing a new community. There is a sense of personal inefficacy, a questioning of self-worth, that makes rejection seem a thoroughly plausible anticipation. Every social venture is felt to carry risk, even attending a gathering of other single parents:

> When all of a sudden you realize you are single, you say, "I can't go here because I'm alone." You're afraid. And then you say to yourself, "I have to get out and I have to go and do these things." I walked in cold at a Parents Without Partners meeting because I made up my mind I had to do it.

Where do the new friends come from? Some are old friends: men or women known from the days before marriage, perhaps from school. They may have been only rather distant friends when known in the past; now some perceived similarity of situation, together with the trust that comes from having been acquainted for years, provides a basis for sympathy and closeness. Or the new friends may be parents of the children's friends, or neighbors, or people met through other friends, or through an organization like Parents Without Partners. Or they may be married acquaintances whose problems are different but who live nearby and whose schedules fit and who are, in addition, amusing or helpful. Most important is that the initial exploration reveals a mutual sympathy or shared outlook that facilitates easy interchange, liking and respect: reasons for each to feel interest in the other. A woman reported:

> It wasn't through work that I made friends. It was through going out and just meeting people and being compatible with them. You start going out together a little bit and start doing things together. These are all friends that have been in similar circumstances who understand probably a little bit more and know a little bit more.

Some single parents report having been recruited into friendship by someone who had previously been only an acquaintance. They had little to do with the initiation of the friendship, although it may soon have become important for them. A widow reported:

> Marie is six years older than I am. Her husband was a friend of my husband, and I knew her vaguely from working with her. Then they moved away and moved back, and we knew them just as friends in a group. Then, it was the first day that I was alone, about a week and a half after my husband died, and I didn't think any day could be worse.

> Everything was a mess. The baby was sick. He had vomited all over everything. The house was a shambles. And the doorbell rang and I thought, "This is the final straw."
>
> I wasn't even going to go to the door. But I went, and it was Marie. She came in, and she gave the baby a bath, and she cleaned up the bedroom, and she told me to put the tea kettle on, and she sat down and talked to me. She said, "You must make arrangements to go back to work, even if it is one day every other week. You've got to get your mind into something else." And she stood by me through thick and thin. She has been the greatest help that anybody could have and I feel very fortunate to have her.

A single father reported a rather similar story, although the friendship that developed did not become so close:

> I have a friend—I grew up with him, knew him for close to forty years. There were times when we never saw each other. But when my wife left, about four days later there was a knock on the door, and he was there and he said, "What are you going to do now?"

Gradually these new relationships, together with some remaining from married days, provide the single parent with a new community. The community is not one that can be located geographically; it cannot be identified with a particular neighborhood, although with one or two exceptions most members will be within easy reach. Rather, the community has a conceptual basis. It exists in the single parent's mind and feelings. It is a group of friends, some of whom know each other, some of whom don't, but all of whom are people the single parent likes and feels liked by, among whom the single parent has a place.

With the reestablishment of community, the single parent need no longer feel beleaguered. Now there are others in the same boat with whom to make common cause. A divorced mother said:

> The single-parent friends that I have, I think we help each other by talking. You know, you'll start to say, "Oh, wow, this just happened." And then they'll say, "Well, look what happened to me." And we're kind of all in the same boat. We all don't have enough money, we repeatedly run into guys that want to take you home and go to bed, we're trying to run a family and work at the same time.

Within this community the single parent maintains friendships of various kinds. There will be friends to go out with—the style of going out may itself vary with the friend—friends with whom to do things with the kids, and friends who are intimates, with whom it is possible to talk about worries, moods, plans and hopes. A widow said:

> I think it is wonderful to have friends to go out with and other friends whom I can go and see and knit with. I think it is good to have a diversified group of friends, different friends with different interests. This is what I have and I fill my life with this.

Establishing a Community

We asked one divorced woman to describe in detail her community of friends. It included a good many women whom she liked and kept up with by a telephone call or a luncheon date once a month or once every six weeks; a smaller group of women, not all of them single parents, whom she saw fairly often and felt close to; and two women who were confidantes and for whom she served as a confidante. The two women with whom she was closest were, like her, single parents.

> The girls I run around with, we talk on the phone and sometimes we get together for coffee. I see all of them quite a bit. I don't see them every day, but I see all of them. Three of us are single: me, Marie, and Terisa. Dotty and Cathy and Charlotte are married. I've never been able to figure out what we have in common. We have different tastes. Marie and Terisa are pretty liberal about men. So is Dotty. I'm more conservative. So are Cathy and Charlotte. We all have children, so we are all going through the same things there.

> It could be that once you are a mother, you can't do the things that other people do, whether they are married or not. You can only get together when the kids aren't putting on the pressure. So if you happen to have five minutes, it is nice to get together with somebody that can understand why you are so rattled. And we've always got the kids with us, too. I can't take my kids to my girlfriend June's house. She is married, but she doesn't have kids.

> I like Cathy very much, but we aren't that close. Marie and Terisa will call me late at night if they are upset. Marie calls about one of her children. She'll ask, "Am I handling this right?" She's aware of the fact that she's totally overreacting. She just has to have somebody to talk to, and there are very few people you can call at midnight. She never apologizes, "Oh, my God, it's midnight." And she can't say she's upset. She'll start in by saying, "Well, it has been one bitch of a day," and then somewhere in the middle of the conversation she comes out with what's really bothering her. Terisa will call at midnight, too. That would be about a man.

> I have another girlfriend, Thelma, that I have been very close friends with for a number of years. Thelma is married, and she and her husband are having trouble. She has started to call me; once a week she calls, because the marriage is getting hard for her to handle. And she'll say, "I'm just calling in my I.O.U.'s," because I used her many times. I think that's how it works.

> Many times friendships have intruded on other parts of my life. If I have a night clear where I have things to do, and my friend June stops in and she has a problem—it may not be a big problem, but she's just fed up—well, fine, I can't turn her down, because I have already committed myself to her life. I'm not living it for her, but I'm helping her through, just like she has committed herself to mine. And if it's not super pressing, what I have to do, I'll talk with her.

> You know, you're not aware of the time friendships take because they're so integrated into your life. It is like breathing. If I'm sitting on the

couch reading a book and am bored with that chapter of the book, there is the phone. I just pick it up and call. I just called June last night. I haven't talked to June for six weeks. I just wanted to get in touch with her, to see how she was, what was going on. I wasn't thinking, "Who can I call?" When I got off from calling June, I realized I hadn't talked to my girlfriend Peggy for six or seven weeks. But Peggy and I don't get along that well right now and I didn't want to call Peggy. So that was fine.

Of special importance in the single parent's network of friends are the small number—usually only one or two—of intimate friends. These are the friends to whom the single parent feels closest, who are regularly used as confidants, whose understanding and support play critical roles in maintaining the single parent's emotional equilibrium. Here is a comment by a woman who had just one intimate friend:

> I'm very fortunate in that I have Catherine as a sounding board. And then, too, she always has some kind of a problem or something, and you listen to her and it takes you out of your own. And before you know it, you've forgotten what you were feeling so low about before.

Some friends work as intimates and others do not. The friends who do not work are not understanding enough, are oversolicitous, or have too few or too many problems themselves. They are not able to maintain the needed mix of identification and objectivity, to be at once ally and dispassionate listener. One woman became pregnant while in the midst of a rocky affair. She felt that the friend to whom she had turned had been of little help:

> She's really nice and she tries to support, but she really doesn't know how. When I was going through this thing about a pregnancy, the next thing I know, she is saying, "Gee, I missed my period, too." You know, she was trying to relate to it and say, "I understand. We can share this thing." But I didn't need somebody to share it with. I needed somebody to support me.

Of great importance to a friend's functioning as an intimate is that the friend question the single parent's ideas tactfully, if at all. It is understood that kin become overinvolved; friends are expected to be sympathetic but to respect each other's autonomy:

> When we were on the phone she was telling me that her son had done something really wrong, and she had told him he was going to have to stay in. But her ex-husband was due to come down and take all the kids out to a baseball game. She could have told her son, "You can't go." But I didn't tell her what to do. I was very smart. I kept my mouth shut and didn't say a word.

An intimate who becomes actively engaged in a single parent's situation—who acts as a brother or sister might—is likely to introduce stress into the relationship. For one thing, the single parent may act in a fashion contrary to the friend's wishes. But, more important, the friend's intrusive involvement moves beyond the underlying assumptions of the relationship:

> You know how you confide in your girlfriends? I confided in this girl-friend and she saw me through a lot of tears and all this other stuff. So when this man started coming back into the picture, she sort of re-sented it. And she just came out and told me, "Don't even mention his name to me if you go back with him." I said, "All right, I won't." So I've been seeing him for a few weeks now and I haven't mentioned it to her. And I see her almost every day. She knows, like if I have his car. But I don't talk to her about him, and that puts a strain on our relationship, because we are really close.

Friends, even intimate friends, can be counted on to be available only to the extent that their lives permit it. And although friends will often set aside other engagements for each other, it is generally recognized that work, the children, and family demands, along with a satisfactory sexual relationship, actual or potential, all have precedence over the friendship. Single parents tend to accept, although sometimes only grudg-ingly, that a close friendship may become less close if the friend's ener-gies have been appropriated by a boyfriend, a marriage, or a job. Friendships can contribute much to one's life, but they are expected not to deflect its course:

> I have a girlfriend that I go out with and we just have great times to-gether. I think it is wonderful to have a friend like this. But if we have a date, we understand that that comes first.

Still, an intimate friendship cannot be easily relinquished. Should events in the friend's life make the friend less accessible, hurt feelings may accompany a sense of loss:

> I've known Lillian a long time. But it wasn't until she got married, and then after she got pregnant, that we were close friends. And it seems to me like after that we became closer than two peas in a pod. We really were each other's confessors. I spent more time in her house than I spent in my own. After my husband died, I could call her any time. But then Lillian didn't have time to talk on the phone and chat. I think I was getting sorry for myself because I figured, here she is, my best girl-friend, and she doesn't even call me. So I went to see her and just said to her, "Did you forget my phone number? Where have you been?" And she said, "Working." And that cleared the air, right there. I didn't know, but she was working from nine until three or four, would go home for supper, and then go back from six until ten.

Sometimes single parents establish two intimate friendships. It ap-pears to be too difficult to find the time and emotional energy to maintain more than two such relationships, but two appear possible, although to keep them going may require evenings devoted to telephone talk first with one friend and then with the other. But with two such relationships, the single parent need not be overly dependent on either; should either friend be lost the single parent would still have the other.

> I have really two girlfriends. I used to see one of them quite a bit. She was my best friend. But she got married, and you know, the relationship changes. She's with her husband more, which is kind of depressing, because we were always together.

The most important things provided by friendships appear for single parents to be of a psychological or emotional nature: a sense of support, an opportunity to match experiences, a feeling of acceptance within a valued community. Friendships also can be sources of quite substantial help—a place to stay in an emergency, the loan of a car if needed—as well as all those favors that constitute the small change of friendly relations: babysitting, or passing on clothes a child has outgrown.

The helpfulness of friends is different in several ways from that of kin. It has in it more of the spontaneous, less of the obligatory; there is no hidden reproach in friends' helpfulness: "If you had managed properly, my help would not be necessary." Instead, there is recognition that mutual helpfulness is important for all. There is, too, a responsiveness to emergency or to special need. A divorced father who was a member of a group of single parents commented:

> I have found as a single person that we single people band together and help each other a lot more than married people. When you know somebody's going to move, boy, there is always someone there to help you. If you are sick, they are there. Someone may show up with a meal or someone may take your kids out for a day, and you take it easy.

But friends expect favors to be returned for favors given. Failure to reciprocate would be interpreted as absence of gratitude or as exploitativeness, and in either event it would put the friendship in question. Knowing this, a friend unable to reciprocate for a favor would feel uncomfortable, would want somehow to communicate a sense of indebtedness. Reciprocity need not be exact; friends don't keep count of who has done how much for whom. It is enough if each friend feels good about the relationship, though often it happens that temporarily one friend feels indebted to the other. But reciprocity must take place, and utter failure to reciprocate is apt to lead to a friendship's fading. The readiness of kin to continue helping despite limited reciprocation may be too much to expect of friendship.

Friends do more than simply help each other. Friends enrich each other's lives. They provide information about things going on, about movies or plays or places to take the kids; they are company for an afternoon at the beach or an evening at a bar; they produce social events, parties, and outings. But the most important single contribution friends make to the life of a single parent may be simple, nonintrusive, relatively uninvolved, sympathetic understanding:

> When things aren't good I turn to friends. I don't think you can turn to family because it puts a strain on family relationships. I've turned to my sister emotionally, and that has put a strain on our relationship because now she feels left out. She knows I'm dating, but she doesn't know just what I'm up to. And she resents it. So I don't think I would turn to her now. Your friends love you, regardless.

Neighbors

If the single parent's marriage was ended in a way that marked the single parent as victimized, and if the single parent's neighborhood was one in which neighbors were aware of each others lives, the neighbors are apt to have rallied around to help. One widow told of neighbors cooking food for her family during the grief-filled days just after her husband's death. Neighbors were solicitous also of a woman whose husband had deserted her, leaving behind a stack of bad debts including an arrearage on their apartment, and what seemed like a battalion of persistent bill collectors. This woman's next-door neighbor provided her with housing until she could make other arrangements. In contrast, a marital dissolution in which the single parent was not so evidently free of fault is much less likely to have been followed by neighbors rallying around. Instead of support, the single parent may have been made to feel disapproval.

> I've had the usual remarks from some neighbors who think they're on equal terms with God. You know the remarks. There was one occasion when my closest girlfriend had moved to another part of the country. The day I decided I wanted the divorce, her husband flew in to drive their car back, and he called and stopped in for lunch. I was really happy to see him because I was so upset and wanted someone to talk to. When he came in for lunch I told him about the divorce, that I was going for it, that I had had it, that I couldn't take married life any more. And one of the neighbors across the street passed the remark to this girl that we both know, "I wonder what he got for dessert?"

Once the change in the single parent's marital status has been absorbed by the neighbors, the single parent's relationships with them seem to return to whatever is normal for the neighborhood. In some neighborhoods people want to have rather little to do with each other; in other neighborhoods people try to be friendly:

I've been in a neighborhood where—even being married like everyone else on the block—I was not taken into that neighborhood, because it wasn't a neighboring neighborhood. Where I am now, almost everyone on the block is a teacher. Most of them are stuck to their mortgages and they're not going any place. They are going to be there forever. It is very much a community neighborhood, and luckily I've been taken into it.

There can be nasty neighbors, of course. Neighbors can speak harshly to the single parent's children, perhaps drawing the assurance to do so from the absence of a second parent in the home. Or the single parent, especially if she is a woman, may find herself the target of a neighbor's bullying:

My neighbor downstairs has been on me. He had been making trouble for the girl next door to me until she got her boyfriend on him and then he switched to me. I had no reception on my television set, and there were three antennas over my living room up in the attic, so I hooked on to one of them. And I got terrific reception. Well, my downstairs neighbor went up to the attic to get his Christmas ornaments and he noticed my wire, so he cut it. I had been shopping, and I was just coming in, and here he comes. Always I have a knot in my stomach, what is he going to pull? And he starts right in, "What's this about wiring your set to my antenna?" I said, "I didn't think it would bother your reception." He said, "It bothers my reception." I said, "That's funny. I did it in September and it just now bothers your reception." So he started ranting and raving.

But for the most part, once neighboring relationships settle down, they are rather like relationships with relatives: neighbors are people who can be relied on to help should there be need, but with whom it is desirable to maintain a certain distance. And, since neighbors are by definition people who live nearby, distance can only be maintained by tempering one's friendliness. One divorced woman said:

You want to be friendly with your neighbors, but not too friendly, because then they are over all the time and you don't have teabags because the next-door neighbor's borrowed them. You want to be friendly enough so that if there is an emergency there would be help. And if you're fighting with them, if you have a next-door neighbor that you absolutely don't get along with, that can be difficult. But if you get along with them really well, it can almost put too much of a burden on you. I've met most of the parents of the kids my kids go around with, and we've had tea. They are nice enough. It is good to know them because their kids come over. But I would never want to have more to do with them socially.

Single parents are much more likely to need to ask favors of neighbors than married parents are. The neighbors may regularly be asked whether they would mind keeping an eye on the children when the single parent has to go out briefly, or whether they would accept a package the single parent has ordered but cannot be home to receive. In respect to helping, neighboring relationships are rather like friendships: help from neighbors must be reciprocated. To accept help from neighbors and fail to reciprocate would produce the same sort of discomfort that would be produced by failing to reciprocate for the help of friends. Another divorced woman said:

> I've gotten to know my neighbors better since Bill left. I would never ask them for favors before, when Bill was here. But now I find I'll ask people for help. I won't be demanding or anything like that, but if I'm really stuck, I'll call a woman down the street and say, "Can my son go to your house? Such and such has happened." My neighbor next door I'm friendliest with; she's the one I go to for help first, because I know I can always reciprocate. Oftentimes she needs favors, and I'm more than glad to help her. She doesn't have a car, and when she really needs a car, I'll say, "Take my car." Or, "I'll drive you there." I wouldn't ask people to help if I didn't think they'd ask back, because then you just feel like you're taking advantage of someone.

A few of the single mothers with whom we talked had constructed social lives in which neighbors played a prominent role. These women seemed to live somewhat more restricted lives than the women who gave more weight to friendships. They gave much thought to maintaining their neighbors' respect. But more than anything else, their social activity seemed to be directed not so much toward satisfying talk or doing interesting things as toward maintaining relationships in which people helped others and were helped by them in turn.

Weak ties

All of us, single parents included, make some use of "weak ties." A weak tie is a relationship with someone who is neither a friend nor a near relative but who can, nevertheless, be asked to provide information or, to a limited extent, help.[1] A relationship of this sort might exist with someone who works in the same organization but who is only infrequently encountered, or with a distant cousin, or with a friend-of-a-friend. It is possible to telephone someone known in this way and, after introducing oneself and perhaps exchanging a bit of news, to ask a favor, if the favor is not too large. A woman who was looking for an apartment said:

> I called this girl that I had known ten or twelve years ago who I had heard through the grapevine was divorced now. I said, "Hi, Nancy,"

and then I told her my name and said, "Do you remember me?" And we talked small talk and then I said, "I'm looking for an apartment in your area. Could you keep your eyes open for me?"

Single parents reported using weak ties for information about jobs, for help in getting a child into summer camp (the person called was a distant relative who knew the camp director), for information about the Welfare Department, for information about whether a particular school was a good one.

The single parent may have no more need for weak ties than would a parent in a two-parent household; anyone responsible for children has need for information about many kinds of services. But the single parent is without the resources of the spouse to add to his or her own. The single parent is dependent for weak ties on only one set of friends-of-friends and one set of distant kin, whereas the married have two sets of each. This is one argument for single parents' residing in a community in which they have roots, since in such a community they are likely to have the sort of connections that can function as weak ties.

Work and community

Work provides an alternative to the social world organized around home and family. As such, work can be a welcome relief for those single parents for whom the tasks of caring for home and family are tedious, without challenge, and isolating. It can be a relief, too, from reminders of distress, from relationships—like that with the former spouse, and to a certain extent those with the children—that can absorb energy endlessly and return not a bit of recognition. Work often provides a community walled away from the rest of life, with concerns and engagements of its own. Here is a comment by a mother of two school-aged children, separated from her husband for a year or so, in her thirties:

> I work as a bartender, and I work with a lot of waitresses. And the girls I work with—there's a couple of them who are in the same position as me, separated with kids. We don't talk about our problems that much. Sometimes we'll say, "Oh, yeah, what a bummer babysitters are!" But work is good. It gets you out and you're talking to people. You're out of the house. It's a different attitude. It is just really good.

And then this woman adds: "I've made friends through my job and we've gone out a few times. But I don't see them much when I'm not at work. I just don't have the time." For work does not, ordinarily, provide relationships that are carried over into the community of friends. Work mates are to apt to live at a distance from each other. And the basis for the kind of friendship that would survive outside the workplace, in which mutual sympathy and shared concerns sustain companionship, is often lacking in relationships formed at work. There are variations, of course. Some occupations and professions are so engaging that relationships outside the field are without savor. But for most, work is an encapsulated world, located in a place and time separate from the rest of life. At work job-related matters provide shared concerns. Away from work there might be very little to share. Here is a comment by a woman in her forties, employed in an office typing pool:

> I'm friendly with a lot of people at work, but I don't socialize with any of them. I'm in an odd situation over there. The women are either older women or they are kids. There is no other woman there in my situation—well, there are a couple, but I don't socialize with them at all.

In addition, for co-workers to carry their relationships outside the workplace would require not only that they feel the requisite mutual sympathy, have adequate shared concerns, and live near enough to each other, but also that each be ready to make new friends:

> Where I work as a cashier there is one girl who likes to go to the beach, and I said, "Here are the directions, come and meet us at the beach." What the hell, a few more kids isn't going to bother us. She enjoys the beach and she has children. And because she only works a few nights a week, obviously she has a block of free time. But I would never say to her, "Would you like to get together and go to a show on Saturday night?" I'm not that friendly, other than seeing her at work. You know, at work the people are very nice, but at quitting time you go your own way.

The single parent's responsibilities at home also tend to impede participation in the after-work sociability that in some settings provides a transition between the world of work and the world of home. Here is a woman who worked in a candy factory, on the packaging line:

> Right after work, at five o'clock, the girls would just go out together to a barroom and have a good time. They would say, "We're going out. Why don't you come?" One other girl, about my age, was married and living with her husband, and she'd say, "If you go, I'll go." But it was hard for me to go. At five o'clock I have to come home and cook supper. So I kept my private life at home. I didn't mix the two.

Many single parents, along with others in the workforce, feel it to be a bad idea to mix their private lives and their work lives. Work, they believe, requires the maintenance of friendly, even relationships. And this is more easily accomplished if just enough, not too much, of personal life is shared with co-workers. Better not to become too involved with people at work; better to maintain some barriers.

This does not mean that single parents may not have friends and confidants at work. And some single parents report that at times of stress in their homes or on their jobs they have consulted a supervisor or colleague. But ordinarily none of these relationships extend beyond the workplace.

While work can be of great value as a setting within which single parents can achieve membership in an alternative community, the work community cannot serve as a replacement for the community of friends and kin. The concerns of those known at work are too little related to the issues emotionally important to single parents: issues of parenting and personal life. And the work community exists only five days a week, eight hours a day. Those single parents who rely too much on work for sociability are isolated on evenings and weekends.

How are things different for men?

In large measure the discussion of this chapter holds equally for men and for women. But men who become single parents may have more difficulty than women in constructing a sustaining community. Men often are accustomed to organizing relationships with other men around shared masculine interests: work, sports, sometimes the sociability of the barroom. The responsibilities of a single parent bring with them need for friends who can understand the problems and tensions associated with bringing up children alone. Most men will not know other men who have such understanding, nor feel comfortable revealing their uncertainties to other men, nor have a relational style that would permit them to do so without making the other men uncomfortable. Sometimes men who are single parents say that it is much easier for them to talk with women. One single father said:

> I think men in general communicate less often and have fewer confidants than do women. I think men have been programmed over the years to be strong, and they particularly want to be strong among men. It's not a good thing, but I thing it's a fact. Men in general prefer to talk to women.

Another single father, commenting on the relative isolation of men, was determined that his situation would be different. He recognized it would take special effort:

> Women relate to each other on a friendly, emotional sort of basis. I think that men are brought up in a different way, to relate to people so

they don't let their feelings and emotions out. They bury them. I don't like it, and I'm not going to do that. I like the way women do it more. It's something I've made a decision about as far as relating to people. It means carrying on a relationship with close friends in a similar way, as far as talking about emotional things and letting my feelings out.

Some men who become single parents move rather quickly to bring into their households women who may provide emotional substitutes for their former wives, and with whom they can once again become household heads able to delegate some of the chores of child care. Men who do not do this may find themselves either trying to raise children without the social supports developed by most women who are single parents or, alternatively, developing kin ties and friendships with women that together begin to resemble the sort of community maintained by women who are single parents but that are quite different from those maintained by childless single men.

Conflict between the need to get out and parental responsibility

Without another adult in the household, failure to maintain linkages with friends and with kin produces a life barren of companionship, afflicted by boredom, without engagement, and without access to the help and information and support that friends and kin can supply. Yet after an eight-hour job together with the tasks required by home and family, those single parents who work outside the home are left with little time and little energy for maintaining ties to other adults. Nor is there anyone else with whom to leave the children. And given that they have already been away from the children through the day, how can they justify also being away from them through the evening? Still, the companionship of other adults is not easily relinquished. One divorced mother put the matter in this way:

> Because there isn't another adult in the household you have to get out. Because there isn't another adult in the household you *can't* get out.

The conflict between the children's need for their presence and their own need for relationships with other adults may seem to single parents to be beyond resolution. One woman said:

> I wish I had more time for my kids, because I know how hard it is for them. But sometimes I resent not having any time for myself, too. It

> bothers me that I have to go to work to support the family and I have
> to come home and keep working at home and I'm not able to spend
> time doing things with the kids and I'm not able to just get away. Some-
> times I find myself sitting down to cry. If I didn't cry, I don't know
> what would happen, but I've got to let it out.

The single parent may find there are moments when the children,
though loved, are also resented. For, if it were not for the children, the
single parent would not be isolated; if it were not for the children, the
single parent could get away, could do things with others. A father of
three school-aged children said:

> The hardest thing for me, when I first got divorced, was getting over
> the resentment of being stuck with the kids. There are a lot of things
> I can't do because I have the children. I can't go off for a weekend, even
> if I have the money, because I have these kids and I can't leave them
> too much.

A divorced mother of a seven-year-old boy said:

> When I get lonely I think, well, I do have Alex, and he's a lot more
> than other people have. But if I didn't have Alex I could go visit other
> people.

Parents may attempt to suppress their desire for the company of
other adults. But the desire is likely nevertheless to break through:

> I'm going to have to suppress Nancy-the-single-woman until Nancy-the-
> single-parent gets a better grip on herself. Like, I spent yesterday at a
> Little League game and I had to forfeit what I might have liked to have
> done for me. That's part of being a parent. But Nancy-the-single-woman
> was thinking of what she would have liked to have been doing that
> night.

Those who have been single parents for some time are likely to believe
that only if their own lives are satisfactory can they meet cheerfully
and wholeheartedly their responsibilities to their children. Having other
adults in their lives is seen by them as necessary if they are to meet their
parental responsibilities. They accept that they must reconcile themselves
to remaining at home most evenings. But they also believe that they
must have time with other adults, away from their children. And so they
try to find a workable compromise. They strike bargains, perhaps with
the children, perhaps silently with themselves. For they want neither
to resent their children nor to neglect them. One divorced mother of
three said:

> I do have these children to raise. And it's not being fair to them if I
> constantly just devote time to myself. So I don't, that much. I'm learn-
> ing to live with it and it doesn't bother me. Thank God, I'm not one of
> these types that really likes to step out a lot, because then it might
> bother me more. But I did have resentment in the beginning. And it's
> still constantly making bargains and balancing things off.

Establishing a Community

Probably most parental arrangements undergo change over time. As children grow older it becomes easier for a single parent to get out. And the parent's policies and priorities may shift as the parent attempts to compensate for earlier deficiencies. Parents who feel they left their children alone too much when the children were younger may try to make it up to the children. And parents who feel they sacrificed too much to the children may try to make it up to themselves:

> I have two children nineteen and twenty-one and a young son nine years old. And I think I treat the young one differently because I have seen the two older grow up and go their own ways, live their own lives. I don't always put myself first, but I don't always put him first either. I fill my own needs more often, before I do his, because I have been able to watch the older ones break off and go away.

The compromise between their own needs and their children's seems often to be uneasy. The parents may wish they had more time for themselves and, simultaneously, worry that their children see too little of them. With so little time left after working and meeting the demands of the home, it may simply not be possible for single parents adequately to meet both their children's needs for them and their own need for linkages to others.

Nor are needs for others limited to the kinds of social ties discussed in this chapter. In addition, parents are almost certain to be needful of a relationship with a reliable, accessible, cared-for figure: the sort of relationship that might be referred to as "being close to someone." It is to relationships of this kind, and to the problems associated with both their absence and their presence, that the next chapters turn.

CHAPTER 8

Loneliness, Sexual Need, and the Problems of Responding to Them

Loneliness

Some among the separated and divorced say that for them loneliness is nothing new; they were lonely even when they were married. A few say they were lonelier then, for the marriage prevented hope of other relationships. Yet most became fully aware of loneliness only with the ending of their marriages. So long as they were within the marriages another figure was accessible to them—a troubling figure, perhaps a burdensome one, perhaps one toward whom they felt hostile, and yet a figure to whom they were attached. A divorced woman said:

> I was lonely when I was married, but it was different. There was another adult there. And I was always busy. My mind was busy thinking about what I had to do and what I should do and what he was going to do. I was just too involved in him to worry about loneliness. I didn't even realize half the time that I was lonely. It was there, but not the way it is now, because I was too involved with him.

Without marriage and without an emotional partnership like that of marriage, intermittent loneliness appears nearly inescapable. Nor can the children effectively serve as emotional partners, despite their participation as junior partners in the management of their households. Although at times a sorely distressed parent and an anxiously solicitous child may engage in role reversal or an intensely lonely parent find comfort and security in a child's presence, parents ordinarily recognize that their children are too young, too in need of reassurance themselves, to be asked to sustain the parent's sense of security. If this is not immediately evident to a parent, it will become so as the children complain about responsibilities, press for treats, or in other ways display their conviction that the parent is a *parent* and not someone to be cared for. In addition, a parent's respect for a child's developing autonomy and awareness that the child must eventually establish an independent life are likely to discourage a too heavy reliance on the child's continuing accessibility. And so, although the parent's life may be entirely devoted to caring for the children, the presence of the children ordinarily will not allay the parent's loneliness. A widow said:

> I get kind of lonely home alone. There should be somebody sharing something with me—somebody on my level, not kids that I have to be responsible for all the time or that I have to always look out for what's happening to them. Somebody I can just share something with on an equal level.

Parents may actually blame their children for their loneliness. A parent may feel that if it were not for the children, he or she would be free to leave the home, to move among others, perhaps to find that missing true partner. A mother of two boys, the older aged thirteen, the younger aged ten, said: "If I didn't have kids, I wouldn't have as much loneliness, because then I could go and do anything I felt like doing." And a divorced man who had won the custody of his two sons, one seven, the other four, felt that loneliness had turned out to be an unanticipated consequence of his victory in court:

> You quickly learn the difference between the love of a child and the love of another adult. I mean, you love your children, you spend a great deal of time with them, and you feel a great deal of love for them. But there isn't the feeling of communication you have with another adult. At night, knowing that I couldn't leave the house because of the kids' being upstairs sleeping, and that I couldn't really afford to hire a baby-sitter if I could find one, I was trapped. I couldn't go anywhere. I was stuck. And I was lonely. I thought, "I brought this on myself. It was my choice. Boy, am I dumb."

Studies of loneliness suggest that there are great differences in individual vulnerability. John Bowlby, whose work has been fundamental to our understanding of loneliness, has suggested that loneliness may be most acutely felt by those whose earlier lives left them with an inheritance of insecurity, and also by those whose recent experiences have made them doubt their own capacity to meet challenge.[1] Other factors, too, have been shown to affect at least reports of loneliness. The extroverted, while they may feel loneliness as sharply, may be quicker to remedy the condition. And, although men may be as susceptible to loneliness as women, they may be somewhat more reluctant to admit they experience it.[2] Yet despite these variations, loneliness seems to occur regularly when emotional life is unshared. Loneliness appears to be a quite normal signal of an emotionally unsatisfactory state, the state of being without emotional partnership.[3] Why humans should be so constituted is unclear, but it might be surmised that in the evolution of the human organism, loneliness proved a guarantor, desirable from the standpoint of progeny, that parents would remain bonded to each other.

Lon:liness appears to include several distinct components. First is a feeling of inner insufficiency that may be characterized as emptiness or hollowness, a sense of deep ache as from a pervasive sorrow. Here is one description of this inner feeling:

> It isn't a pain. I don't think there is anything in physical pain that could really explain it. It is an ache that is deep, that you really feel, that is inside of you.

A second component of loneliness is anxiety. The lonely person may feel the world to be threatening, and the resources available for meeting its threats to be entirely inadequate. There may be nothing in the single parent's life to justify feelings of anxiety, but nevertheless there may be a foreboding that something awful is about to happen. One woman described her loneliness as progressing through stages of anxiety until it reached sheer panic. Another woman said that she felt it was like being alone with a hurricane in the offing:

> Loneliness is lousy. It is kind of like we are going to have a hurricane and you are all alone. It is like I'm the only one left on earth or something. And it's terrible; it's terrible, this feeling.

The feelings that are part of loneliness often are accompanied by physical tensions that may express themselves in restlessness, in a need to keep busy, or in random, uncoordinated activity. The present situation, whatever it is, is felt to be unsatisfactory, nearly intolerable. Lonely people may walk aimlessly, drive without destination, or experience a compulsion to go where there are people, whether they know them or not. Tension may be great enough to prevent easy sleep; lonely people commonly find that sleep is elusive and easily interrupted. The drive to escape loneliness can easily overpower other kinds of anxiety, and even rather shy individuals may find themselves actively looking for someone new. One woman said:

> You look for something to fill that emptiness. You start going out. You go out with the girls meeting people. Wrong people, right people, it doesn't make any difference. You start dating, just to get out. When

> you're not going out, you sit, you talk on the telephone, you read a magazine, but you get tired of it, and you get disgusted with it. It all builds up inside, and then you go.

Among some single parents, especially widows and widowers, feelings of loneliness are associated with yearning for the lost spouse. Their distress may be more accurately characterized as separation distress than as loneliness, insofar as they are pressed toward rejoining a particular figure rather than finding someone as yet unknown. A man who had been a widower about two years described separation distress when he said:

> Do I ever feel lonely? Yeah, I miss my wife a lot. A whole bunch. All of a sudden missing her just flashes through my head like a railroad train. It can happen any place. It can happen in the middle of a ball-game, in the middle of a meeting, in the middle of a conversation. I can get up in the greatest mood in the world and just drive down the street and it can happen.

Friends and relatives, like children, at best provide distraction from loneliness and from separation distress. No matter how understanding the friends and relatives or how sympathetic, their lives are removed from the single parent's. A divorced woman commented:

> You know you've got family and you've got friends, but sometimes you just feel like you are alone.

Being with married friends or family may exacerbate a single parent's feelings of loneliness by making evident the single parent's isolation. In addition, especially with married friends, there may be a sense of marginality, of no longer being part of things. Single parents sometimes speak of being made to feel like a fifth wheel. To be marginal is to be more vulnerable in a situation already felt to be threatening.

For a few single parents, loneliness becomes a chronic condition. It becomes a part of their lives, itself a kind of companion. It is with them constantly. But now it no longer expresses itself as restlessness; instead it makes their step heavy, slows their responses, moves them toward depression. They do not believe it will ever end. Other single parents prevent this development by distracting themselves with some sort of occupation. A woman who had been divorced for several years said:

> The beginning was really bad. In the beginning it would be all the time. Then it was once a week I'd get lonesome. Now I'm so busy with everything, it's maybe once a month.

Still, for even the most self-controlled single parent, awareness of loneliness may be brought on by an encounter with married friends, an observation of a neighborhood couple returning together from a shopping trip, or the recognition that everyone else in the neighborhood is a member of a two-parent family. A woman who had been divorced about eight years said:

> I feel lonely when I'm outside with the kids, just sitting. I look around and everybody around here has a family, and they are all out together doing something. I just want to hide, because I'm a single mother with two kids and that's it.

And a divorced woman who described herself as relatively free of loneliness said that there were times when she could not prevent herself from recognizing that, in contrast to others, she was alone:

> I really don't have a lot of time to think about being lonely. But it hits you at weddings. Weddings are a good time to feel, "Shit, I'm really out of it." Or any sort of reunion, even a class reunion, it hits you.

Certain times of the day can be especially difficult. The supper hour is a time when a single parent may imagine couples getting together after the workday. For some it is the later hours that remind them they are alone, despite the children. Weekends, too, are difficult, since families are together then; so are children's birthdays. A divorced woman with two adolescent children said:

> During the day it is not too bad. I go out, have coffee with some of my friends. Suppertime is all right. We get through that. But then there is that big gap from suppertime until the time you go to bed. You can just watch so much TV, you can read so many books, and you just don't want to listen to the children all of the time. You just want to talk to somebody your age. And then you think of the lonely nights ahead for the winter, the holidays coming up. It is just a lonesome, lonesome, feeling.

The family holidays of Thanksgiving and Christmas can be harrowing. Single parents are likely to have memories of warmer, better Thanksgivings and Christmases past. As the holidays approach, they can hardly escape encountering family scenes, in newspaper advertisements and on television, of excited children and above them their two beaming parents. For those who are divorced, the holiday itself may be divided with the children's other parent, and some holidays may be spent quite alone. A divorced woman said:

> I hate holidays, especially Christmas. That seems like that's the loneliest time. What my husband and I have been doing the last two years is, I have Christmas with them on Christmas Eve and he has them Christmas Day, which means I'm by myself Christmas Day. So usually it ends up that I go to my brother's house. And that's lonely.

There is a remedy for loneliness: establishing a new attachment. But until this happens, the single parent will now and again be reminded that evolution has ensured that we humans are not content to be emotionally alone.

Sexual need

Virtually all single parents, excepting those who moved directly from marriage to a new attachment, report at least occasional experiences of loneliness. Sexual need appears more variable. While some single parents report almost intolerable sexual need, others disclaim having experienced a specifically physical need distinct from loneliness. Because the single parents with whom we have talked do not in any way constitute a representative sample, we cannot say whether one or another response is the more frequent among all single parents. But among those with whom we have talked, it is more nearly the rule than the exception that there has been sexual tension. And, for some, the tension has at times been intense.

We have found little evidence for the traditional belief that sexual desire in men is impelling while in women it produces, at most, a state of passive responsiveness. Women do appear more diffident in reporting sexual need and perhaps more resistant to accepting that this is what they feel. But among the women and men with whom we have talked, sexual desire seems as likely to be impelling in the one sex as in the other. A divorced woman, for example, said:

> Oh, God, I've felt sexual frustration. I was, like, climbing the walls. I would wake up during the night and I didn't know what in God's name was going on, that I had this sexual desire. I think if I had been another kind of a woman, I would have gone out in the street and God knows what I would have done. But I couldn't do that. The feeling was through my—well, say my stomach—just a yearning, but very bad.

Perhaps because they are unaccustomed to thinking of themselves as possessing strong sexual needs, some women at first fail to identify correctly the nature of their discomfort. One woman said that only by talking with other women was she made aware that she was experiencing sexual deprivation:

> In the beginning, I wasn't aware of being sexually frustrated. But then, talking to other divorced women, I identified with them. And, yes, I was frustrated.

Another woman spoke of regularly failing to recognize sexual need until the feeling had become so intense that she could not avoid attending to it:

> There is this inability to concentrate, this tension. And it grows and grows. It's wicked. I can't concentrate on anything. I'll say, "Why can't I concentrate?" And then I'll know what it is. And sure enough, once I've isolated it and said that's what it is, I'm aware of it.

Men seem entirely to accept that sexual deprivation should produce sexual tension. But women seem often to separate themselves from their physical needs, almost to take toward their physical selves the role of a no-nonsense older sister, telling themselves in firm tones that this is what it is and this is *all* it is. It is as though they need to introduce distance between the selves with which they identify and their physical selves; then, this distancing accomplished, they can admonish their physical selves in a sympathetic, blunt, rather patronizing fashion. One woman, for example, said:

> I found myself looking at men and sizing them up. And I said, "Oh, shit, you are getting lonely. You just need some male company."

Another woman described a very similar distancing of the self with which she identified from the physical self that experienced sexual feelings:

> I can feel me getting frustrated. I can feel my stomach getting tight. I can feel it building up. I get short-tempered with my kids. And I say to myself, "You just need a good screw. Right now you don't have a good screw."

Splitting and distancing can be used to blunt the impact of sexual yearning. First the parent separates the self identified with from the physical self. Then the physical self is treated condescendingly, like a child. A woman who had been divorced several years said:

> Over the years it has been easier. I'd say maybe half a dozen times a year, I've got that feeling. But now when I get it, I figure to myself, "Okay, now, God gave you feelings. So the feelings are there. There is nothing you can do about it." Then I'd have these fantasies, which don't do me a damned bit of good. So I'd say, "Okay, you'd like to go to bed with a man. Where the hell would you go?"

Like loneliness, sexual tension, for women at least, may occur only intermittently; as several women put it, at "certain times of the month more than others." Those are the times, one woman said, when she gives her house an extra good cleaning.

Keeping busy appears about as useful in distracting attention from sexual need as it is in distracting attention from loneliness. One woman said:

> It isn't that you feel it all the time. I mean, you've got other things on your mind, like getting out to work and making sure there will be a supper for the kids.

Experience with sexual tension, just as with loneliness, enhances abilities to deal with the feelings. The feelings are less strange, their existence is less distressing, and their course can be more easily predicted. A woman divorced about five years said:

> I guess life is all right the way it is, except for sexually. I don't handle this sexual frustration too well. I get very depressed. But I come out of it in a few days. I guess you get used to it after a while. I don't have it as much as I did.

Just as some single parents may feel separation distress rather than loneliness—that is, yearn for the person to whom they had been married rather than simply feel a need for an as-yet-unidentified emotional partner—so do some single parents continue to feel sexual desire focused on the person to whom they had been married. Widows speak of dreams in which their husbands return, and sometimes the dreams are sexual in content. Among the separated and divorced, sexual tension is sometimes associated with thoughts of the former spouse. One woman, separated from her husband for several years, considered reestablishing a relationship with him limited to sex. She did not want to live with him again, but she continued to yearn for him. Some separated and divorced couples do maintain sporadic sexual relationships for months or years after the ending of their marriages.

Sexual tension can provide additional force to other desires. Loneliness, in particular, may become more impelling because it is intermeshed with sexual tension. Or sexual need may become intermeshed with a wish for someone who could help deal with the problems of home and family, or with yearnings for another child. The result may be a curious, confusing mixture of feelings:

> I think, in a way, I'm lonely for a man, just the thing of having your head on his shoulder or having his arm around you to comfort you, or just having him give you a squeeze or a hug. I'd love for somebody to put his arms around me. So I guess it would have to be said I was lonely for a male. And yet if I went and met some stranger, that wouldn't be enough. I can't explain it.

And so sexual need—perhaps intermeshed with loneliness, perhaps associated with still other feelings—provides the single parent with still further evidence that unswerving dedication to the welfare of the children is likely to be accompanied by feelings of deprivation.

Thoughts of the future

In survey studies, single parents appear much less satisfied with their lives than either married parents or childless single people. In one survey, among women forty-five years of age or younger, 41 percent of married mothers and 26 percent of childless single women described themselves as very happy, but only 16 percent of no-longer-married mothers described themselves as very happy. And, while only 9 percent of married mothers and 16 percent of childless single women described themselves as "not too happy," about 31 percent, almost a third, of no-longer-married mothers put themselves in this least happy of the available categories.[4]

Loneliness and sexual deprivation are reasons enough for dissatisfaction with life. But, in addition, single parents are liable to all the troubles of raising children alone: worries about money, more work than can be done, unremittant responsibility. No wonder, then, if single parents permit themselves the belief that there are better alternatives.

Most single parents hope that at some point their lives will be shared. Some have daydreams of happy endings in which the perfect person appears and together they enter the perfect marriage. One divorced woman said:

> Sometimes I have dreams of what might be. Like everything's all going to come together for me; it's all going to work out. There will be marriage and everything I thought marriage was supposed to be. People tell me it isn't real, the "happily ever after," the knight in shining armor. But why bother going on if there isn't something to look forward to? If this is what it's going to be for the rest of my life, I give up now. The hell with it!

Some single parents, more skeptical of marriage, have somewhat different daydreams. And yet they, too, want more than they have. A divorced woman said:

> You know what I think ideally I would do? Meet a man who has been married and has some kids, so he knows what it is all about. Fall in love and all that goes with it. But, "You live in your house and I'll live in mine—and don't get under my feet."

With few exceptions, single parents want their futures to be different from their present lives. Even those who feel they are managing well enough want, some day, to share their lives. A divorced woman in her thirties with small children said:

> I can get along without a man. I'd rather have one, but it's not a trauma if I don't. But every once in a while, I'll think about what it's going to be like in twenty years, when the kids are gone and I'm sitting here by myself.

For many, unwillingness to remain alone becomes stronger as time goes on and memory of the grief and pain that accompanied the ending of the marriage recedes. The divorced regain confidence in themselves and in their ability to maintain a satisfactory relationship; the widowed feel less obligated to continue to observe their earlier vows and more willing to risk new commitment. A woman widowed several years said:

> I would like to remarry. The only negative thought that I might have would be that I could really care for somebody again and the same thing would happen. And I don't know if I could stand that again. That would be uppermost in my mind. But I really hope to have the companionship and the closeness again that I had. I wouldn't want to go through my life being alone.

Single parents may, despite their hopes, postpone the point at which they become involved with someone new. They may feel that, just at the moment, they have their hands quite full, that the children need to regain their equilibrium first, that they themselves are not ready. But they do not want to go through their lives alone.

Hesitancies about dating

The remarriage rate among widows is far lower than that among the divorced. In the early months of bereavement, a new relationship may appear to widows to be uncomfortably close to adultery. Widowers, although their grief is as great, are more willing to contemplate finding someone new who might, perhaps, help them with their grief. But widows generally feel themselves not ready to consider a new person for some time, even though loneliness and sexual need may make them question themselves. A woman widowed about a year said:

> I'm not ready for going out with other men. I have been called to go out and I'm not interested. If someone that I knew and that I liked called, I suppose I'd go out and I'd have dinner or something. But not a romance. I'm just not interested right now. I still think he's coming home. At other times I say, "What in blazes am I doing sitting home? Why aren't I going out?" Just mixed emotions.

Both widows and widowers may share, as a reason for hesitancy to form new relationships, the fear that no new marriage could compare with the marriage that they have lost. A woman widowed for several years said:

> I have been saying that I would like to meet somebody. Then this man called me, and I will be seeing him tomorrow, and he is everything I would like. He is very wealthy and so forth, and he likes me. And all of a sudden I'm building a wall around me. I don't want him to get too close to me. I think to myself, "Would I make a good wife?" I was a

good wife the first time. "Would I love him as much? Would I compare?" I had a fantastic marriage. I'm afraid another won't be as good.

The separated and divorced, far from worrying that a new marriage would be different from the marriage they had earlier, are likely to worry that it would be only too similar. A woman whose husband had left her for another woman described her continued wariness:

> I saw a movie where there was this scene where the husband was telling the wife he was having an affair. And it was like it was five years ago, like I was her, and what this actress was doing, I was doing five years ago. And I remember saying, never, never would that ever happen to me again. I just don't want to take the chance that it won't work. I don't want to go through being rejected again.

Mothers who have not been married may nevertheless have been hurt enough in earlier relationships to be hesitant about new ones. They may not share the sense of betrayal of the divorced mother whose husband left her for another woman, because for them there had been no vows. And yet they, too, can have been made distrustful of men and relationships with them. The following comment was made by a never-married mother in her late twenties:

> I had this terribly bad experience with this man. He was under the assumption that I had so many things to do with my job and my kids that whatever he did outside the house, I would never know. But I found out. And it made that time really rough. I have this terrible fear that I just really can't deal with that situation again.

Those who have been hurt in earlier relationships may find that their anger has generalized and they are now angry with any representative of the other sex. Or they may be fearful of the other sex or convinced that all members of the other sex are exploitative and untrustworthy. Or they may feel compelled to demonstrate to themselves their invulnerability, or their ability to diminish any representative of the other sex they become involved with, and then may be dismayed that they should feel this way:

> In the beginning, I didn't date. And it was just as well because, I think, in those days I would have castrated the man. That's how much hatred was embedded in me.

Even should all these feelings be surmounted, it can be stressful for the widowed and the divorced to contemplate entering dating situations. For while they were encapsulated in their marriages, the world of single people was changing. Single parents may feel themselves entirely unprepared for what they understand to be new values and new practices. A divorced woman said:

> You live with one man for twenty or twenty-five years and all of a sudden you're in a permissive society and you are part of that permis-

sive society. I hadn't had a date since I was nineteen. Meanwhile, we had been through the sexual revolution.

Single parents recognize, too, that not only has the society changed, but so have they. They are older. They may be less attractive. They worry about their bodies. Women think of sagging breasts and stretch-marks. Men worry about pot bellies—and about impotence.

And now they are parents. They come as a package deal: adult with children. What might that mean in the dating marketplace? A widow said:

> I can't imagine anybody that's never been married wanting to take on somebody with three children. Their whole life style would change com-pletely. Perhaps somebody that has been divorced. But then again, maybe they wouldn't want to take on someone else's children when they were still supporting their own. I think a widower, more than any-body—if they weren't taking you just to bring up *their* children.

It may be especially important for a single father that whoever he becomes involved with get along with his children. If the relationship should lead to marriage, the woman might be expected to assume much of the responsibility for managing the household and caring for the children. A divorced father with custody of his children said:

> I want someone who has had experience with children, who can take care of my children as well as I can take care of my children. And I feel that the only kind of woman that would *want* to be involved with a man with two kids would be a woman who had had children or knew a lot about children.

Single parents, both men and women, can easily despair of finding the right person. Single fathers may have an easier time meeting some-one. But those they meet, they complain, are too young or, if older and never married, then career-driven or spinsterish. If they are widowed, they idealize their former husbands, and who can compete with that? If they are divorced, they are embittered toward all men. Single mothers who are themselves beyond their twenties voice parallel complaints. There may be men around, they say, but not the right sort. If the men have never been married, then it is because something is wrong with them: they are unwilling to settle down, still tied to their mothers, or homosexual. And if the men have been married, then they are likely still to have responsibilities to their former families, still to have wives to whom they must furnish child support and children whom they must see. Many single parents, male and female, feel themselves drawn to the conclusion, "Why bother?" A divorced woman about forty said:

> It's really hard at my age, because the man who is still single and is in his early forties is married to his job or so set in his ways that he's impossible to live with, or he's a little bit odd, or he has various prob-

lems. He's single for a reason. And divorced men have usually got responsibilities.

Then there are all the practicalities of dating to worry about, the costs in time and energy and money. If the children are small, dating requires finding and paying a babysitter. A man must, in addition, be prepared to pay for tickets or dinner or drinks. Both men and women will need clothes in good order. If funds are limited, there may be competition between these needs and the needs of the children. A mother of four said:

> Dating is hard if you have to worry about babysitting, because babysitters are expensive. And if you want to look nice when you go out, you have to have new clothes. And that puts a limit on me. I have four kids and I have to think of them.

Nor will a parent who gives the weekdays to work, the evenings to home and children, and the weekends to all the things that couldn't be done during the week have energy to spare. Going out imposes a cost in fatigue. It means less time to get other things done, and less time to rest. A divorced woman said:

> There is the problem of exhaustion. If you stay out half the night, you're going to pay for it the next day. You're still going to have to carry out the same routine. And you were already tired before you went out. So it's two or three days later that you finally get back on your feet.

Going out means less time for the children. Single parents who work may feel they already are with their children too little. But the date means the children must be left for yet another evening with a babysitter and the television set.

> There's a conflict between going out and being a mother. I work four nights, and here is another night I'm going out. I say to the kids, "I'm going out tonight. I have a date. I'm going out to dinner." And my son says, "Not again!" Then he says, "Oh, all right." And I feel guilty.

Some women—perhaps especially those who are living in family neighborhoods in very traditional communities—worry about their reputations and about protecting their children from the jibes of friends. One woman, a divorced mother of two latency-aged children, said:

> Why should I give the impression to my children and to other people that I'm running around? My girlfriend thinks there's nothing wrong with this. She feels, "Why should people condemn me? They never saw me with anybody." She feels like you actually have to be caught with a man in a motel; otherwise, they don't condemn you. I told her, "Talk does more damage." And children are very cruel. When the children become older, a friend might say to them, "I know about your mother. Your mother isn't so good."

Most single parents worry about their children's reactions should they begin to date. They are likely to be aware that their dating will require their children to stop seeing them simply as parents and to recognize that they have sexual needs. They may worry about their children's reaction to the people they go out with. One woman agreed to have coffee with a man she met at a church supper. But then, although the woman had planned to return home to get her own car, the man insisted on driving her to the skating rink where she was to pick up her fourteen-year-old daughter. The woman worried through the drive about what her daughter's reaction might be to seeing her with this strange man. She said:

> I said I had to pick up my daughter from skating at ten o'clock. And this fellow said, "We'll go and pick her up together." I kept saying, "No." But, no, he had to. So we pulled up in front of the skating rink and my daughter was there. I didn't know what she would say. I was afraid she would say, "Isn't he horrible-looking." What she actually said was, "Oh, *no*."

The children may actively discourage parents already uncertain about entering into dating. And although parents may feel it a relinquishing of their rights as independent adults to permit their children to control their personal lives, and, in addition, inadvisable from the standpoint of its effect on the children, their children's objections may nevertheless increase their hesitancy. A divorced mother of two adolescent children said:

> I had this problem with my kids when they were younger. My son used to say, "Don't ever have a man over to this house." And I would say, "Who the hell are you to tell me that?" But I kind of did what they wanted.*

On the one side, pressing the single parent towards finding a new partner, are emotional, physical, and social needs. But on the other side are all these reasons for hesitancy, including the costs of dating and concerns for dignity and self-respect. In family neighborhoods, there are the neighbors to worry about and what they may think. There is the recognition that an appropriate new figure may be very hard to find. And—another issue for someone separated or divorced—it is just possible that the former spouse would use the parent's dating to malign the parent to

---

* The following story told by a woman in her thirties, now herself a single parent, suggests that children may later have second thoughts about having kept their parents from dating: "My parents were divorced when I was eight. And we played a lot of scenes for my mother, not to get another person. You know, 'We don't want to have to change our names,' and how could this be guaranteed? We did a lot of things to make her feel guilty. And she said, 'Okay. I'm not going to date. I'm going to devote all my life to you children.' And now that we're grown up, we're just so guilty. Now she's old, and we take turns taking care of her, to pay back what we took from her. How we wish that she'd married! We really feel so guilty." As is noted in chapter ten, children often are ambivalent regarding parental dating, whatever they may say.

the children or to argue in court for renegotiation of support or custody: "There's someone she's just about living with, Your Honor; she doesn't need my support."

Where there are so many strong contradictory forces, there is justification for a variety of policies and reason to anticipate that no policy will be entirely satisfactory.

Managing alone

Some single parents choose, for any of the many possible reasons, to make themselves unavailable to new relationships, perhaps only for an interval, perhaps indefinitely. Or it may not be the case that a single parent chooses to be unavailable; there may be no one of interest in sight, or the single parent's ambivalence may make others wary. In any event, with no new attachment the single parent will have loneliness and sexual tension to cope with.

Many find loneliness to be manageable, so long as there are tasks to be done or others to talk with. The loneliness is not ended—it remains, at the edge of awareness—but it is not so painful, not so near to being overwhelming. A divorced woman said:

> I think I'm finally learning to cope with the loneliness and everything. When I feel lonely I pick myself up and go visit somebody or go to a meeting or go out with the kids. I try to fill my days and I try to fill my nights. I have no interest in TV any more. At first all I did was watch television, night after night after night. But now things are quite hectic here.

The strategy of keeping busy is easily adopted by a single parent whose normal state is overload. But at times it becomes important not just to be busy, but also to be out of the house, among other adults. It is prudent to avoid situations in which being alone would become a reason for feeling marginal: dinner alone at a restaurant, for example. An evening with married friends can also send a single parent home lonelier than ever. It may be best if the friends visited share interests that have nothing to do with private lives or, if private lives are to be discussed, if the friends are, like the parent, alone. For example, a widower, living with his sister, could feel community among other lonely men:

> When I get to feeling lonely on the weekend, after we put the kids to bed Saturday or Sunday nights, I'll go out and talk to somebody, or I'll go

> visit a friend. I might go up to the tavern, have a couple of glasses of beer with a couple of guys that are in there, that maybe are in the same boat as myself. I mean, they have no connection.

The telephone may provide both an activity and a means to companionship. One mother, never married, said: "When I'm lonely I get on the telephone and I run up my telephone bill." Just the reassurance of engagement with another person can temporarily allay loneliness. A divorced woman said:

> I'll call somebody up on the phone, just to talk. I don't even talk about the way I'm feeling. I just get into the kids and what they are doing in school and stuff like that. And it takes my mind off of it.

But after the receiver is replaced, the single parent may again feel lonely and again need to do something to manage the feeling. Some single parents, when in this mood, make one long telephone call after another, filling the evening with talk until it is time for sleep.

Permitting oneself to telephone because that is what is needed is a way of caring for oneself. Some single parents are even more direct in their self-nurturance. One woman said: "When I'm lonely, I'll go out, just go shopping, buy myself a new outfit, have a hot fudge sundae. I'll be good to myself." A few nurture themselves with alcohol. But here is danger, for alcohol, when used to blot out anxiety, can be addictive. A woman who had left an alcoholic husband found herself, in an ironic development, drinking to cope with her loneliness:

> The nights are long and very lonesome. And sometimes I drink to forget. I drink too much and I hate myself in the morning. For the time being, you do forget, but the problems are still there in the morning, and you feel worse about it. And the children don't like it either. My husband was such a drinker. And I hated it. I hated it, hated it, hated anything to do with it. And now I find myself sometimes drinking too much.

With time, as single parents' lives become more nearly routinized and they become more confident of their ability to manage in other respects, there may be longer intervals during which they are entirely content to be by themselves. And, should they nevertheless be visited by loneliness, they are likely to have techniques for dealing with it. It can be helpful for them just to recognize the feelings and to remind themselves that they recovered from them in the past.

While loneliness may sometimes simply have to be endured, sexual tension has at least one obvious remedy: masturbation. True, the satisfactoriness of masturbation may be diminished by a feeling that it is immature or morally wrong, and coincidental loneliness may be worsened by recognition that this is now how one is dealing with one's sexual needs. Yet for some, masturbation, at least for a time, takes care of some part of their need. One woman said:

> I was feeling frustrated, so I masturbated and I was fine. Christ, I hadn't masturbated since I was two. And it was great. Who the hell ever needed my husband? I went to bed with my husband for how many years and played games; Christ, I fantasied myself with Paul Newman, anybody, just to turn myself on. Now I don't have to bother. I'm all set. I don't have to mess the sheets up, the pillows aren't on the floor, it's great.

Some find in masturbation not only sexual relief but still another way of providing nurturance for themselves. One woman spoke of masturbation's becoming so gratifying that she worried that she would have little interest in a relationship with a man should one become possible. She said:

> You can do a better job yourself half the time. But I was afraid of doing it so much; it was taking energy away from putting it onto a person. So I consciously decided to back off for a while.

But even if individuals could find in masturbation a satisfactory response to sexual tension, loneliness would preclude foregoing a partner indefinitely. Indeed, sexual need is so intermeshed with need for an emotional partner that masturbation is likely to be of only limited satisfactoriness.

The urgings of others

Sometimes it appears to single parents who desire, despite the discomforts of remaining alone, to settle for what they have and to give their energies to their children and their homes, that others in their lives have entered into a conspiracy to unsettle their resolve. Their friends and relatives admonish them to become active socially, to get out and meet people, to look for someone new. Co-workers feel it is a kind of friendliness to suggest that so attractive a person need not be alone, and that it would be good for the single parent to find someone nice. And there may be passes, subtle or blatant, that carry the same messages. A woman in her mid-thirties, divorced and with four children, worked in the purchasing department of a large firm:

> I have guys at work that will come up and say, "You know what you need? You need a little loving. A little good Irish loving." What they mean is a night out in a cabin. One of them, he kind of pressures once in a while. I say, "Look, I'm going in the convent. Just as soon as these kids are grown up, I'm going in the convent."

All this affects the single parent's resolve to remain alone by continuously confronting the single parent with its alternative. In addition, younger, more attractive single parents may be made to feel that remaining alone is a withholding of oneself from life. The same woman said:

> Somebody made the comment that I'm very friendly, but there is always that reserve. So they know I'm not going to get involved with anybody. I could only lose and I've been selfish enough to know it. I'll go out to dinner, go to a show; I'm content with that. I suppose somebody could say I'm frigid or cold or something, but most of my affection is on the kids. Sometimes I get depressed, lonely, sitting here, or late at night, the house is quiet; but I wash something, go get a book and read, take the dog out.

Insofar as others' urging that the single parent go out, meet someone, and become involved implies that the single parent's loneliness is a problem that could easily be corrected if the single parent would only act, it is a form of blaming the victim. Single parents are likely to respond defensively. A divorced woman reported an interchange with her sister:

> My sister said, "You've got to go out. You're young, you're pretty, you're attractive." And I said, "I don't want the hassles. All men want is just to go to bed with you. They're all assholes."

Another woman, also divorced, had invited her mother to live with her. At one point a man called to invite her for dinner, and she declined. Her mother was critical, and the woman, in response, became angry:

> Somebody called me up to ask me out, and I said, no, I wasn't going to go. My mother heard me and said, "What are you going to be? A fucking hermit?" And I started yelling, "I'm not going to be a fucking hermit! You want me to go out every goddamned night?" And then we both kind of shut up and we let each other alone. Except that she kept saying to me, "I wish you would go out and have some fun," and I kept answering very sweetly, "Why don't you mind your own business?"

Relatives, like single parents themselves, are likely to be of two minds regarding the parents' dating: both distressed by the parents' isolation, and concerned that their grandchildren or nieces or nephews be properly cared for. Sometimes the same relative who earlier urged that a single parent get out of the house will later criticize the parent for neglecting the children. Single parents may end by feeling that the less their kin know about their private lives, the better.

The same ambivalence may be displayed by the single parent's children. Children often do not want a new figure to enter their household: it would mean having to adjust to the new figure; it would end whatever hopes the children might have of their parents becoming reconciled; it almost certainly would mean that the parent with whom they live, already too little accessible to them because of other demands, would become still less accessible. But on the other hand, the children are likely to recognize the parent's need for another adult; they may already have learned that when another adult is around, the parent is easier to live with. A mother of two children, both in early adolescence, said:

> My children say, "Why don't you go out? I think you should go out." If I'm down and they know it, they'll say, "Why don't you go out? It might do you good." I think they probably see that I give them a rough time when I'm in a bad mood. So they are really saying, "Why don't you get out. Then life will be easier for us."

It is difficult to know how much impact these urgings of others—self-interested, ambivalent, implicitly critical though they may be—have on parents' behavior. But it seems likely that if parents are uncertain about what they should do, the urgings of others to find someone new would carry some weight. Certainly others' urgings remind parents that the way things are is not the way they have to be.

CHAPTER 9

Someone New

Is there anyone around?

Should single parents decide that they are available for new relationships, they may wonder how to form them. Are eligible people really around? And if they are, where are they?

Sometimes, not as often as some single parents would like, friends provide introductions. They invite a single mother or father to a dinner at which there will be another guest, someone of the other sex, also single. Or a married friend says to a single mother, "I suggested to someone that he call you; I hope you don't mind," or to a single father, "There's a friend of ours I think you would like."

Single parents may feel uncomfortable about these introductions even as they are grateful for them. They may worry about being obligated to their friends to have the relationships go well. A single parent may imagine that the friends will be curious about what happens on the date and so feel under scrutiny. And good friends are not necessarily good agents. The introduction may be to someone entirely inappropriate. The single parent may suspect that the friends' first commitment is to the other person. And why does the other person need the friends' sponsorship? A divorced woman in her mid-thirties said:

> First they fix you up: "Have I got the perfect guy for you!" And then after, it's, "Oh, gee, what happened? He was a wonderful fellow. Didn't you like him?" People that your friends want to introduce you to, there's something wrong with them. Otherwise they wouldn't want to be pushing them onto somebody all the time.

But most single parents report that their married friends, perhaps after one or two half-hearted efforts, make no attempt to introduce them to anyone. The married friends may recognize the awkwardness of match-making. In any event they rarely do much of it. A divorced woman said:

> I haven't met anybody from my married friends. Either they don't know anybody or they would feel they were pushing. But they have never said, "Hey, have I got a guy for you," that kind of thing. We never talk about it.

Single friends may not be much better than married friends. Someone found interesting by a single friend will hardly be passed along. More likely, the single friend will try to establish a nonencroachment agreement. Very occasionally, a single friend who is already going with someone may extend an invitation to a double date. Or, should the single friend's own liaison end, there may be some possibility of seeing the friend's former boyfriend or girlfriend. But most often, the friend will have said so much about what was wrong in the relationship that the single parent will feel warned off. And, should anything develop, there may well be problems with the friend. One single father began to see his best friend's former wife; the friendship, understandably, cooled.

Relatives, particularly siblings, appear a more promising source of introductions. Indeed, single mothers describe the introductions made by their brothers or by their sisters' husbands as among the most likely of all to work. A brother or a sister's husband can be assumed to be identified with the single mother, and so his recommendations can be trusted. And, although there may be some joking about fixing her up, the single mother's happiness is likely to matter to him. A divorced woman about thirty told this story:

> My brother Vic comes up with ideas occasionally. One night he came over to my house and I was playing this record, "Find Me Somebody to Love." I like the arrangement and I wasn't thinking about the lyrics. But Vic says, "What's this? Your theme song?" And that was his introduction to, "By the way, I have the perfect man for you." This is the new chemist that has come to work with him.

Even when brothers or sisters' husbands do not intentionally arrange an introduction for single mothers, men met through them have some likelihood of being appropriate. For the taste in friends of their brothers or brothers-in-law tends to be similar to the single mothers' own. A divorced woman in her late twenties described meeting the man with whom she was currently living:

> My brother was living with me over the summer. He invited his best friend, Gary, down for the weekend. And Gary just fitted in beautifully. Then Gary came for another couple of weekends. Then my brother moved away, and Gary came just to see me. And it has turned out that we are really in love with one another.

Single parents' own parents seem less often to become involved in matchmaking. Usually they restrict their efforts to urging the single parent to be more active or to encouraging the serious consideration of someone the single parent has already decided is hopeless. A divorced woman in her early thirties said:

> My mother has come up with this fellow who lives in my neighborhood. I used to go out with him when I was a kid. He's very, very handsome. And my mother says, "He's an electrician. That's decent pay." Well, I had gone with him when I was a kid and I didn't like him then, so I'm not going to like him now. But I ran into him last year and he came to my house on Christmas day to wish me a happy Christmas. My mother was there and she says, "That man is interested. Go get him." But I know he isn't, and I'm not.

An extensive social network is helpful to single parents even though no member of the network may assume responsibility for out-and-out matchmaking. A friend may pass on the news that someone of potential interest is now alone, has returned to the area, or has expressed interest in the single parent. Or a relative may provide a casual introduction after church services or at a party. Just because these casual introductions are easily neglected, single parents are apt to feel comfortable with them.

Acquaintances may also provide casual introductions, and here the single parent is likely to have still less sense of being under scrutiny. In consequence, the new relationship, should one develop, will carry less of a burden of sponsorship. One woman, mother of a nine-year-old girl, described meeting her boyfriend through the parents of one of her daughter's friends:

> My daughter and some friends were going to put on a performance one night at the house of one of her friends. All of the parents were invited, but I was the only parent that showed up. And this girl's mother and father bought pizza and we had a few drinks. Then they sort of put their heads together and said, "Let's invite our friend over." So they said to me, "We just invited a friend over. He's bringing the salad." So that's how it started. And we've seen each other since.

The same freedom from the burdens of sponsorship is obtained by meeting people at parties or other social events. Although the people have all been invited by friends and relatives, the meetings themselves have not been arranged; it is up to the people there to discover each other. One divorced mother met her current boyfriend at a wedding reception for a friend's older son; she and the man both arrived late, each was relieved to have company in tardiness, and it was natural to talk. A mother who had not previously been married met someone in the course of helping her neighbors to move. The woman's own mother was looking after her daughter at the time.

> The people next door were moving and they had everybody they knew up helping them. I came up the stairs, coming home, and this fellow

says, "Don't stand there; grab a box and take it down." After we worked a while, the girl next door said to me, "We're all going over to my new house. Why don't you come?" So I called my mother, and it was all right with her. So I went over, and we sat around the kitchen table, voicing opinions on all kinds of subjects. I found the fellow very interesting, and he found me interesting. And the next day he came and knocked on my door and said, "Hi."

So long as the person met is a fellow member of the single parent's own community, the single parent can feel initial confidence that a date cannot go too badly. A single mother, for example, can be assured that if the man she has met is known to her friends and family, she will not be victimized by impression management; she will not be "fed a line." She may already know a good deal about the man and, if she wishes, can learn more.

I was at this party with this couple. And this man was there and I was talking to him. He was divorced, too. A couple of evenings later, I got a phone call from the girl in the couple who said that the man I had met would like to take me to dinner. I said, "What is he like?"

The single mother can assume that a man known to her friends or relatives is as aware as she is that each can affect the other's reputation within their shared community. In addition, insofar as she and the man are from the same social milieu, she should be able to understand what the man is about; she should be able to compare him with others of his background, interpret his comments and behaviors, and assess his goals and life chances. And there should be enough similarity in understandings of the proper roles of men and women, as well as in other areas of values, to provide a foundation for their relationship's continuing should she and the man decide they want it to. For all these reasons, meetings between the single parent and someone within the single parent's own community hold most promise for developing into something more.

There are, to be sure, drawbacks to these meetings. The pool of eligibles within the single parent's own community is likely to be severely limited. And friends and relatives may not be entirely comfortable with the single parent's wish to find someone new. A divorced woman said:

When I was first separated I was invited to parties. I didn't dare talk to anybody else's husband because I had a feeling that they would think I was trying to take him away. I went to a Halloween party, and I wasn't doing anything that I wouldn't ordinarily do at a party. And yet I was feeling very vulnerable at the time and very lonely, and I guess you come across in a different way. And people sense it. And I got that reaction from the women there. After about an hour or so, I decided I would stay away from dancing and stuff. I'd just sit down and just talk to the women.

If the single parent were to meet someone outside the parent's community, he or she would be less constrained by concern for the responses of others. But, by the same token, the new relationship would lack the assurance of trustworthiness provided by membership in the same community. Thus a general rule: the farther the single parent moves from his or her own community in looking for someone new, the more freedom there is to behave in a variety of ways, but the less confidence can be placed in those encountered. And this leads to a fairly obvious corollary: the farther the single parent is from his or her own community, the more likely is a new meeting to offer opportunity for sexual adventure rather than for a continuing and reliable bond.

Sometimes single parents form relationships with people whom they meet in the course of their daily rounds but do not otherwise know. One man began seeing a woman who was the secretary in an office adjoining his. A woman became involved with the mechanic who worked on her car. But relationships based on casual contact easily go awry. A divorced woman told the following story:

> The guy who put in my phone in the apartment where I am living now, he called me up the next day. He says, "This is Artie." I say, "That's nice. Who is Artie?" So he tells me he was there the day before, installing the phone. So I asked, "How did you get my number?" And he says, "I installed the phone, right?" So I say, "Oh, yeah." And he says, "I'd like to get to know you. Would you meet me for lunch?" He was pleasant, so I met him for lunch. And he says, first thing out of his mouth, that he's ready for a relationship and that sex is very important to him. I say, "I think it has it's place." I mean, not that sex isn't important, but don't you want to find out what I'm like? I ate lunch and left.

Entirely removed from the single parent's community are acquaintance-ships struck up in places open to virtually anyone: tennis clubs, folk dance societies, evening classes for adults, singles' groups, and the dating bars.

Single parents tend to evaluate these settings partly in terms of the kinds of people met within them. One issue is, are the people like one-self? Many single parents attend an open meeting of the local chapter of Parents Without Partners and decide not to return because the members appear to them too much older or too much younger, of a different social class or too bold or too shy. Another issue is the number of unmarried, reasonably attractive members of the other sex. A tennis club proved disappointing for one single mother because the men she met there were for the most part married and for the rest unattractive:

> I joined a couple of tennis clubs where I thought there was a potential for meeting somebody you would want to date. Well, one of the clubs is a family-oriented club. The men are interested, sure, but if you play tennis with the wife in the morning, who wants to date that man? For-get it. Now I've started going to another club that is supposed to be singles-oriented. And yet what I've run across there are men who are

married. The few that I've met who aren't married, I wouldn't want them anyway.

Another woman described in similar terms her disappointment with a church group:

There's a young adult group in my church and I'm fairly active in that. They are very nice people. But I don't think I'm going to meet anyone there. Everyone is too good. The ones that aren't married are very, very Christian. The Lord's will is in everything. And I just can't take a lot of that.

Dating bars represent an extreme in absence of shared community. One woman who did not especially like them described being taken to a dating bar by a friend:

This was a fairly big bar, and it was super-crowded. My girlfriend sprung for a first round of drinks. I would have sprung for the next, but she said, "Now we've got to circulate." I said, "Okay, I'll circulate." And I started walking around. I met a foreign guy and we got to talking about children and the differences between child-rearing practices in Europe and here. He was all right. Then a man said, "You're a very nice girl." I didn't know what to say, so I said, "I don't know what to say." And he came back with, "You're a very nice girl." And I said to my- self, "Fuck this. I'm not a great circulator." And I sat at the bar.

It's sort of an unspoken rule, if you go with a girl, you leave it open as to what happens, but you don't leave if there is a doubt. So I had to wait until two in the morning because my girlfriend had met a guy and we had come together and I was driving. She did come over to tell me, "I don't know if this guy's going to ask me home with him. Will you wait? Are you angry about it?" And I said, "No, I'm not angry. When you know, let me know." And then, at two, she came over and said, "He asked me to go home with him. Do you mind?"

Those who have gone to dating bars alone report that their first re- action, once inside, has been anxiety. It is not only that the newcomer is uncertain about how to respond to an approach or how to provoke one. It is also that there are few supportive gestures from others; no one makes the newcomer feel welcome; there is no one whom the newcomer can feel is a friend. A divorced woman said:

I decided one day I would drop in on a few of those places and see what they looked like. I went in one place, and I sat for a few minutes, and I was absolutely terrified. I got up and left and went to the place next door, sat for a few minutes, got up and left and went back to the first place. A few minutes later I got up and left. It was ridiculous.

But some learn with time to manage dating bars and to find sociability within them. A single father said that he would go to dating bars when he was lonely because he could be assured of at least finding someone to talk with. And one single mother said that once a week she took a night off from looking after her fourteen-year-old daughter and, if she had nothing better to do, visited a dating bar. She said:

> The first time you go there, you feel like you are not going to make it. You go in and you say, "What am I doing here? I want to leave!" You feel like everybody is looking at you, and you just feel so awkward and everything. But then, as you get to know the people, you realize that there are so many other people in your situation, and they are just trying to be sociable, like you are. And you find it comes very easy after a certain time. People come up and talk to you and so forth.

Still, dating bars are unpromising settings for establishing reliable relationships. And yet many women visit dating bars hoping to do just that. Men seem less often optimistic in this respect. As one woman, herself an habituée of dating bars, said: "On the bar scene the men are looking for sex and the women are looking for a relationship." There are, of course, men who go to bars who are lonely and would like to meet someone with whom things might work out, just as there are women whose aims are limited to a single night. But the reverse would seem more frequently the case. Women, though they appear to have sexual needs as strong as men's, seem to value forming a reliable relationship more highly. Some women who tried dating bars gave up on them because there was so little promise in the relationships formed there. A divorced woman in her mid-thirties said:

> When you go into a club there's all different kinds of men there. But the young ones I don't want. And the older ones are married. And they are all out for one-night stands. And emotionally I don't need that.

There are many, both men and women, who find an evening of conversation with strangers to be a struggle. In any event, an evening spent with strangers, some of whom may prove unpleasant, can be an unhappy experience. Instead of producing a date, the evening may only reaffirm feelings of isolation. A divorced woman of about thirty said:

> My girlfriend and I would try different singles' bars. Most of them were for younger people. Weekends were a mad scene; don't even try going out those nights. And some nights there would be a lot of couples, and that makes you feel more alone. There were many nights that the two of us cried going home in the car.

Dating

Some single parents are fortunate enough to form a new relationship without undergoing the preliminary experience of a date. Someone is met at a party, or an old friend not seen since high school days is encountered while shopping, and an invitation is extended to stop by for coffee, or to share dinner. Then further meetings are arranged and, in an entirely natural way, there gradually develops a sharing of lives. But, often enough, things proceed less effortlessly. The first meeting must be followed by something more formal, and so there is a telephone call in which the man proposes an evening's entertainment and the woman agrees to embark with him on a date.

For parents who were previously married, beginning to date constitutes a statement to themselves and to others—particularly their children —that they now define themselves as single. The first date after the ending of a marriage is a milestone in that it establishes this new definition of self. But a first date can also be an occasion of much tension. Because the status of single person is so new, the single parent may not yet be comfortable in it.

> My first date, I was so unsure of myself, I thought it was going to kill me. I was carrying around this handkerchief because my hands were so wet it was like I was just washing them. I was so nervous, because I didn't feel that anybody would accept me. And my husband never danced, so it was the first time in a long time that I had to dance with someone. God almighty, I thought I was going to die.

The partner on the date presents a challenge: is it possible to please this person while yet being true to oneself? The single parent's desire for the partner's regard and fear of new rejection makes authenticity— behavior that is faithfully expressive of the single parent's values and feelings—particularly difficult to achieve. And hanging over the date and adding to its tensions may be the question of what will happen when the evening moves to its conclusion and the couple return to the woman's home. For some single parents, the gratifications of a date are entirely realized when the date is made; the date itself is given to the masking of uncertainty and anxiety. And should the compulsion to gain the partner's approval lead to behavior that is felt to be false, the single parent may end by feeling diminished.

> You find on the first couple of dates, you're saying what the person expects. I find I'm really a chameleon. That is what I am trying to overcome; I'm trying to be what I am, not what I think other people want me to be.

Someone New

One single parent said, wistfully, "If you can get to know someone before you date, you feel so much more comfortable." And yet dating is intended to be a way of getting to know someone.

There are almost endless ways in which dates can go badly. The other person can be dull, or overly aggressive, or rejecting. The single parent can feel wearied, or out of place, or misunderstood. Nor is the cost only an evening wasted. In addition, the children have been left with a baby-sitter yet another time; the babysitter will have to be paid; and there will be fatigue in the morning.

But even though a particular date may fall flat, just going out helps sustain a single parent's morale. For if dating does nothing more, it enables a single parent to be among other people and to be free, for a time, of responsibility. The following comment was made by a divorced mother of five children, the oldest adolescent, the youngest a physically handicapped five-year-old boy:

> If I didn't go out at all, I'd be ready to climb the wall from just plain boredom and doing the same thing over and over again. But going out breaks up the monotony. It keeps me half alive, to at least see a little bit of the outside world besides work.

Being admired by someone can feel marvelous. A divorced woman in her late thirties said:

> It was just so different, to have someone fall over you and think you're great. It was just what I needed. And the first guy I met, he was like that. I just ate it all up. I just thought it was terrific.

For some women, the sense of being "taken out," of being cared for instead of having to care for others, is gratifying. To be taken to nice places, to be treated well, and not to have to worry about the cost provides them with reassurance that they are receiving as well as giving.

The result of all these contributions of dating can be a dramatic improvement in mood. A divorced woman in her early thirties said:

> My personality changes when I'm going out. I'm happier. I'm not so picky at home, not so irritable, not so grouchy. Because there is more happiness in my life, things run smoother in the house.

There is always the chance that a date will turn into more, that the date will be marked by that intense rapport which is felt when an attachment is forming: that sense of having found someone who understands and empathizes and is so admiring that it is impossible not to participate in the admiration. The evening may be one of deep satisfaction in presenting and listening to autobiography, so that the charmed present is provided with roots in a newly shared past. Each is sorry that the evening must end, and each will want to extend it, to bring it home:

We started going out and it just seemed as though—it almost seems crazy to say we hit it off as well as we did. I just can't believe how I feel about this guy and how he feels about me. Can you believe it? Honest to God, I'm really crazy about him. I can really, honestly, truthfully say that.

With dating potentially providing so much, many single parents cannot resist the gamble that is posed by an invitation or an indication of interest. For while it is possible to lose by dating, it is also possible to win. And there is no way to know how it will turn out without trying it.

Dating policies

Some single parents, especially those who have been widowed, establish on entering the single-parent status what amounts to a program for themselves. They want first to get their lives in order. Then they will consider a friendly, companionable relationship. Only later will they be available for more. One widow said:

I have taken everything slow. I've jumped into nothing. I'm trying to get everything organized, straightened out, the best I can. Now I think I'm ready for male companionship. No physical involvement—just companionship. Just to get my feet on the ground a little bit.

And some single parents, more experienced, are reluctant to go out with someone just for the sake of going out. A divorced woman said:

I had a chance to go out this weekend. The guy is all right. I've met him before at parties. But I just wasn't that thrilled, because I have to really like someone in order to enjoy myself. I said I really didn't want to go out.

But many single parents discover that having once become accustomed to dating, the possibility of staying home can seem drab indeed. During the first year after the ending of their marriages they may have stayed home most of the time, but once they began going out they could no longer tolerate empty weekends. A divorced woman said:

It took me a long time to date. I think it took me almost two years to really date a man. I just had no interest in going out. But once I went out, I couldn't stay around the house any more. Now I have to get out.

Some single parents describe dating and the social life associated with it as almost addictive. Getting out of the house, going somewhere, doing something produce an excitement that lessens awareness of problems and concerns. Staying home, on the other hand, is like missing the party. One woman in her late twenties lived near her mother and so could ask her mother to look after her small son. It was not long after her husband left that she began going out:

> I started going out all the time: five, six nights a week. If I could get my hands on a dollar, I'd go out the door. I would go out with my girl-friend. We'd go to a bar and have a few drinks, and my son would go see his grandmother for the night. Or if a fellow I was seeing was taking me out, my girlfriend would mind my son. I was in a fantasy world. I wasn't thinking about the future. I was just going day by day.

This level of activity outside the home, added to a single parent's other commitments, severely reduces the single parent's accessibility to the children. This was ruefully recognized by a man who had custody of his two boys, aged eleven and eight, during the summer:

> Fatherhood is very important to me. But my life is kind of schitzy, be-cause on the one hand I'm into a sort of bachelor life style, which I really enjoy, and on the other hand I'm into being a father. And boy, they just don't match.

A few single parents seem to be able to maintain a fairly hectic dating life without feeling overwhelmed. One woman who worked as a secretary in a high-rise office building met a succession of men around the elevator, by the newsstand, at the lunch counter. Several of her boy-friends were married; that made them easier to manage. She was generally pleased with her life. But another woman, also involved with more than one man and also out of the house more evenings than not, found her life to be more than she could cope with. There were too many calls when she was at home, too many demands on her for emotional response. And at the same time that she was trying to apportion her time among her men friends, sometimes lying about why she could not see one of them and having to remind herself to remember the lie, she was carrying on a dispute with her former husband, worrying about money and about where to live, and trying her best to respond to the needs of her two small children. The man with whom she was most involved moved in with her. An earlier boyfriend appeared and there was a fight. The first man left her. In despair, the woman became involved with still an-other man. And now the first wanted to return. The woman finally swallowed a few less than a lethal dose of sleeping pills, was hospitalized, and in this way extricated herself from her confusion.

This is an extreme case of a life out of control. Ordinarily, single parents' other commitments would limit the number of evenings they could go out and, in this way, would limit the number of people they could see. Most single parents have not the time nor the energy nor the desire to maintain more than a single close relationship.

Sexual policies

We are a society in which a great many different value systems coexist, with enclaves of people maintaining one system of values living beside, or among, enclaves of people maintaining others. Nevertheless, among single parents who define themselves as accessible to sexual relationships, one of two different sexual policies appears most often to underlie their behavior.

The first is phrased somewhat differently by women and by men and may lead to a double standard in the sense that proper behavior for women is somewhat different from proper behavior for men. The essential idea of the policy is that sex is all right if there is affection. As it applies to women, this policy holds that a woman may justifiably establish a sexual relationship with a man if she truly cares for him or is in love with him, or if the woman and man are committed to sharing their lives. The point is that the woman is not frivolous in her sexual choices; the man whom she accepts sexually is the one man, the only man, she wants. Sexual accessibility, for her, connotes emotional commitment. Here is an expression of the policy:

> I would rather feel a little bit uptight every now and then than go out and get myself involved. If I got into a situation because I was sexually frustrated, I would feel bad about it because it wasn't the individual that I wanted to be with. I would rather be a little uptight every now and then than do that.

The same policy as it is interpreted for men, however, is somewhat different. It is all right for a man to enter a sexual relationship so long as the woman is emotionally important to him. The woman should not be "used," treated simply as a means for satisfying his sexual needs. She need not be the one woman, the only woman, he wants.

The general statement of the policy, that sex is all right if there is affection, seems to be shared by more conservative single parents. But because it gives rise to a double standard when interpreted for women and for men, it permits the kind of conflict that occurred in courting couples of an earlier era as a result of a different double standard:

> I have this one male friend who would like to have our friendship be a sexual relationship. I'm finding it difficult to work through the possibility of having a friendship-type of relationship where you are just very comfortable and easy with somebody and you call them up when you have nothing to do, and then having sex come into that relationship, and you still have a casual relationship, where you each go out with other people.

Someone New

Women who subscribe to this sexual policy tend to equate respectability with remaining sexually inaccessible except to the one man to whom there is emotional commitment. And while they might not think less of the man if he did not quite commit himself fully to them, they would be hurt. Though the word is no longer used, they would agree with the idea that a woman "cheapens" herself by accepting a relationship that is solely sexual. Should they themselves do this, their respect for themselves would diminish, and they would fear the loss of their children's respect. Though they may experience sexual desire, they are not the sort of women who behave in such a way.

> I am not the type that would go out with a man with the intention of going to bed with him. I think I have a lot more to offer. I haven't put myself in a position where that could happen, but I'm sure it could happen easily. But, having been married and having known only the one man, it's not my conditioning. And I have to watch out for myself and my children.

But there is another policy, one that is sexually more liberal, whose ideas are competitive with the first. And that is a policy based on the idea that if you know what you are doing, if you understand both your needs and the potential of the relationship for filling them, and if you are in some measure considerate of the other person and not exploitative, then sex is all right. This policy leads to a single standard for both sexes, the standard of "act on your feelings." One woman who felt herself to have a firm grip on her life phrased her policy in relation to sex in these terms:

> If I feel the vibes and I want to do it, then I do it. It's not every man, but when I find the vibes, I do it. You live according to your standards, regardless of what your standards are, and I see no reason why I should hang my head down because I have a need at a certain time and I choose a certain person for fulfilling my need.

It is essential, in this outlook, that one not delude oneself into equating a sexual relationship with love. To do so can only lead to asking more of the other person than is justified, and to feelings of hurt and loss. A woman who had been divorced about three years, and who now subscribed to this policy, said that she earlier had been confused about what might be found in the relationships she formed:

> When I was first divorced I was promiscuous; I was going to bed with anybody that I dated. It was, "Somebody please love me." I was looking for affection. It would always come out lousy, lousy, lousy.

The theme of this policy is know what you want; if something really is what you want, and you won't hurt anyone by taking it, then take it.

Don't look for affection in sex; but if it is sex that you want, then that's all right. Another divorced woman said:

> It wasn't until I was able to separate affection and sex and say, "All right, I have to sleep with someone for physical reasons," that it worked out for me. My frustration level would get high and it would grow and grow, and finally it would be like that was the only goal in the day. There is something icky about going to a bar, but if you go in with the thought, "I'm not going to get picked up, I'm going to pick somebody up," there is a big difference. I don't care if they are really terrible people; it is just a matter of having a physical attraction towards them. And I don't care what they think of me, because I'm doing it. They can think they are picking me up, but I'm picking them up. And if they think, "Wow, I scored last night," they didn't. I did.

But another implication of this policy is that when there is no desire for a sexual relationship, it would be wrong to permit one. Nor does a single sexual encounter imply continued interest in the other person. This same divorced woman said:

> There was this guy I had known from work. He had been to the house occasionally for coffee. This one particular time I was giving very blatant messages. So we started this thing up. Well, once I was satisfied, I didn't want anything more to do with him. But he kept calling me and calling me. He'd say, "How about if I come over? I'll bring a bottle of wine or something." And I would say, "Jesus, I'm loaded. I've got eight million things to do." I didn't have a thing to do. But I wasn't going to say, "Look, I just had to be serviced."

There are other policies single parents adopt as well as these two. Some single parents choose celibacy, at least for a time, because they already are coping with all they can manage, because they feel they have moved beyond the point in life when sex was appropriate, or because they cannot accept sex without marriage. But most single parents seem to follow one of the two policies described above.

Sooner or later, so long as a single parent is going out, a relationship of some commitment develops. It may be exactly what the single parent had dreamed of, making it possible for the single parent to anticipate its further development into shared lives, perhaps marriage. It is a relationship that gives hope of a shared future. Or the relationship may be with someone not deeply cared for, someone who was nice to go out with, who after a while became a sexual partner, and who now, without the single parent's intending it, is a part of the single parent's life. As one woman put it: "All of a sudden you wake up one day and find yourself in the middle of something." There seem to be these two polar types of committed relationships: relationships of hope and relationships that form for want of anything better. Let us consider the latter first.

Relationships for want of anything better

As a single parent and the person the parent is dating become accustomed to seeing each other on weekends and begin to see each other during the week as well, the other's presence may begin to be important to each, not because of deeply rooted affection, but rather because the other makes life seem more nearly complete, less empty. Attachment may develop without full acceptance, perhaps without liking, and with it a relationship, ambivalent, understood as temporary, but preferable to no relationship at all. As one divorced woman put it:

> When you enter into something, you think to yourself, "Well, at least I'm not alone any more. There will be somebody. Anybody is better than nobody."

Even if the other person isn't entirely right, it is good to have someone there: someone to go out with, to have around. One woman maintained this sort of relationship with a man who was much more committed to her than she was to him. But he had a car and she did not, the children seemed to like him, he was company, and he asked little of her. Infrequently, she permitted him to go to bed with her. But then the man began to suggest marriage, and she wondered whether she should not send him off. And yet there she was, in the suburbs, with two small children and no car.

Some single parents, perhaps particularly those who have survived destructive marriages, appear willing to accept thoroughly unpromising relationships if nothing better is available. A divorced mother of an only son became involved with a married man whom she had earlier rejected, just so that she would have someone in her life:

> This fellow used to see me when I was out with my girlfriend. He was older and he was married. He started making passes that I'd ignore, because I thought he was a jerk. And anyway, I was still a married woman. Then, when my husband and I broke up, he got word of it, and he would call me and we'd go out for a drink or something. And we started going out. It wasn't so much the sexual thing as it was just to have someone around. Although you really couldn't say he was around that much, because he was married.

Relationships for want of better alternatives are apt to be heavy going. The reservations each participant has regarding the other can hardly fail to be expressed. Awareness that the relationship is a stop-gap is itself frustrating. And there may be questions regarding how it will end.

> Kenny and I have been together two years. I'm content with the way things are right now. But Kenny aggravates me. I know, inside I know,

it is not going to last. You feel a certain sense of frustration, like, "Gee, I just wish he was somebody just a little bit different." But I've given up hope of ever changing anybody. I'd never attempt to change anybody. So I wonder if I'll end up getting hostile to him.

The single parent may want to limit the other person's expectations. One woman, going with a man she had no intention of marrying, said: "He makes me guilty when he says he cares. He makes me feel guilty when he says, 'Why don't you get a divorce?' " And another woman reported advising the man she was seeing to go out with other women as well.

In these essentially uncommitted relationships, a pregnancy, should one occur, produces a crisis. One woman, divorced, with a six-year-old daughter, became pregnant by the man she was seeing:

> I told Gordon that I was pregnant. "Get an abortion," he said. "I don't want it. If you have it, it's all your own." And I said, "Here I go again. I've got one kid to raise on my own. Here I go again with another one." And after a while I agreed to get the abortion. I decided that it would be the best thing because financially I couldn't handle it and emotionally I couldn't handle it. My daughter was finally old enough to go to school and I would be back in the house again with another baby. It would mean going right back down to full-time welfare, no work, no nothing. And I couldn't go through another pregnancy by myself. The last time, even though I was married, it was alone. There wasn't any way in the world I could do it again.

> So I had to go in for the abortion. It was a nightmare. It was the most horrible experience I have been through in my life. When I first came out of the anesthesia, after having had the abortion, all I could hear was babies crying. Gordon stayed with me in the hospital for the first day. He was supportive, but mostly he was glad that I had had it done. He didn't react emotionally at all. It was sort of like an abortion is nothing, everybody does it all the time.

Yet even unsatisfactory relationships augment life enough to make a single parent reluctant to return to empty evenings and solitary days. A single mother, not previously married, said about her boyfriend:

> My sister says that she doesn't understand how I can continue my relationship with him the way it is going now, why I find it so difficult to terminate it. I think it's a need to have someone, to have some kind of relationship, whether it be weekend dating or a live-in situation, just someone to go to, someone to have there. I'm less depressed because he's here. When we broke up for a while, it was depressing. I had a whole sadness. I imagine that is why I'm having such difficulty terminating it.

It is a fairly common experience among single parents, especially those who are younger, to have a succession of relationships, each in its own way limited, each in its own way gratifying, each ending for its own set of reasons. Between relationships there are intervals in which there is no one, during which the single parents become reacquainted with loneliness. Or there may be people to date, to go places with, perhaps someone with whom a sexual relationship can be established, but not anyone to be taken seriously. The following history is a fairly typical one. It was reported by a woman of about thirty, attractive and outgoing, mother of two school-aged children, employed as a secretary.

> My husband was extremely tidy and meticulous. He wanted everything neat. After we broke up, I went with Arnie, who is just a total slob in everything he did. A slobby personality. You can't live with somebody like that. So I flip-flopped then to Rolf, who was very much like my husband, but better-looking and much sexier. The thing with Rolf was the sexual thing, which was very exciting to me, because I had never had that before. It was really fun. But that never became a live-in relationship and it could never possibly have been, because of Rolf's objection to the way I do things. We would have been incompatible. It was never discussed or considered.

> I broke up with Rolf and I didn't go out for about a month and a half. Then I was seeing this fellow Eddie, off and on. It was sort of like my relationship with Arnie. I enjoyed his company. The sex wasn't bad. But Eddie wasn't a real pleasant person to be around when he drank, which was frequently. He wasn't an alcoholic, but he had a drinking problem. So that automatically eliminated the possibility of ever living with him. But he treated me nice, and I craved the companionship. I broke up with Eddie about a month ago. Now, I'm not looking for Prince Charming, but I don't know how to meet anybody.

Relationships of hope

In a stop-gap relationship, when the single parent's attention is directed to ways in which the relationship is unfulfilling, there is reassurance in anticipation that the relationship will end. In a relationship of hope, problems have to be dealt with so that the relationship can continue. Doubts are apt to be resolved in favor of the relationship: "Let's give it a chance."

The intensity of feelings in these relationships is unmistakeable. The other person is seen as quite special, entirely different from the general run. Quite quickly there develops a sense of being linked to the other person. A divorced mother, about thirty, said:

> John is an unusual individual. I've been by myself for quite some time now, and I really haven't run across anyone quite like him. If I was going to get remarried with anybody, it would be with him, because I

have feelings for him that are going to last for more than just a few months.

Sometimes a relationship that had been maintained for want of anything better changes toward one of hope. One woman, in her late twenties, had been going with a younger man for some time. She had almost ruled out the possibility of the relationship's being permanent, partly because her older son and the man did not get along, partly because the man gambled and she did not want to give him control of her finances. But then she became ill and the man not only cared for her but cared for her children as well. She said:

> Warren showed his true colors. I wasn't sure of marrying him, but I am now. We might have our differences and he and Patrick don't hit it off. They don't argue; they just don't talk. But I figure I can make it up to Patrick because I need Warren. He was just wonderful. He stayed with me day and night.

Possessing a relationship of hope, the single parent can feel comfortable remaining at home in the evening. No longer is home isolating; no longer do the responsibilities of child care appear to be barriers to participation in social life. One woman, for example, had maintained an active dating life before entering a relationship of hope. She said:

> When I started up with Stuart, I started staying home. I might go out one night a week with my girlfriends, but basically I was staying home. I didn't want to go out. I felt like there was nothing out there.

Loneliness disappears. There is someone to talk with and to do things with. It becomes easier to deal with the house and the children. The single parent may feel augmented. A divorced woman with two children, one a teenager, the other a few years younger, said:

> It's an awful, lonely thing, to bring up children by yourself. You can talk to your children, but there are problems you really can't speak to them about. I can talk to my boyfriend about these problems or anything. We talk everything over. We kind of work things out together. I don't have to shoulder all the responsibility and be completely independent. And yet he doesn't want to take away my independence either. He wants me to be the best of what I can be.

In this relationship sex is free of the disappointments and angers that burdened it during marriage. It is free, too, of the feeling of emotional isolation that often accompanies sex in more superficial postmarital relationships. A woman in her forties, with three children, said:

> I feel much more comfortable with sex now than I ever did all the years I was married. And I have one person to thank for that, the man I'm going with. I'm just sorry that I didn't find out how nice it really can be back when I was married. But I just didn't. I was a prude. It was more or less of a duty. And it's funny, here I am almost forty-four

years old and enjoying it more than I ever did being married. I've been going with my boyfriend for a couple of years and it's just as much fun today as it was at first.

The relationship of hope provides a structure for life. There may be a feeling of having returned to the community of those with mates. Daily tasks regain meaning. Now there is another adult to do things for. A woman in her early thirties said:

I'm an altogether different person—I'm smiling, I'm happy—when he's around. It gives me a lift. It makes me want to live. He makes me want to clean and cook. I cook and cook and cook: stuffed peppers, stuffed eggs. When he's around I love to cook.

These relationships may or may not move to marriage. In either event, they are understood as potentially permanent. Although the single parent is likely to insist that the children continue to come first, the relationship of hope becomes of fundamental emotional importance for the single parent. A woman in her late thirties said:

I have known Michael a long time. We probably act like a married couple. When I first started going out with Michael my mother asked me, "Are you thinking of getting married?" I said, "No, Mom. I don't intend to." I wanted no part of marriage after what I went through. I love things just the way they are. But this is permanent. Definitely. On my side, and as far as he is concerned, too.

To go together, to live together, to wed?

As a relationship becomes established in a single parent's life, the question arises: Should the single parent and the other person remain in their separate residences? Or should they live together? Should they, perhaps, marry?

So long as a couple maintain separate residences, their relationship can be presented to others as just a friendship, perhaps a welcome addition to each of their lives, but not of vital importance to either. Then, should the relationship end, there will be little loss of face. And the new figure can be kept at a distance from the children.

Respectability may demand that the single parent and the new figure not live together. Indeed, a single mother living in a neighborhood of traditional families may require a man who has slept over to leave early in the morning, before the children and the neighbors are up. And both the woman's kin and her older children might be made uncomfortable should the couple live together. One woman reported that her eighteen-year-old daughter, a college student, was willing to accept that her ex-husband might live with someone but not that she might. The daughter raised the issue after a Thanksgiving dinner with the mother and the mother's boyfriend:

> She said, "Are you two getting married?" And I said, "No." And she said. "Oh my God, you're not going to live together!" And I said, "We're not planning anything." Her father lived with somebody at one point and she said to me then, "I hope you don't ever live with anybody. I can take Dad's doing it, but I couldn't take your doing it." I don't know why she feels this way, but my morals are very important to her. She sets up standards for me.

Mothers themselves often feel that they must uphold moral standards in their behavior. It is difficult enough for them to reconcile their own acceptance of sex without marriage with their concern that their children not become sexually active before they are truly mature. They feel they would fatally weaken their ability to serve as moral arbiters if they were to live with someone. One woman, for example, said that although her two college-aged sons had both lived with girlfriends, she could not herself live with the man she was seeing without betraying what she had always stood for:

> I have two nearly grown boys. They have both lived with girls. They've shared apartments. I condone it to a certain extent when I visit with them, because I don't want to lose them. But when they come to my house, there is no sleeping together. And I could never live with a man, no matter how old my kids are, because it would change everything I have said to them.

Some single parents are simply unwilling to share their living space with another adult. They want someone in their lives, but not cluttering up their homes. One man described becoming angry when he discovered that a woman with whom he was involved, as it happened in a relationship for want of anything better, threatened to invade his living space. Whether he would have felt the same way if the relationship had been one he entirely wanted is impossible to say.

> There was this woman with whom I started having sort of an affair. And I got sick once, with a very high fever, and in the course of it I was aware that she was doing something out in the kitchen. Then I got better and I noticed all kinds of changes in the house. New things were hanging from my walls and all kinds of pots and pans were in the kitchen. And she had pretty much moved right in. She had decided I needed somebody to take care of the house and the kids. And I didn't want that.

A final argument for maintaining separate residences is that living together would impose further constraint on the single parent's freedom.

Someone New

One woman, not at the moment going with anyone, said this was something she would want to avoid:

> It would seem to me that if you're living together, in some way you're sort of semitrapped, because you're sort of still responsible for getting home for a meal. You can't just go wandering off by yourself, because there's someone else to consider. If you want to go out for an evening, you can't just take off. It's more constraining than just having a relationship.

Indeed, single parents who have tried living with someone report that they did feel constrained and in addition found themselves constraining the other person. One woman said that within a week after her boyfriend moved in with her, she was as overbearing with him as she had earlier been with her husband. And there may be still other problems in living with someone. The new person may fail to carry a reasonable share of housekeeping tasks. Another woman said her boyfriend expected to be treated as a guest, albeit a semipermanent guest. And, beyond this, he competed with her children for her attention:

> It was like having a third child, because he demanded as much attention as they did. I was split three ways instead of two. Occasionally he would play with the kids, occasionally he would reprimand them, and he would do things for them like get their baths ready if I was busy doing something. But he wanted my attention as much as they did. He was worse than they were, I think.

Yet there are advantages in living together that may outweigh all these reasons for hesitancy. Living together may just be easier. True, the new person's role in the household would have to be established. There might have to be a shakedown period for putting in place the new household organization, when new understandings would have to be worked out between the two adults and between each adult and the children. But it would be so much easier to know there will be someone in the household to talk with, to know that the new person will be there for dinner and through the evening and through the night. And there always is the possibility that the new person will be truly helpful and will lighten the burden of the household:

> Michael is very good about doing things in the house. He thinks nothing of getting up and doing the dishes, making a bed, sweeping a floor. He just does it, not all the time, but I don't have to say to him, "Do this or do that." If he's out in the kitchen and there are dishes in the sink, he just does them. You'd think with all the kids in the house, somebody would do dishes besides me and Michael, but nobody does. And, naturally, he takes care of all the garbage, which I love. He and the older boy do it. And if somebody's coming, he'll help out. He cooks Sunday dinners so I can stay in bed Sundays. He gets up and puts a roast on, peels all the potatoes. The only thing I do is make the gravy and mash the potatoes.

At best, the new person in the household can be a genuine partner: not another parent, to be sure, but a partner in the sense of someone who shares the single parent's responsibilities. One woman said about the man with whom she was living, "Gene seems to take a burden off my shoulders." To some single parents, living with someone appears to have all the advantages of marriage with none of its risks. A divorced woman, not going with anyone, said:

> I've had girlfriends who are on their second marriages, and that one isn't working. I'd end up in the hospital if that ever happened to me. Going through one divorce, I don't plan on going through another. If I lived with a man, and he walked out, it would probably be just as painful, but there wouldn't be the legal hassles and everything else that goes with a divorce.

For widows there is a practical, sometimes weighty reason for preferring living with a man to remarriage: the Social Security laws are written in a way that would end a widow's payments if she remarried.

As cohabitation is more widely accepted, it will be easier for mothers to make this choice. It may at this point be mothers' own discomfort with so unconventional an arrangement that makes them anxious about their children's reactions. Interviews with children of single parents suggest that the children are not nearly as moralistic as the mothers believe. The parents may be told this themselves. One woman said:

> I've been widowed two and a half years, and I've asked my kids, "What would you think if I ever lived with a man? Because then I wouldn't have to give up my widow's benefits." My daughter said, "Mom, don't ever get married." And my boy said the same thing. But if it really comes down to it, can I do it?

Many single parents do set up cohabitation arrangements. They may worry about the reactions of their children, their kin, the neighbors, and their children's other parents, but they tell themselves that they are adults and can do what they want with their lives. And it may make no sense to a single parent that someone the parent wants to be with must maintain a separate residence for appearance's sake, nor, knowing what the parent knows of the trauma that accompanies marital dissolution, that marriage should be the only alternative.

Much of the attraction of cohabitation for single parents stems from a desire to live with someone together with an aversion to marriage. For some, the problem in marriage is that it would require relinquishing freedom and independence. Many women feel that by far the most important benefit of having been on their own is that they have gained the confidence and the skills needed to direct their own lives. Marriage, for them, might mean retrogression. The following comment was made by a woman who waited three years after her separation from her husband before filing for divorce. She had been living with her boyfriend for about a year.

> Jim keeps asking me to get married. But I'm not ready to. Actually, the first summer I went out with him, I'm very happy I wasn't free to get married, because I think I would have gotten married. But the more I got a taste of freedom and independence, the more I realized that I didn't want to get back into being married again.

For men who are single parents, remarriage has attractions it may not have for women insofar as marriage promises to provide someone who will look after their homes and care for their children. Women may fear that marriage would require them again to assume wives' responsibilities for scheduled meals and ordered households and responsiveness to husbands' wants. For both men and women whose previous marriages ended in divorce, there is likely to be a fear of going through it all again. A divorced woman said:

> It's not marriage that I fear; it's getting divorced again. I would love to get married again. But what if it doesn't work?

Despite reasons for hesitancy, if a relationship seems reasonably permanent, it may make sense to get married. The relationship may then be easier for the family to deal with, have less potential for embarrassing the children, and be more understandable to teachers and bank mortgage officers. And, for whatever it is worth, there would be the reassurance of a formal pledge of permanence, even though, the last time around, the pledge didn't prove all that effective.

CHAPTER 10

Personal Life and Parental Responsibility

THE SINGLE PARENT who contemplates forming a new relationship that may eventually provide the emotional and sexual satisfaction of marriage is almost immediately confronted by a dilemma. Dating someone new implies directing still more time and energy away from the children. In itself this seems a failing of parental responsibility. But what if the relationship should become important? Would not investment in a new relationship result in neglect of the children? The single parent may argue, reasonably enough, that a happy person makes a better parent. But the single parent may fear that the argument will leave the children unconvinced. And it may not entirely convince the parent.

As we have seen in an earlier chapter, some single parents, because they anticipate conflict between the demands of a new relationship and the needs of their children, hesitate even to begin dating. But most go ahead, perhaps telling the children that they have to have lives of their own, or reassuring the children that the children will always come first. In any event, they say to themselves that while they hope there won't be problems, they will be alert to the possibility that there may be, and will deal with whatever happens when it happens.

The children's initial reactions

Often children do object to the parent's dating. Dating is yet another activity taking the parent away from the home and competing with them for the parent's time and energy. But dating also competes with them for the parent's emotional commitment and so, more than other activities, threatens them with the parent's total loss. And, if the parent should bring someone home, there would be another person with whom they would be required to share their space, a stranger whose relationship to the parent is disturbingly close and disturbingly competitive with their own. A father of two adolescent daughters said:

> When I first started to date, I am sure there was some question in my children's minds as to how much time this was going to take away from them. And there is a degree of jealousy. There was another female to rival the affection they had been getting all along.

The appearance of someone new requires the children to accept that the parents have indeed separated, and that the parent with whom they live is free to see new people. It suggests that the other parent may be entirely replaced, at least as a figure in their households if not in their lives. This can be a lot for children to absorb. A divorced mother of three children, the oldest fourteen, said:

> I had told the children I was going out but not really talked about it. And this fellow walked into the family room. He told me later, "Those three kids were sitting on that couch, and I never saw three such scared kids in my life!" You know, Mommy had been with Daddy and now she's going out with somebody else. Maybe that's when it really hit them. Granted they knew that we were separated and everything, but now Mommy's going out with somebody else. And for them to see him and meet him, this really brought it home.

Younger children of divorced parents often harbor hopes that their parents will yet reconcile; this fantasy is attacked by a parent's interest in someone new. Children who have not established a secure relationship with the parent out of the home may fear that if the parent with whom they live becomes involved with someone new, the parent out of the home will be lost forever. Some children feel that loyalty to the parent out of the home requires that they be unfriendly to the custodial parent's dates. All these are reasons for children being cool to a new figure. The following story was told by a mother of two, the older a nine-year-old daughter:

> Toni—she's a very emotional little girl, and she has such great love for her father—it was hard on her when I started dating. If I had a man

over for supper, or for the evening, she would get very upset. We lived near one of her aunts and she would say, "I want to go up to Aunt Mary's." So I'd say, "Go ahead." What I think it was, she was afraid that her father was going to find out that there was a man in the house and that was going to hurt her relationship with him.

Although a first encounter with a parent's dating can be upsetting to children of any age, it seems to be children of latency age or preadolescents who voice opposition. These are children old enough to hold to a position independent of the parent's, yet not so old that they take the parent's dating in stride. Among the children who seem most unsettled by the parent's dating are those who have reason to believe the parent not in the home was lost to them because of a new attachment. The possibility of the remaining parent's going the same way may then seem quite real. A mother of three children, the oldest ten, said:

My children will ask me a lot of times, "You're not going to get married again?" It's not that they dislike the idea of marriage itself, but that they think they are going to lose me, because when their father left, he told them, "Mommy and I don't want to live together any more. We don't love each other. But we do love you and things will not change in our feelings for you. Daddy will always be around. But Daddy is going to get married again." That is why our marriage broke up: he had fallen in love with this other girl and wanted to marry her. He told them he would still love them and see them. And things have all been the opposite. The new wife doesn't particularly want the children around. She puts up with them when she has to. They think that if I got married again, they would lose me.

Even without the experience of losing a parent because of that parent's new attachment, a child may suppose that if a parent should marry, the parent will form a new family and move to a new home, where there may not be a place for the child. Since dating leads to marriage, dating, too, becomes worrisome. One divorced mother of a nine-year-old girl described how her daughter's concern burst forth when a man came for dinner:

I had someone over for dinner and my daughter all of a sudden said, "Are you getting married?" And then, before I could answer, she said, "Are you moving out of the house?" She was worried that if I remarried I wouldn't take her with me.

Children, of course, may also have positive feelings about a parent's dating. They may have recognized the parent's loneliness or despair and be pleased that the parent has become happier. They may experience a certain vicarious excitement from the parent's increased vivacity as the parent prepares for a date. They may feel pleasure, as well as dismay, at the prospect of an evening without the parent to limit television and insist on an early bedtime. They may anticipate that a new person will come with candy or a gift or will play with them or take them for a ride.

Nor must the new person be seen as entirely beneficial or entirely troublesome. Instead the new person may be liked for providing outings and a new source of attention, and disliked for displacing the other parent. Or the new person may be liked by one child and disliked by another. One child may compete with the parent for the admiration of the new person, while another child competes with the new person for access to the parent. Or the same child may display a succession of reactions to the same person or to different ones. A mother of two children, a girl of about ten and a boy of about eight, described the different ways her children behaved in response to two men she brought home:

> This one date that I had, I brought him home, and my daughter went absolutely beserk because she didn't want me showing anybody any affection. And then I was dating this fellow who was a gym teacher so my son started tumbling and standing on his head in the corner. He was really taken with this guy. I think he was more in love with him than I was.

Younger children may express ambivalence by acting up, so that they both unsettle the new person and engage his or her attention. A mother of two rather precocious children, a girl of ten and a boy of nine, said that her children were determined that she not replace their father but, at the same time, would compete with her for the attention of anyone she brought home. They created a tumult and so ensured that they were not left out. And if the new man was angered, well, so be it.

> Normally my kids are very quiet, reasonably sane people. In the evening they read or watch TV. I brought this guy in for the first time, and they went running through the room, screaming nonsense syllables. I dated that fellow for about six months, and the kids were awful all through that time. He thought I had the most rowdy children. And the more they saw that it bothered him, the more they would do it.

Somewhat older children may express ambivalent feelings more clearly. They may be able to encourage the parent with whom they are living to go out while making it clear that they do not want to accept another figure in their own lives. A divorced woman with two children, a girl about thirteen and a boy about eleven, reported:

> My daughter will say to me, "I wish you had a boyfriend. He could take us places. And I think you should get married. But don't get married while I'm living in the house." My son said that, too. One time I made a remark, "I may be getting married someday." And my son said, "Well, I'm not going to live here. He's not going to be my father."

Parents do well to reassure their children, no matter how farfetched the children's anxieties may seem. A flat and simple statement of the way things are may suffice. One mother said:

What you have to do sometimes is to say, "Look, I'm only going on a date. I'm not getting married and moving to Texas. So don't get scared. Our life is not going to change. And if I start to think about changing it, you are going to be the first to know. So don't get scared."

One woman entered into dating only after first establishing for the children that friends, both men and women, would frequently call on her. By the time she embarked on her first date, the children were accustomed to having new people in their home:

> I joined an organization of single parents and became very active, which meant that there were a great many people coming in and out of my house constantly, men as well as women. So if the kids found a man sitting at the kitchen table drinking coffee, it didn't faze them, because they could come in tomorrow and there might be somebody else there. So my kids never flicked an eyelash when I went out on a date. And I think it is because there were people in and out constantly.

Another divorced woman with children aged thirteen and nine, brought her children in on the question of whether to date, just as she might have had the children participate in other decisions:

> I used a little finesse with the kids. I said to them, "Gee, I met this guy and he asked me out." And they said, "Well, why don't you go out with him?" And I said, "I don't know. I think it's a little too soon." And they said, "Oh, Ma, you got to start going out sooner or later and having a good time." So I said, "You guys think you wouldn't mind?" And they said, "No, we wouldn't mind."

But many single parents feel that, at least at first, they will be most comfortable if they keep their dating and their parenting separated from each other. They may tell the children that they are going to meet someone, but they don't have the someone come to their homes. Or, if they are to be picked up at their homes, they make sure they are ready and waiting so that they can, as one woman put it, "zoom right out the door," with dates and children never meeting. In this way the parents postpone confronting some of the problems their children might have with their dating until they feel readier to deal with them.

The compartmentalization of dating as protection for the children

By sequestering their dating lives, parents hope both to avoid having to answer the children's criticisms of their dates and to shield their dates from the children's scrutiny. But their primary reason for sequestering their dating is to protect their children. Parents can feel less guilty about dating if their children are not made to suffer through uncomfortable introductions and, especially, if their children are not permitted to grow fond of someone who may soon disappear. Their children, they feel, have already suffered enough loss. One woman said:

> I've never been involved with anyone that really got involved with my kids. I just haven't let it happen. I'm not ready for that. I haven't met anybody that I think I'd like that to happen with. So it just hasn't happened.

When a relationship is still tentative, a single parent is likely to want the children to understand that the relationship is between the parent and the new person and that only incidentally are the children involved. And so, if the woman friend of a single father should help the father's adolescent daughter shop for clothes, the father would define her help as a favor to him, and not an act of friendship towards the child. Similarly, should the male friend of a single mother admire her nine-year-old son's stamp collection, the mother will want it understood that he is doing so simply as might any guest of the mother's, and that he is making no special overture to the boy. The mother of a seven-year-old only son said:

> It is sort of a strange thing to say, because you feel if you are going to become involved with someone and he becomes a part of whatever living situation you have, that means your child is involved too. But I think it's just a matter of protection for Jimmie. I'm more or less making it a point to keep Guy and Jimmie apart. Because I don't want Jimmie to become involved with Guy and then have Guy leave and have Jimmie experience what might be a greater loss than he is able to deal with. So if Guy comes over, I tell Jimmie to go watch TV.

Some parents have witnessed their children become close to someone who then disappeared from all their lives. They are unwilling to have this be a recurrent experience for their children:

> The children can accept the fact that there was this man that we all loved for the three-year period that he was here. But to have this happen frequently in their lives I think would be too much. So now when I do date I rarely have the man come to meet me or pick me up. And if he does, it's just an introduction and then out we go. I don't get the men involved in any family stuff.

A single parent may be annoyed should someone just met fail to cooperate with the parent's deliberate failure to sponsor his or her relationship with the children. Some parents keep their children out of sight just so that no new person will be tempted to cultivate them as a means toward winning the parent:

Something else I've learned is that you don't really expose your children too much to someone unless you really feel it is genuine, because some men will come in and they'll bring gifts, and they will really play up to the children, hoping that will attract the mother. And the children can become attached and, consequently, get hurt.

Single fathers may be somewhat less concerned than single mothers about these issues. The following comment, made by a divorced father with custody of two teenaged children, expressed a point of view that several other single fathers with whom we spoke, but very few single mothers, would have agreed with:

My children have known every woman I've ever gone out with, every woman I have had a relationship with, and when the woman and I broke up, the children and I have talked about it. Lately they have agreed that it helped them understand that just because two people like each other, they may not be able to get along. So both of them feel it has been helpful to them to see what happens.

Children themselves, as they become accustomed to a parent's dating, learn to be cautious with whomever the parent is seeing. A mother of two children, both teenagers, said:

At one point, after I broke up with somebody they had learned to like, they were cool to somebody, and I made a remark about it and they said, "We don't want to get to know anybody until you are sure."

Even after a parent has begun to hope for permanence, the children may feel more comfortable maintaining a friendly distance, aware that this person, too, may only be passing through.

The parent, the new person, and the children

Should a new person prove accepting and acceptable, the resulting relationship is likely to become central to the single parent's emotional life. No longer need the single parent cope with loneliness and its accompanying discomforts, nor feel isolated by responsibility for the children. For the children there may be losses: the single parent will be a bit more distant from them; the children will have to accept loss of their roles as the parent's companions and confidants. Now, too, there is another person whose interests and tastes affect how evenings and weekends are spent. And at times, perhaps for an entire day or entire weekend, the single parent may be away, and so entirely unavailable to the children. But balancing these losses, the single parent is less short-tempered, less harried, more energetic. There is someone else for the parent to worry about and, as one adolescent girl put it, "She has someone else to nag." And, for older children, the parent is less of a concern.

Yet while the parent's morale is likely to depend on how things are going in the relationship with the new figure, the parent's deepest commitment remains to the children. What if the children would prefer that the new relationship end? What if the parent must choose between this vitally important new person and the wishes, perhaps needs, of the children?

Generally parents reassure the children that they come first. If there is any possibility of the new person's joining the parent's household, the parent is likely first to seek the children's approval—although it may be clear to the children that the parent hopes to obtain it. One mother of three described the sort of consultation with children that tends to precede a new person's entering the household. The children consulted, Mike and Larry, were eleven and nine respectively. There also was a five-year-old who was not consulted.

> I talked with Mike and Larry about Ward being here. Larry and I had a long conversation. I think he likes Ward. Mike is the one that I was really kind of leery about. I asked him if he would object to Ward being here and he said, "No, I like him." And I asked how he would like to have Ward around all the time. He didn't answer me for a little while and I didn't push it, but around twenty minutes later he came up to me and he said, "Ma, remember you asked me if I'd like to have Ward around?" I said, "Yeah, would you?" "Yeah," he said. "I think I would at that."

If children are not yet of school age, the single parent may assume that the children will accept a new person easily and need not be consulted. Parents sometimes underestimate the need of small children for preparation before a new adult becomes a member of their household. In one extreme example, a child with whom we spoke said that it took him and his brother a while before they could stop thinking of their mother's new boyfriend as a robber. The boyfriend had been unknown to them until they returned from the home of a neighbor, who had been looking after them, to find the boyfriend's car in the driveway and the boyfriend in their home, suddenly a full member of the household. They were then six and four.

Once a relationship with a new figure gives promise of permanence it becomes of critical importance to the single parent that there be mutual acceptance between the new person and the children. Now the single parent may feel grateful rather than alarmed should the new person reach out to the children:

> The first thing Wally did was suggest we do something with the kids that weekend. We all went to the park, and the kids thoroughly enjoyed it. I appreciated his doing that. He did it because he cared about me.

It can be most helpful to the single parent if the new person is sensitive to the children's needs. One mother of three, not yet divorced, had begun living with a man. She said:

> Marty, my youngest boy, is a little jealous of Vince. Every time Vince and I are together, all of a sudden there is this little six-year-old between us. I tend to baby Marty a little more than the other two. He was the child I had alone when the older children were at school, so we did a lot of things together and we got very close. Last night we were all sitting on the bed watching TV, and Marty's nose got a little out of joint because he wasn't the center of attention. And he went into the other room. But Vince got up and said to him, "Why don't you sit up there for a while? I have something to do." And Marty sat beside me and I had my arm around him. He just wanted the extra attention. And I think it might have meant a little more, not having Vince there.

If the children, too, welcome the new figure, the single parent need feel no conflict between commitment to the new figure and commitment to the children. An incident like the following can be most reassuring to the single parent:

> My son really likes Michael. A few times Michael had to go places and he took him by himself, and that's what my son wants. My son brought home a registration blank from school. I filled out everything on it— my name, his father's name, the responsible people to call in case of emergency, except where my son's father is working. So my son said to me, "Can't you just put down Michael's name, and his work?"

But either the new person or the child may be unwilling to accept the other. Then the single parent is tugged each way. One woman described a man she had become involved with as appallingly competitive with her small son:

> Arthur was in competition with my son for attention. When I first met him, my son was about three, and I'd tuck him into bed and read him a bedtime story and give him a kiss and everything, and that would take forty-five minutes. And Arthur would say, "Aren't you doing a little bit much?" Or he'd find an excuse to come into the room and mention something to me. He would sort of interrupt. He was always doing that and he never realized what he was doing. But he was definitely in competition with my son. They were like two little boys.

This woman found the man's behavior intolerable and soon ended the relationship. To another parent in a similar situation the new relationship might be too important to relinquish. Then the parent might take the role of diplomat, shuttling between the new person and the child, encouraging each to feel friendly toward the other, trying to mollify each while limiting their interaction, and hoping that sooner or later something would change.

No parent would want a child to suffer hurt or unhappiness as a result of the parent's new relationship. Yet sometimes a child does feel resentful of a new person's presence in the parent's life and in the child's own home. The child may dislike the new person, may be embarrassed by the new person's relationship with the parent, may be angered by having been displaced or by being unable to have time alone with the parent or by being unable to command the parent's undivided loyalty. Very occasionally an adolescent whose parents separated or divorced will choose to live with the other parent rather than continue to live with a parent whose new involvement is intolerable. Or the adolescent may choose to live away from both homes:

> My teenage son and I don't get along on account of the guy I go out with. My son lives with a family. He comes to see me once or twice a week. When he sees the guy's car, my son won't come in. He goes back. I am hurt, because I do love my kids.

Single parents can find themselves in a cruel dilemma should it appear that a new relationship that is for them a relationship of hope is for their children an irritant or worse. Most single parents who are going with someone new do what they can to avoid having this happen. Even so, some worry:

> I just hope that what I'm doing now doesn't harm the kids. That's the only time it would bother me, is if I thought it bothered the kids. It doesn't seem to. They don't say anything or ask questions. But that's the only thing I worry about.

Sexual activity and parental responsibility

Parents who are married need not consider how their children view their sexual lives. For all they know, their children believe they are sexually inactive. But single parents cannot so completely keep their sexual lives to themselves. Dating is very obviously motivated in part by sexual interest. And, while married parents need provide no explanation for their living together, should the single parent have someone move in or, for that matter, stay overnight, the children may wonder why.

Men find it easier than women to take the position that they need not hide their sexual natures. The following is a not atypical masculine view. It was voiced by a father of two girls, aged fifteen and twelve.

I figure I have a life of my own. My daughters have never questioned me, and I have never explained it to them. I don't feel I am under obligation to. When I was married, my bedroom door was always locked, and it was really none of their business what went on behind it. I feel like I can be a good parent and still have a life of my own. If I'm going to go away with somebody or something, I don't flaunt it. As a consequence, there's no embarrassment. I don't feel that I have to discuss it with them.

Women, in contrast, often feel more comfortable if they can limit their children's awareness that they are sexually active. And so a woman may require that the man not stay the entire night with her; should the man sleep with her, he must awaken and leave before the children are up. Or the woman may restrict her sexual activity to the man's home. A mother of two children said:

> I seem to have a double standard that is accepted by my children, and that is if I stay overnight at Richard's apartment that's OK. We don't need to talk about what's going on or anything else. But I would never in a million years have Richard stay at my house.

Yet the single mother may slip, and the children may come upon a man in her bed. Though women to whom this happens are likely to be embarrassed, the children invariably appear unperturbed:

> I told this fellow I was seeing that I couldn't go out with him because I couldn't get a sitter. I said, "Why don't we have a cookout in my backyard? Come on over." So he came over, thoroughly enjoyed the kids, the kids thoroughly enjoyed him. He gave them a lot of attention. And he ended up staying over. He fell asleep in my bed. And the kids got up in the morning and woke me up, and he was there sleeping. Since then, he's picked me up a couple of times, and the kids say to him, "Hey, Mr. Norris, when are we going fishing?" I think, as far as they were concerned, nothing happened.

Single parents who have experience in the matter agree that children are in no obvious way disturbed by someone's staying overnight. A mother of a thirteen-year-old girl and an eleven-year-old boy, for example, said that neither of her children seemed to take special note when her boyfriend stayed over:

> Ben has stayed overnight. The kids don't resent it. Sometimes he's here when they come home from school, and they say, "Hi, Ben." They've never said anything about it.

Parents report that their children exhibit rather little curiosity about the parents' sexual lives. And this is as true when parents frankly share their bedrooms as it is when parents inform the children that the person who has stayed for breakfast spent the night on the living room couch. Why children should be so little questioning of a parent's bed being shared is unclear. It may be that their speculation is repressed. But children act as though the matter of where a guest sleeps is pretty much the parent's business and, once they know, no further concern of theirs.

This is not to say that children are never moralistic. If parents have a hectic dating life, children are sometimes made uneasy. Although what may be most upsetting to a younger child is a parent's emotional inaccessibility, the child's discomfort may be expressed as a feeling that the parent is doing something risky or, perhaps, wrong. A man who had custody of his eight-year-old son said:

> My son is a little confused sometimes. He doesn't understand my life style at all. He's seen me with a lot of different women. His mother has been married for the last four years, and he sees what is a fairly stable home environment there, with his mother and his stepfather in the home, so he doesn't understand that I should be seeing so many people. It isn't right for me to be seeing two people at the same time, for example. He would feel better if I were married. I wouldn't get into trouble then.

Adolescent children sometimes do hold parents to fairly stringent moral standards. Adolescence is a time when children are developing their own moral codes and they may then be especially critical of parental failings. But, in addition, moral criticism is a convenient channel for expressing tensions based elsewhere. So one sixteen-year-old girl, uncomfortable at home for other reasons, accused her mother of acting like a prostitute by going out with several men. And an adolescent boy, angry at his mother's attempt to restrict his evenings with friends, asked his mother why she was seeing a married man.

When parents are confronted in this way they may defend themselves by saying that they are not answerable for their behavior to their children, or by saying that they will explain when the children are older. But they are bound to be shaken.

Single parents can be troubled by the discrepancy between their own sexual policies and the policies the want their children to adopt. They are, for themselves, willing to accept nonmarital sexual relationships; some will accept sexual relationships that are without implication for long-term commitment. But they want their children to behave differently, and so they worry about the model they are presenting. Men as well as women feel this way. The following statement was made by a man, father of a boy and a girl:

> Some of the things that I do are not really what I want my kids to know or think or adopt as a pattern. I have difficulty in explaining my sexual style to my children because I have a double standard.

Women, more than men, may also worry that their behavior will result in social disapproval and that their children will be hurt. If they live in a neighborhood of two-parent families, they may do what they can to protect their reputation for their children's sake as well as their own. The following comment was made by a divorced mother of two children, living in a stable low-income neighborhood:

> By the time I started going out, my children were going to school, and they were old enough to be hearing things from other children that the children heard from their parents. You know, "Their mother is no good because she has this one over the house or that one. She goes out with this one or that one." So I've always been very careful.

A woman living in a middle-income neighborhood also did what she could to minimize her neighbors' awareness of her dating:

> I've always been careful. I feel that my personal life is my own and I'm not hurting anybody in what I do. Well, I'm not hurting anybody but myself. I do it at the times when the children won't know about it, and it won't wash back to where the kids would find out about it. And I make sure I'm home when the kids get up. And I know that if people do see me occasionally on a date in a restaurant or something, I'm conducting myself in a manner that's very acceptable. And I won't go where people that live close by will see me.

It may be in this area that men as single parents and women as single parents are most different. Men are quite willing for their children to realize that they are sexually active and appear less concerned about their reputation in this respect. But neither men nor women who are single parents want their own sexual policies to become models for their children's.

The new person's rights in the household

Although parents' sexual lives appear not to be of great importance to their children, children are manifestly concerned about the roles new figures will play in their households. In particular, a child will want to know to what extent the child must be deferential to the new person. What are the new person's rights? Can the new person tell the child what to do? Punish the child? After all, it is the *child's* home. And, whatever the new person's relationship to the parent, the new person is *not* a parent.

Single parents generally agree: the new person is not a parent, and, while the children should be as respectful of the new person as they would be of any adult, that is as far as it should go. Only rarely will a single parent permit someone new to assume real authority in the household. Even though he or she is a member of the household, the new person has authority in relation to the children that is strictly circumscribed and dependent, in part, on what the children will tolerate. The understandings described by a mother of two children, the older about eleven, are typical:

> Gordon would never interfere with the children. If the kids want to stay up a half hour later, they'll ask him; they won't ask me, because they know I'll say, "No, this is bedtime." So they'll ask him, and he'll say, "Well, you can stay up a half-hour more." And I've asked him for advice, and he's given me advice. But he wouldn't say to my son, "Jonathan, you'd better get in your room, and you'd better stay there." No way. He would never do that. And, as far as laying a hand on them or anything like that, he would never.

Many single parents pledge to themselves, if not to their children, that under no circumstances will they permit anyone else to punish their children. Punishment is *their* prerogative; *no one* else has that right. And if the relationship is one maintained for want of anything better, the parent will be willing to act on that principle, even though the relationship is thereby endangered. A mother of a seven-year-old only son described the following incident:

> Paul likes Joey, but one night Paul slapped Joey on the ass. I was doing the dishes, and Joey had a friend staying over, and they were getting out of line. I was going into Joey's room, but Paul beat me to it. He had no right going in that room. He wasn't watching the children. He was my guest. Those two were *my* children for the night. I told him, "Don't you ever do that again! And if you don't like that, leave!"

But if the relationship is one of hope, the parent is likely to try to smooth things over, perhaps tell the children that punishment was deserved—although the new person should not have been the one to punish them—and perhaps, as in the story that follows, remind the children of all the new person has done for them. The mother of the following account had been seeing a man, Harold, for about two years. Harold was separated from his wife but not yet divorced. There were two children in the household: Helen, aged eleven, and Timmy, aged seven and described by teachers as overactive. The mother said:

> Last Saturday Harold got upset with Timmy. Timmy said he wanted to use Helen's skates outside. Harold said, "Why don't you go out and ask Helen's permission?" Later Helen came in and was mad because Timmy had her skates. And Harold said, "Didn't he ask your permission when he went outside?" And Helen said, "No." When Timmy came in, Harold stood up and gave him four slaps on the behind. Timmy was shocked. He ran into his room. Helen started to cry. She said, "I didn't want you to hit him!"

> Helen still brings it up, that Harold hit Timmy. I have to talk to her. I say, "What about all the good things he does? He takes us out to

dinner, brings us things. Whose idea was it to buy you a hat? You forget all this. You want to take all of it, and yet you don't think he has a right to yell at Timmy!"

But note that as this mother reported her defense of her boyfriend she was defending his scolding her son, which would have been acceptable, rather than his spanking her son, which was not.

One single mother said that her boyfriend complained that having only limited rights in relation to the children made him feel marginal to the life of the household. The mother tried to have her son accept her boyfriend as a second parent, but she herself questioned her boyfriend's right to parental authority:

> My son has said to me, "I don't have to listen to Vince. Vince's not my father." And I said to him, "Well, your father isn't here, and I can't always handle things." And Vince has said, "I'll never be the kids' father. I'll never have the right to yell at them." And I've said, "No, that won't interfere." But a couple of times he did yell at them, and I've said to myself, "He shouldn't be doing this. This is my responsibility. He's got no right to do this."

Given an already well-established relationship that has every likelihood of continuing, some single parents do permit the new person to play a parentlike role. Even then they need the justification that the children benefit:

> The kids were little when their father left, and it was about six years before I got involved with Cal. Then Cal came in, and he really made it a family unit. The three children and Cal and I would sit down and have family conferences about homework and the dishes and chores, and the children would take discipline from him because he was fair. And he was good to them and generous and loving.

No matter how important the new relationship is to the parent, the parent remains committed to the care and protection of the children. Should a mother on her own be joined in the household by her boyfriend, the boyfriend will not ordinarily become a quasi-parent. He may be granted increasing rights and privileges as the relationship becomes ever more established, but always the mother is the parent and the boyfriend only the mother's boyfriend. Similarly, a father's girlfriend, no matter how caring she may be towards his children, is in the last analysis only the father's girlfriend.

Money and authority when a new person enters the household

The issue of financial responsibility for the household may arise between mothers and the men they are seeing, as the mothers' relationships with the men become established. To what extent should the men be permitted to "help out?"

With money goes control: the role of provider brings with it the power to withhold and the ability to require deference to one's wishes. Because of this, single parents ordinarily refuse to permit a new person to assume financial responsibility for their households. They do not want their children to have to defer to anyone in the household besides themselves.

It is acceptable for the man to bring gifts: that can be simple reciprocity for being invited to dinner and for the woman's home serving as the setting for their relationship. It is acceptable for the man to provide entertainment; indeed, this is one aspect of courting. And, of course, it is acceptable for the man to replace food and drink he has consumed. For the man to fail to do so might constitute exploitation of the woman. But for the man to go beyond this, to assumption of responsibility for the woman's expenses, would not be acceptable. As one woman said:

> I can't think of a guy just handing you $20 for something. That kind of thing doesn't sit well with me. If he had been eating with me regularly, I could see his going to the grocery store and buying groceries, or taking what I have picked out and going up to the register and paying for it. My question would be, "Has he eaten that much coming over? Is it kind of paying it back?"

A woman may, perhaps, borrow money from a man she is seeing to meet an unexpected bill. But most women are reluctant to do this and insist on repaying the money as soon as they can. One divorced woman said that her boyfriend didn't especially want repayment, but she returned the money anyway:

> I borrowed $300 from my boyfriend so I could buy a new car, and I made sure I paid it back.

Another woman moved into a flat owned by her boyfriend but insisted on paying rent, although she could have lived rent-free. And still another woman, about to move into a new house with the understanding that her boyfriend might move in with her, would permit the boyfriend to pay only a small part of the redecorating expenses:

> When we moved in here, the house needed a lot of work, and there were a lot of things Roy wanted to do for the house. And I said, no, I would do what I could afford to do. We were going to try to strip the

wallpaper, but Roy spoke to a friend about coming in and doing it, and I said, "Roy, that's a real luxury, to pay somebody to strip the wall-paper." And that was the one thing I conceded and let Roy pay for. That was about the only thing I did accept from him.

Discussing the matter further, this woman distinguished between the kind of help that she considered appropriate and the kind she would not accept. In general, exchange was acceptable and benefited both. But she would not accept money:

Roy does help me, just by the fact that he takes me out all the time. That's an expense I don't have. And he pays for a lot of the liquor. If we've entertained his friends, he'll buy two or three bottles of whatever we need. And there are a lot of times he'll take us out for the day, the kids and me. And we've gone for Chinese food a few times. But to actually take money from him, no. No.

To accept a man's money would reduce the woman's independence. It would obligate her to consider the man's wishes when she might not want to. So long as the money a woman uses is her own, the man cannot tell her what to do. The following story was told by a woman who had been together with her boyfriend for more than five years:

Charles had taken me Christmas shopping. I had $45 left over, and Charles said, "Go and buy yourself a new dress." I said, "No, I want to buy the girls slippers and to buy the boy a proper man's bathrobe." He said to me, "You're foolish. After Christmas they won't wear those things." Which is true. The girls forget to put their slippers on, and the boy doesn't wear the bathrobe. So Charles said, "You're wasting the money!" And I flared up. I said to him, "It's not your money! It's my money! And I can do what I like with my own money!"

Acceptance of money from a boyfriend—and, especially, reliance on a boyfriend's regular financial contributions—would mean that not only the woman, but her children as well, would have to accept the boyfriend as a figure with legitimate rights in the household. No longer could the woman claim that though she might ask advice of the boyfriend, she alone decided what would happen.

Some women, a very small minority among those in our study, did rely on boyfriends for a significant part of their incomes. One woman, divorced and with three children, became involved with a man she met while working as a waitress. The man, as it happened, was married, although the woman did not discover this immediately. It is instructive to observe the way in which the man's financial contribution to the woman's household established a basis for his assumption of authority.

When I first met my boyfriend, I was waiting on table, and he was a customer. I got the regular routine from him, if I was married or divorced, and I just completely ignored it. Except that he was an extremely good tipper, and you don't forget a good tipper. And he came in again and asked me if I was married or divorced. I said I was divorced. He wanted to know how many children I had. And I said I had three children. He said, "Do you and the children like lobster?" I said, "Yes, we do." And he gave me his business card and a big tip.

The following week he came in and he said, "Are you going to be home Sunday? I'll bring you some lobster." So I gave him directions on how to get to my home, and he did indeed come to my house about eleven on the Sunday. He had a big box full of lobsters and bags of frozen shrimp. And he made himself right at home in my kitchen.

I thought, OK, this is nice of him to bring me the lobster and the shrimp; he can leave now. I have absolutely no attraction to this man. But he doesn't leave, and I can't be rude and say, "You can't stay," after $50 worth of stuff, maybe more. So it ended up he stayed for the whole afternoon. And my children are coming in and out of the house. I didn't care whether I saw him again or not, so the kids did what they damned well pleased: screamed, hollered, just their normal selves. Ordinarily, if I met somebody that I liked, I would try to keep my kids subdued. But I wasn't trying to impress him. And he just took it all in and fit right in.

The relationship was begun by the man's providing the woman with money in tips, a form that permitted it to be understood by her as earned, and then following this with an extravagant gift. Perhaps if the man had said to the woman, "I will provide money and gifts for you and your family as a way of purchasing your company," she would have refused. But the man simply provided the tips and treats, made himself available to the woman and her children, and seemed to want very little in return. It would have been difficult for any woman who had long been struggling just to meet her bills to turn away attention of this sort.

Now if he came in when I was working, he would ask me what I was doing on my day off. And I would say, "I don't know what I'm doing, but if you like, you can call me the day before, and I'll let you know." And, if nothing better had come along when he'd call, I'd say, "Yeah, fine." Because there was nothing better to do and he was a good date, and he was good to the kids. And he would bring things. If he came over to the house, and it was suppertime, he would either treat the kids to hamburgers or take us all out. And because he was so good to them and was providing things that I could not get for us, I allowed him to continue to come.

After a couple of months, the man offered to provide the woman with a vacation.

This went on for two months, and I was very tired. I had been working for almost seven years, sometimes two jobs, to support myself and the children. I had too much pride to go on welfare. I was very exhausted, and he knew this. He would say things like, "You need a vacation. You should get away." And I would say things like, "Yeah, that's true. I do need a vacation. But I can't afford a vacation." And he would say things like, "Well, I'll take you." I didn't believe that. But he got two tickets to Puerto Rico.

Now up until now, there had been absolutely no contact between us. That's probably why I tolerated him, because I didn't *like* him. I would go out with him because I knew there wouldn't be any pressure from him, and he was really good to the kids. But now he gets tickets, and we're going to San Juan! Well, I know there's going to be a bedroom scene in San Juan, and I'm wondering, how am I ever going to get through it? But I needed the vacation badly enough to accept.

Beginning with the vacation, the man became more and more part of the woman's emotional life. And more and more, the woman depended upon him financially.

We did go, and the bedroom scene was bad. It was out of obligation, and I think he knew it. But the rest of the vacation was so good. We enjoyed each other so much, and it was so relaxing. I know that he would have liked the bedroom thing to be more than it was, but out of the bedroom, out on the beach or whatever it was that we did, we enjoyed each other.

When we came back, we went back to the old routine: once a week, maybe twice a week, and only if nothing better came along. But he was getting pretty tough to top. I may not enjoy him for sex, but I was enjoying him as a person because he was so good to me. I was feeling that even if I did have a chance to do something else, it wouldn't be better than being with him. And a close relationship was growing with the children. It was my daughter's birthday, and she wanted a tape recorder for her birthday. And he brought the tape recorder. And I had a party for all of her girlfriends at the house, and he helped out with all of the expenses for the party, and he was there for the whole party.

When things came up, I would ask his advice, like, "Where do you think I should go to buy this?" or "Where do you think I should go to have my car fixed?" The next thing I'd know, he'd come to the house with what I wanted to buy. Or if it was the car, he'd say to me, "Let me drive the car and see what I think." And then he would suggest where I should go, and he'd tell me what had to be done. Or I would say, "Well, I can't have that fixed right now because it's too expensive. I'm going to have to wait until I have the money in my budget." And he would say, "Go have it fixed," and he would pay for it. I never asked him for money, but I got so I was hoping he would offer, and he always did.

The woman stopped accepting other dates. And although the man did not move in with her—somehow he kept his marriage intact while spending much of his time with her—he did assume a role that was very nearly that of head of the family.

By summer, the relationship was completely different. I was enjoying him so much that it was easier for me to have sex with him. Then it got to a point where I enjoyed sex with him. And then we were like a family. He was always fair with the kids if there were problems. And he was loving. There was a lot of warmth. It got to a point where, if the children would talk back to me, he would say, "Listen, that's your mother, and don't speak to your mother in that way, especially not in front of me," and the kids were more respectful to me. It was getting to be a pretty enjoyable scene.

If we had a meal, and it was time to do the dishes, he'd say to my daughter, "OK, it's your turn to do the dishes tonight. Your mother has been working. She is tired. Let your mother rest and relax." The following night he would say to my son, "Well, tonight, it's your turn." We would have family meetings. We would sit around the table, and it was open conversation. Everybody would have their turn to say, "Well, I have this gripe." Like if my daughter said, "I don't feel like doing the dishes tonight," he would say, "Well, after the dishes are done, we'll sit down and we'll have a discussion and try to work something out that is fair." And everybody had their chance to talk and to say what they were feeling. We would have this type of meeting about once a month. It was something that we never had before.

It was now established that the man contributed to the woman's expenses. At the man's suggestion, the woman reduced the hours she worked. Now, although the woman could pay her rent and buy her food with the money she herself earned, she depended upon the man for everything else.

After I had been going out with him for about a year, he gave me money almost on a regular basis—maybe every two weeks he'd say, "Here's some extra money to take care of the bills this month." And he would give me money for extras. If my daughter would say, "Ma, I want to take dance lessons," I would say, "I'm sorry, we can't afford it." And he would say, "When do the lessons start? Go sign her up." And he would give me the money for her.

Although the man described himself as essentially separated from his wife and living, temporarily, with his parents, he sometimes could not be available to the woman because his wife and his own children required him. Unexpectedly, he suffered a business reverse and began to find that the expenses of two families were more than he could manage. He was less often with the woman and provided her with less money. His authority in the woman's family diminished accordingly.

Over those last six months, the relationship went downhill pretty fast. I didn't see very much of him, and there was really no financial help except maybe once or twice. By the end of that time, I was handling everything financial myself. But he was trying to hang on to his relationship with me and the children. He was trying to keep the same authority over the children that he had had before. He would telephone me and he would say, "This is their reading hour, and they should be reading now." And I'd say, "When you're here to help me, then we can keep up your rules, but now you're not here, so I am the authority." I said, "You're not here to be an authority. You're dictating over the phone. You're acting just as you do with your employees." He was treating me like somebody that worked for him. I tolerated that only for a certain amount of time, and then I didn't take it any more.

So there were arguments, and the whole thing just crumbled. As a matter of fact, it was my son's birthday, and he said to me, "Do you have presents?" And I said, "Yes." And he said, "Well, I'm going in town and I should be picking up some money, and I'll stop by the house and drop some off and make sure that there's enough for a party, for ice cream and a movie and whatever." And he never did show up, and I never heard from him since.

Many women, raising children alone and chronically worried about money, allow themselves to daydream about how nice it would be if only a man would come by to take care of things, to pay the bills, and to share responsibility for the children. Indeed, looking back, this woman felt that all in all the relationship had been a fortunate one for her. The man had provided her with a breathing spell during which she could call on resources beyond her own. Also, she felt that she now managed her family a bit better, because of him. Even knowing how it turned out, she would do it all over again. But the bargain she had made was one few mothers on their own would agree to: in exchange for the man's financial support, she had ceded to him authority in her family. Undoubtedly she did so only because she could believe that her children were benefited. And the gradualness of the man's movement into her family made it possible for her to accept, little by little, changes she might not have agreed to all at once. But other mothers in her situation might still have balked at the diminution of her authority in her household, and its replacement by the man's.

Endings

When relationships end, whether they were maintained for want of anything better or were truly relationships of hope, the single parent again experiences loss and again is vulnerable to loneliness. And there may be, again, a questioning of self for having entered something that ended badly. One woman, interviewed about a week after the ending of an affair, said:

I was up last night until three. I never stay up that late. But I was very, very blue yesterday. I'm not a happy soul today, but last night I just sat there, very depressed and morbid. I don't know if I'm feeling so bad about Vinnie and me splitting up or about the fact that I was stupid enough to get into the affair in the first place. I don't know what my feelings are. But I think constantly, I cry easily, and it doesn't do any good.

Personal Life and Parental Responsibility

Children, too, are apt to be upset. If they had not gotten on with the new person, they may feel uneasy, despite relief that the relationship is now over, because of concern that they may have contributed to its end. And if the children, like the parent, had been attached to the new person, they as well as the parent will experience loss. To the extent that the new person may have served as a substitute for the absent parent, the children can be expected to be the more distressed when the new person, too, departs:

> I had a serious relationship with a fellow for three years, and my boys, of course, were older than when I got my divorce, and they were much more visibly affected by the breakup of that relationship. But the fellow did show them an awful lot of attention.

Yet there is a critical difference, in the families of the separated and divorced, between what follows the breakup of a marriage and what follows the breakup of a new relationship. When a marriage ends, the children retain their relationships with both parents. Mother and father may become antagonists, but the children remain loyal to both. And this means that the children maintain relationships with the parent outside the home that are very different from their custodial parent's relationship with that figure. But when a *new* figure leaves, the parent and the children are together in their feelings of loss. They may both be angry or both regretful, but in any event the parent need not leave feelings unexpressed out of respect for the different feelings of the children, nor need the children learn to be silent because to refer to the new figure would create tension. On the contrary, because their feelings are similar, parent and children can draw support from each other.

> Cal had a good relationship with the children and I'm sure they were as hurt as I was when it all ended. About six months after I broke up with him, my younger son came home one time and said, "I wish you were still going with Cal," because he was having a problem with the neighborhood children. He said, "Boy, he would handle this." I guess I knew they missed him too, but it really didn't hit home until he said that. And every so often we speak of Cal, and there is still a lot of love there when we talk about him.

In other ways, too, the ending of a new relationship is not the disorganizing experience that the ending of a marriage is. There is no change in marital status to become accustomed to; no need to find new friends; the household's financing ordinarily remains the same: it is easier for the single parent to go on with life. If the relationship had been a significant one, the parent's unhappiness at its ending may be no less intense than that which accompanied the ending of the parent's marriage. And yet the ending, because it is less disruptive of the parent's other relationships, including the parent's relationships with the children, is easier to move on from.

PART FOUR

*The Good
and the Troublesome:
Valuing the Former,
Dealing with the Latter*

CHAPTER 11

The Benefits and the Problems of Raising Children Alone

NOT LONG AGO I was talking to a group of single parents and, just before we broke up, a woman said, "You make it sound too grim." I said I was sorry, that I didn't think being a single parent was grim so much as it was very demanding while affording few times of relief. Oddly enough, she agreed. But she explained that she thought it was important not to focus your attention on how hard being a single parent can be, because if you did, you would want to sit down and cry. "If you don't stop to think," she said, "you just keep on going from task to task, from day to day."

I am not sure it is all that bad, especially if the single parent has formed a new attachment and so need not cope with loneliness along with everything else. And it hardly needs saying that being a single parent is preferable to continuing in a miserably unhappy marriage. It also can be preferable, as many divorced fathers without custody will attest, to living as a single person away from one's children. Here is a father on this latter point:

> Six months ago my sixteen-year-old daughter came to live with me. She was having a tough time in school and at home, and I suggested she come if she wanted to. She did, and it has had a startling effect on

me. Having another person in the house, creating a home again, the responsibility of having a child, someone depending on me a little bit, it gave me a feeling of having more purpose in life, that I wasn't out there all alone, that I was really a parent again, that I had the responsibility and someone was dependent on me. It was kind of a reawakening type of thing. It changed the apartment into a home, almost. I always saw the children a lot, but having her live with me, it shook me a little bit to realize the change in my outlook that this brought.

To say that there are worse situations than that of the single parent constitutes, to be sure, a guarded recommendation. But the benefits, though their number may not be large, are real. We may do well to begin this discussion of benefits and problems by considering the benefits, for we shall get to the problems soon enough.

It's better than a bad marriage

When a marriage was truly awful, when conflict was open and continuous, so that the parents could hardly talk to each other without contention and evenings were times of rancor, meanness, hostile silences, and now and again a raging battle, there can be no question but that living alone is better. And, when conflict was this apparent, the children are likely to agree. One woman, a survivor of a conflict-ridden marriage, said that it was reassuring to have her children, two adolescent boys and a girl of about twelve, agree that life had been better since she and her husband separated:

> I really think it all worked out for the best. I know he would have killed me or I would have killed him if we had stayed together. And I think it's been better for the kids. They have been much more comfortable around the house. They know that he's not going to come in and object to everything they do or tell them they have to do it his way. My daughter said, "It's so much more peaceful." And my oldest son said the same thing. He said, "It's like a different house."

Another mother of three spoke of a happier home. Tension was no longer present, and a new warmth had developed. She said:

> Since my husband's left it's a whole new ball game. When he was here you couldn't say anything that he didn't jump all over you. If you opened your mouth he had to correct you, the way you spoke, your grammar, all that. When he was here there was an awful tension because the kids couldn't laugh or talk. If they sat at the table, if anybody made a noise, he'd jump down their throat. Someone didn't feel like

eating, there'd be a big argument. Once he left, and after I got back on my feet, the atmosphere was altogether different. Like my daughter was saying a couple of weeks ago, "Gee, Mommy, all that strain has gone completely." The kids had a hard time accepting our breaking up, but I think with the tension gone it has made a big difference. Now they sit down and they eat and they laugh. When supper was over before, everybody would be gone. Now everybody sits around. The kids talk. They feel more free.

Other women describe marriages in which their husbands drank or gambled or were repeatedly unfaithful. Persisting in these marriages, they say, required them to deny problems that were only too evident and to pretend to neighbors, to the children, and to themselves that their homes were like other homes when they clearly were not. They acquiesced in their distress and thought the less of themselves for doing so:

If he and I were still married I don't know what I'd be like today. I know what I was like eight years ago—sick—because my ex-husband was running around. Even if I knew in my heart I was right, he could make me feel I was wrong. But I had to have allowed that man to do that to me. I know I have taught my daughter different. "You don't let nobody, especially a man, make you feel like you're stupid."

Other women escaped from marriages in which they were subordinated, their sense of themselves almost crushed:

My marriage was destroying me. Because if I hadn't got out when I did, if I hadn't finally reached the decision that I did, that I wanted out of the marriage, I would never have become a person. I would always have been my ex-husband's wife, and my children's mother. Because he didn't want anybody that could think on their own. He wanted somebody that would do as he said, with no questions asked.

Still other women, and men as well, count as a blessing that they no longer need spend evenings with someone they found insufferably dull, nor have to adapt to very different standards of neatness, nor wonder if everyone's sex life was as ungratifying as theirs, nor accept the isolation that is one product of a marriage without communication. Ending a bad marriage at least means that some things no longer have to be endured.

It's nice to be able to decide things for yourself

In any marriage, husband and wife must achieve consensus and coordination. The couple have to establish standards for housekeeping, times for meals, rules for the children that both can support. If the marriage is working well, agreement may come effortlessly. If the marriage is not working, there may be quarrels, or one partner may sullenly accede to the other, or one partner may make decisions without consulting the other, and then the other will criticize and object. But with the ending of the marriage, the single parent is able to decide alone, without consultation, without fear of criticism, the standards of housekeeping, the times for meals, the content of the meals, how the evenings are to be spent—absolutely everything. The children must be considered, yes, and, if they are older, consulted. But with the children the parent is a leader, a *parent*. It is not like having to fight everything through with another adult. One woman said:

> I make a decision and that's it. There's nobody to argue with. What we're going to have for dinner, where we're going to go for dinner, when the laundry's going to be done. There's no pressure. Even the financial thing: now I know what's what. I do the controlling.

Some women who believe themselves to have been dominated by their husbands during marriage feel that the ending of their marriages freed them from servitude:

> I feel free; I really do. I can come and go as I want. I can speak on the phone. I can wear whatever I want to. If I don't feel like scrubbing the floor, I just say, "The hell with it! I'll do it when I feel like it." If I don't feel like folding clothes, then I let them sit there until I do. I don't have to rush around and have a perfect-looking house.

The deadlines imposed by a husband's expectations have vanished from the single mother's life. Now she can adjust dinner times to suit herself and her children. And if her children are old enough to take care of themselves, she can come home when she likes. A mother of young children said:

> The good thing about being single is that you can come and go as you please. You don't have to answer to anybody. You don't have to ask permission if you don't want to make supper or if you don't want to do something. You're your own boss.

No longer is there the tension of awareness of another's appraisal, the vulnerability to being told that supper is too late or not good enough, that the house is dusty, that things aren't the way they should be. Another mother said:

> Before, I had a boss over me. Now *I'm* the boss. And that's a good thing. I don't have that worry of doing for someone else. I can go at my own pace. And I have more peace of mind.

Women who had been happily married, and whose marriages were ended by their husband's deaths, are much less likely to find satisfaction in the achievement of autonomy. They recognize the gain, but it does not seem to them very important.

The Benefits and the Problems of Raising Children Alone

> I was a very, very dependent person, completely dependent on my husband for everything. He never made it that way. He was so easy-going. Never once in our married life did he ever tell me what to do. We decided everything together. But I depended on him totally for everything. Gaining my independence was very hard because I am a very dependent person. But I have been forced into making decisions and doing everything alone. Now it has become a way of life. I suppose if I don't want to get supper at five o'clock, I don't have to get supper at five o'clock. But I can't really consider that a good point because I'd give the world if I had to get supper at five o'clock if it was for him.

It is when the marriage had been unsatisfactory, and the woman could see herself as having been an unpaid and unappreciated housekeeper, that she is likely to view her new autonomy as precious.

You think better of yourself

Single parents sometimes speak of having been forced to grow, to mature, or to develop in new ways, by the responsibilities of parenting alone. Men comment on having become more nurturant, women on having become more self-reliant. Women, particularly, seem sometimes to emerge with enhanced self-esteem.

> The winter before we separated, I honestly didn't think I could take care of the children. I was crying to a friend; I said, "There's no way I can bring the children up. I just can't do it alone." And what surprised me is that in the last year and a half, since we've been separated, there hasn't been one minute that I've either needed my husband or wanted him here for any reason. There has been nothing but a healthy, strong, good feeling.

Women who have been able to establish themselves occupationally have a second reason for enhanced self-esteem: not only have they been able to care for their children, but they have been able to make their own way in the world. One woman became an expert in computer programming after her marriage ended. She said:

> I married when I was sixteen. I had four kids, and no professional training. I didn't have any skills. And my husband repeatedly told me that I wasn't going to be able to provide for the children, that I was going to starve. I had a very damaged ego when I came out of the marriage. As I gained in the ability to do things and the knowledge that I had value professionally, and that I was able to take care of my own kids, and that I was able in some ways to do better financially than my ex-husband had done, that was a good feeling for me.

Some women go further than saying that they have merely gained in self-esteem as a result of being on their own. They say that only by being on their own could they have become fully functioning individuals. For some women—and fewer men—raising their children alone was necessary to establishing a self-image that seemed to them both authentic and worthy of respect.

> I think if I was still married I wouldn't be me. I would still be the shriveled-up miserable person that I was. So I have to say thank you to my ex-husband for walking out, because he allowed me to grow. He forced me to become me.

You have a special relationship with the children

As was noted earlier, the single parent is apt to have become closer to the children. This is true for the mother who, before the ending of her marriage, managed her home with her husband and expressed her feelings to him, and it is emphatically true for the father who, before the ending of his marriage, left child care to his wife. Here is a man who had custody of two boys, the older seven:

> When I was married I didn't do any of the things that I needed to do with my kids. I put everything off because of a future goal. I had to provide for them; I had to go to school at night. I wasn't around them, except occasionally. And I found, living with my kids, that I grew very close to them. I found that they were small people, that they had all the same emotions and values and physical needs as big people. And that was very rewarding.

While parents, especially mothers, sometimes complain that it is wearing to try to impose discipline on children without a second parent's backing, at least there no longer is conflict with that second parent:

> You don't have anybody going against your discipline with the children. They can't play a mother and a father against each other. They know there's just Mommy and they can't say, "Well, if I go to Daddy he'll let me do it." There's none of that. You can bring them up the way you want it to be done without quarreling or arguing with another person on what is the right way to bring up the children.

And there can be times when the special closeness of the single-parent household produces a feeling of warmth, of communion with the children, that is quite unique. The children may surprise a parent with a dinner unexpectedly prepared, a skit written and produced for the parent, or a surprise birthday party. Children and parent may sit around the breakfast table on a lazy Sunday morning and talk about issues that would otherwise never have been voiced. A child may express gratitude for something special a parent has done: for regaining a stolen bicycle, in one instance; for canceling a date with a boyfriend so that the child could be taken to a movie, in another. One man told of his six-year-old son's letting him know that he had been a good father:

> I read them a story every night if they were good. If they were bad, we'd skip the story: "That's it. You can't have it." My son had gone to school, the first grade, for a while. He finally came home and said, "OK, Daddy. I'm going to read you a story tonight."

The single parent can find personal meaning, as the children grow, in awareness of being indispensable to the children. There can be no question, for the single parent, about whether the parent is really needed. And, as the children reach their own adulthood and the parent is finally assured that the challenges of raising children alone were successfully met, the parent may justifiably take pride in self as well as in the children.

The fundamental problem: Insufficient support

The fundamental problem in the single parent's situation is the insufficiency of immediately available support. The married parent can rely on a partner, living under the same roof, who shares the parent's aims of maintaining the home and raising the children and who is always available—work hours excepted—for contributions of time and energy and concern. The single parent must make do with the much more limited help available from children, kin, friends, and professional helpers.

To see how support is provided in a two-parent household, let us return to a couple introduced earlier, the Desmonds. The Desmonds' two daughters were aged eleven and nine. While we were in touch with them the younger daughter, Claire, developed an aversion to school. Claire would become so tense in school that her stomach would knot and she would have to race to the girls' lavatory, where she would vomit. She wanted to remain at home, but with both her parents working, there was no one to stay home with her. Mrs. Desmond was repeatedly called by the school or by her daughter. The calls, interrupting Mrs. Desmond at work, upset her severely. She said, later:

I did break down once at work, which is something that I don't like the idea of, the idea of doing such a thing. I was mortified. But the child had called and she was screaming. She had been calmed down for about a week then. And I had had it. I got up from the desk and the phone, and I started towards an empty office, and the tears were coming down my face and all that foolishness. My boss came running over, "Here's a handkerchief." And they drove me home.

Both parents were frustrated. Neither knew what to do. And yet Mrs. Desmond was supported by her husband in that when she felt overwhelmed he could assume responsibility. She, in return, could support him.

Ed helped me a lot because I got to the point where I didn't know what to do. I felt like banging my head up against the wall. Everywhere I looked I was blocked. I'm not emotional. I don't usually cry or carry on. I hold it in more. Anger I do sometimes let loose. But as far as tears or anything, I don't.

Finally I broke down one night. And that, I think, frightened Ed, because he's seen me angry and throwing things, but he hasn't seen me cry. And that bothered him. Then he was at the point where, I think, he resented the child because she had upset me so much. And it seemed like when I got upset, he got strong. Then when he was the most upset, I was strong. So we helped each other out that way.

The school finally suggested that Claire be taken to a social agency for counseling. The social worker, after talking with Claire, suggested to Mrs. Desmond that her husband come with her to a meeting. Her husband felt he couldn't do it. Yet despite his refusal to comply with the social worker's treatment plan, Mrs. Desmond knew she could count on his continued concern.

I was a little annoyed with Ed because he wouldn't go to the agency. But the idea just appalled him. It was all right if I wanted to try it. He is willing to go along with it, and all that: anything to help the child. But, "Please don't ask me to go in there. I don't want to tell them my innermost thoughts and what kind of a father am I and have them ask me if I beat my children." He said, "I can't talk to people like that." Well, I didn't want to push him because he's had problems himself. I figured, why push it? Maybe I can do this without him. But if it reaches the point where I feel I can't, then maybe I can push him into it.

Mr. Desmond did his best to act on what his wife learned. The two, together, found a way of dealing with the daughter's school phobia that seemed to them to work.

They gave me hints and ideas on how to handle Claire. We began really laying down the law, being very firm with her—understanding, but firm. And that seemed to snap her out of it. That helped.

The point is not the particular treatment recommended for the daughter, but rather the mother's awareness that her concerns were shared by the fellow adult at her side. It is this that the single parent must do without.

Some separated and divorced parents say they didn't get much support even when they were married. But most report that, bad as their marriages were, they could count on the other parent for something. They were not the only parent in the household:

> Living with John, as bad as it was—the fights were terrible, the money situation was terrible, everything was terrible—there was still a thread of security there. There was just something about him being there. Maybe it had to do with the kids. He was always good to the kids.

The absence of support means that there are only the single parent's own resources to rely on. The inadequacy of these resources to the demands being made on the single parent may result in three fairly distinct forms of overload. In each case the overload may be chronic or intermittent.

First, the single parent may suffer from responsibility overload. Whatever the children need physically, medically, educationally, or in any other way, it is the single parent's responsibility to provide it. Whatever decisions must be made for the children, it is the single parent's responsibility to make them. For some single parents, at some times, so much responsibility is dismaying.

Second, the single parent is likely every so often to have too much to do. Many single parents function at near capacity under ordinary circumstances. Unanticipated demand then produces task overload.

Third, constant uninterrupted attending to children, perhaps accompanied by feelings of responsibility overload or task overload, perhaps taking place against a background of loneliness or social isolation, can overtax the single parent's emotional resilience. The single parent feels depleted, absolutely unable to give any more. This is emotional overload.

Responsibility overload

Just as the single parent can make decisions and set rules without first having to negotiate with the children's other parent, so the single parent must accept responsibility for the consequences of those decisions and rules. As the children become older, the single parent is likely to share an increasing proportion of responsibility with the children. But with young children and, to a lesser extent, with older children as well, the sense of sole responsibility can sometimes be overwhelming. This is how a father of two children, the older five, put the matter:

> All the obligations you can imagine are on your shoulders. This over-whelming responsibility that includes everything, it's all yours, whether you want to assume the responsibility or not.

Irrespective of the children's ages, the single parent remains responsible for financing the household. As was noted earlier, there is a critical difference between the responsibilities of the two parents in a separation or divorce. The noncustodial parent is responsible for regularly providing a certain amount of money for the support of the custodial parent's household. The amount may be a large or small proportion of the noncustodial parent's income; in any event, it is limited. The custodial parent, in contrast, must meet the needs of the household. These needs may, at the moment, be entirely manageable. But who knows what the future will bring? What medical expenses will have to be met, what educational aspirations, what expenses for household repairs, what needs for money to ensure that three years from now, five years from now, the children will have the same opportunities other children have? It is this open-endedness of the single parent's responsibilities that gives rise to worries about money even among those parents who can meet their current bills.

One mother of older children remembered how she felt when she first contemplated the prospect of open-ended responsibility for her household's financing:

> It's sheer terror when you first break up your marriage. I always looked after the bills, so at least I knew how much my home cost and all this—I didn't have that worry. I sat down and worked out how much I needed extra if I went out to work. But it's knowing that you have to cope with all the other things. And there is the fear, "Oh, my God, what am I going to do? How am I going to support these children?" There is coping with the children, trying to rear them, all the headaches. It gets horrendous, teenagers and the problems and knowing that you've got to pay all the bills and repair the house and get the car and buy this and that. It's sheer terror when you first break up your marriage.

The single parent, as the one person responsible for the household's financing, has to decide, alone, what level of housing can be afforded, what style of life is possible, what purchases can be made. Large decisions and small decisions—they are all the single parent's responsibility. A mother of an only son, about eight years old, said:

> It's a very difficult situation. You have to make all the decisions. You have to pay all the bills. You have to know where the money is coming from. And it's all *your* responsibility. I can almost feel how a man feels who goes out and earns the money for a family and works maybe two jobs to support his family, and there are still bills coming in. Now, all of

a sudden, I'm faced with this situation. That's the fear of doing everything by yourself, all your decision-making and where you're going to
live and how you're going to live.

In addition to the open-ended responsibility for maintaining the
household's finances, there is another sort of open-ended responsibility
single parents have, and that is for the way the children turn out. Whatever happens to the children, there is only one parent who has been making decisions for them, and it is that parent's responsibility. As one
mother put it, "You can't say, 'It's not my kid; it's his kid.' It's *your* kid."
And another said:

X If the kids go wrong, you are the one that failed, nobody else. Not that
you're looking to blame somebody, but it would be the feeling that you
were the one that raised them, and it was completely your responsibility.

X And this means that single parents, even more than other parents,
worry about the effects their child-rearing practices are having on their
children's characters. Are they too indulgent? Too restrictive? They have
sole responsibility for raising their children properly. Are they meeting
that responsibility? A mother of two said: X

I don't really trust my judgment all the time. Like, "What am I doing
with these kids?" "Am I doing the right thing?" Things like that.

And a mother of an only son said:

My child, a lot of times, will ask me to do something and I really don't
want him to do it, but I'm not determined enough. So I say, "Yes,"
with that feeling of, "I'd rather he'd not," behind it and that fear, "Oh, I
hope he does the right thing." But there is no one to lean on, no one to
fall back on.

In two-parent homes parents do consult each other when they are per-
plexed. Here, for example, is the wife of a school principal, mother of
two children, a boy of about sixteen and a girl of about fourteen:

I've come to the point now that, where I know my husband can handle
the kids better, I will say, "Well, I will talk to your father about this
incident and we'll see." I don't usually any more say right there, "OK,
you're in for a week." I will say, "We'll discuss this. When Dad gets
home we'll discuss this and see what he feels." Sometimes I will talk
to my husband first and then we'll discuss it. Or sometimes we all sit
down and discuss it together.

The single parent lacks a partner with whom issues can be discussed.
And, once a decision has been made, there is no other adult to support
it or to question it. The children will gladly offer opinions, of course, but
in matters such as allowances and bedtimes and parental dating their
opinions are affected by self-interest. And in other matters they are

likely to be too little experienced to be helpful. A mother of school-aged boys said:

> I think one of the hardest jobs of raising children by yourself is not having someone to relate to, someone to share with, someone to use as a sounding board, someone to say you're doing the right thing or you're not. You're completely by yourself. Any decisions that are made, you can't talk them over with somebody else. You talk them over with yourself.

Single parents sometimes almost desperately miss a partner who might participate with them in responding to children's wishes. Opposing the children means becoming a minority of one in the household, albeit the person in control; but giving in to the children may be bad for them. A widowed mother of four children said:

> There's nobody to share your decisions with. Every decision is your own. If the kids want to do something, you've got to make up your mind whether you think it is right. There's nobody to say, "Well, do you think they should or they shouldn't?" You just have to make up your mind. Sometimes I worry about whether I'm too strict with them. I don't think I'm too lenient with them, but I worry about whether I'm too strict. I don't know. Every single thing you do, there's no sharing. It's all yourself. It's all on your shoulders.

Should a single parent behave irrationally, become overprotective or impulsively angry, there is no other parent for the children to turn to, no other parent who might buffer the single parent's misperceptions and mistakes. The recognition that the children have no one else makes still more burdensome the single parent's responsibilities. A widower with two children said:

> I'm nervous about the feeling that I'm the only person these kids have to turn to. I don't think that is an ideal situation at all. I think that there should be two people that the kids can deal with, play one off the other, go from one who is kind of difficult to one who is easy, get hollered at by one and seek the other for some kind of assurance or understanding.

These single parents are quite right: in many two-parent households the parents do use their partnership to minimize the impact on the children of parental irrationalities. Here, for example, is a report by a woman married to a machinist, mother of two children, the older a four-year-old boy named Kenny:

> My husband is a pushover. I say, "Art, you're so big, you impress people with just the look of you. As for me, I have a mouth because I have nothing else. I have no muscles. I can't impress people with my look." Art thinks I'm very strict with Kenny. But I say, "Art, you see him for an hour a day, or on the weekends. You don't really have to watch him. So don't interfere. If I tell you to, talk to him."

The Benefits and the Problems of Raising Children Alone

Art doesn't discipline. He tries to. Then he gives in. But then, other times, he won't have any patience. He gets nervous with Kenny and he'll hit him, where, if he's whining he wants something, I'll sit down and explain to him why he can't have it. But other times Art will sit and explain, and I'll be saying, "Kill him!" So it's good. It usually works out.

Widows and widowers who think of their marriages as having been good, on the whole, are particularly likely to miss having fellow parents who might balance their own responses. And all single parents miss someone who might help them carry the responsibilities of raising children alone. If only they could be freed from having to think of everything, do everything! One mother daydreamed about how things might be different if only she had someone to share with. Her son was six, an only child.

If only I was married to the right person, somebody that would take half the responsibilities, half of the discipline, so it's not always me telling Brian: "Brian, sit up straight"; "Brian, use your fork, not your spoon"; "Brian, do this"; "Brian, do that." I feel like I am constantly doing it, and it's because it is only me disciplining him. If I had somebody to share that with, it would be taking off the pressure. And if there was somebody that could enjoy Brian along with me, I think I could enjoy Brian more. I get so caught up in all this discipline that I lose all the good parts of being a mother. I love my son dearly, but I can't feel it a whole lot because I get so caught up, so caught up and strangled by it!

And yet, much as single parents might wish to share their responsibility for their children, or just briefly to relinquish it, they cannot. They cannot because there is no one else who shares the responsibility by right, and to simply hand over the responsibility to someone else, even the other parent, would be irresponsible.

I hate the responsibility, but there's no way to get around it. It's there. And I couldn't stand the responsibility of not taking responsibility, because that's a responsibility in itself!

The idea of deserting, of running away and leaving it all behind, occurs to many single parents. They don't act on it, but the idea occurs to them. Here is a mother of an only son, aged about six.

It's me that's shaping this child's personality. It's all my responsibility. My husband's not helping in any way. Financially, once in a while, he'll give me a few bucks. So what? If I needed money that bad I'd go out and hook. And I just get really tired. Very tired. I'm tired of all the responsibilities. There are times when I feel like just taking my son over to my mother's house and saying, "Watch him for a couple of hours" and just not ever coming back. Just go away and forget everything. No more responsibilities for this child who I am shaping into a human being, who I am going to be giving complexes to.

Being a single parent provides meaning to a parent's life just because the parent is so important for the children. But importance implies responsibility, and there are limits beyond which responsibility is no longer reassuring, when it becomes oppressive.

Task overload

To summarize the argument of Chapter Three, in only a few ways is there less work in a single-parent household than in a two-parent household. If the single parent not only assumes responsibility for housekeeping and child care but also undertakes full-time employment, the parent has become committed to two full-time jobs. The parent may bring the children into the household's division of labor and, perhaps, obtain further help from elsewhere. Sooner or later, some tasks are likely to be dropped or skimped on. In these ways what at first may have appeared unmanageable becomes routinized, and life can proceed. Here, for example, is a brief account by a father of two children, a boy of eight and a girl of six:

> In the beginning I couldn't figure out how I was going to get them over to the nursery school or home for lunch or who was going to take care of them. It just seemed like there were a thousand schedules to arrange, and food, and clothes. It just baffled me, and it took me a long time to straighten that out. But once I had it straightened out, I was doing all the things that a family should do.

It may not be recognized, however, by the single parent who is working full time as well as managing a family, and doing well enough at each, that he or she has very little unused capability. But what has happened is that the single parent, by skimping on a chore here and dropping an activity there, has brought his or her total workload down to the point where it can be coped with—but only just. No room will have been left for meeting new demands.

The two-parent family has a good deal of spare capability. The husband may not regularly help with housework or child care, but he can if there is need for him. If the wife begins taking an evening class, or a child is ill, he can pitch in. The single parent, without this spare capability in the household, is much more vulnerable to task overload. This can happen whenever the single parent takes on something extra, even something that may not seem overly demanding. Here, for example, is a report by a woman with two children, who added to an already full schedule both an evening course and the provision of shelter to a friend in trouble:

> I got a job as a nurse and that worked out really well and I enjoyed it a lot. Then I got ambitious and started going to school nights. And I was taking too much on. I was trying to be mother, full-time worker, and student. Plus my girlfriend was having trouble with her family, and she asked if she could stay with me for a couple of weeks. So I had her and her kid living with me. Then it was just really terrible, just lots of pressure, dealing with all these things together, the school, the work, being a mother, this other family. So it ended up that I practically had a nervous breakdown. I dropped out of school and I moved home to Mommy.

Task overload seems to be produced by the frustration of not being able to complete everything that must be done, and the feeling that failure is inescapable. It can occur when the single parent has been operating for some time at the limits of the parent's capability and has accumulated both fatigue and tasks not yet done. One woman was separated from her husband when he suffered a severe depression that resulted in his hospitalization. She added visiting him to her other tasks. She said:

> Between going to the hospital to visit my husband, visiting my parents, making sure I stay in communication with my family, his family, there's very little time for myself and the kids. Sometimes I resent it. It bothers me that I have to go to work to support the family, and I have to come home and keep working at home, and I'm not able to spend time doing things with the kids or just getting away. Sometimes I find myself sitting down and crying because, if I don't cry, I don't know what would happen. But I've got to let it out.

Anything that demands extra effort from the single parent may create task overload. A child's falling ill is likely to produce overload. If there is more than one child in the family, and the sick child must be hospitalized, the parent is almost certain to be overloaded. But something as apparently minor as moving from one house to another can also produce overload. A mother of two boys, aged ten and seven, talked about this. She had moved to a new neighborhood about three months before the incident she described. She had not yet gotten her new apartment in order when her job became more pressing. She was already giving less attention to her children than they had previously been used to, and the children were responding by becoming more insistent that she attend to them. One Saturday morning it all suddenly seemed too much:

> Saturday my girlfriend called me up and we were just discussing things. I was talking fairly normally, I think. But she said, "What's the matter?" And I started crying and crying and crying. I wasn't screaming, just quietly crying. She said, "Calm down." And I said, "I'm trying." She said, "OK, just take it easy. What has to be done?" I said, "Everything

has to be done." She said, "Look to your right. What has to be done there?" I said, "My plants have to be watered. They're all dying. That's another thing I can't do. I can't grow plants." She said, "It's easy. You just water them. Now when you get off the phone, water your plants. Don't think of all the things you have to do. Just think of that one thing." And then she said, "Can you think of another thing?" I said, "My cat. He has diarrhea. I threw him out. I hate him." You know, I wasn't feeding him or anything. I just threw him out. I wanted to throw my kids out too, but I couldn't. But I could throw the cat out. So she said, "OK, take care of him." Then she said, "Are you OK?" And I said, "Yeah, I'm OK."

I got off the phone and went into the bathroom and I cried for a while. I couldn't cope with it. I wanted to give up. Finally, I stopped crying, and I threw some water on my face, and I said, "Well, I've got to do something." So I watered my plants and then I took the cat to the vet.

Emotional overload

Children can impose stress on parents simply by repeatedly demanding their attention. Parents, on returning home from work, although they want to be responsive to their children, want also to be able to plan their evenings, to relax, to permit their own tensions to subside. Later, they want to concentrate on cooking, or think about the day's events, or watch the television news. The children, on their side, want to be assured that they are cared for. They want their uncertainties resolved, whether the uncertainties are about school or about their relations with their siblings or about the parents' commitment to them. And a child has little capacity for waiting for a propitious moment before calling on a parent's attention.

One mother described in this way coming home to her two daughters, the older eleven, the younger five:

> I always want to come home with a smile on my face and be Mary Tyler Moore because I really figure they need that, this happy, charming person. I start out that way. And right away my older daughter will hit me with, "Sign this. I need a note. I need $4 for something in school. I need this other thing." She doesn't let me rest for one second. She really hits me immediately. And the other one is screaming for food. She's eating everything in the house before it's cooked and I'm trying to keep it out of her face. And if I have left early, all the dishes from the morning are still there. And I'm trying to make something quick, and it really is an insane asylum. I really had full intentions of being charming when I walked in, until: bang!

The Benefits and the Problems of Raising Children Alone

Emotional overload occurs because the parent's emotional resilience proves inadequate for the number and intensity of the children's demands. The absence of relief from constant availability to the children produces emotional depletion, a sense of having nothing more to give. Yet there continues to be no relief, nor any way of turning the children off, nor any prospect that the situation will change.

Here is an expression of emotional overload. It is from an interview with a widow in her early thirties, formerly married to a successful businessman, on her own not quite three years. Her four children ranged in age from four to eleven. She did not work, and the issue for her did not seem to be one of too much to do.

> The most difficult thing about being a single parent is not being able to get away from it. For two and a half years I have had four kids approximately twenty-four hours a day with no way of getting out or leaving them or doing anything by myself. The kids are with me all the time. I wish I could have time to myself. Right now I need a weekend, just a weekend, by myself with no kids. No "Mommy, do this," "Mommy, tie my shoe," "Mommy, find this." It's like you're not you. You're a totally different person. You don't have any time for you.

> Sometimes you wish you were four people so you could handle the four kids. Sometimes I feel badly that I'm not giving them the time. I think that's when I feel the most vulnerable, when it seems like they're all pulling at me and there's nothing left of me. You know, how much more can I give the four kids? They've got everything I've got. And yet they keep drawing on it. It seems like you are going to be completely drained emotionally. There's going to be nothing left of you. Because four kids, they all want you, and it seems like, sometimes, they are just not going to let you go until they get all of you.

Task overload can sometimes be anticipated well enough so that measures can be taken to fend it off. Emotional overload seems more difficult to anticipate. The parent happens to be more tense or more preoccupied than usual; tensions build, as they often do; but now the parent cannot contain them. It may be for the best, perhaps, if the parent explodes, as some do. A man, for example, said: "I explode and say, 'Knock it off. Get out of here and leave me alone for half an hour.'" And a woman said she just would scream, "Everybody get away and leave me alone." More troublesome, both for parent and for children, may be the development by the parent of feelings of not being able to go on, of a bitter or hopeless depression. A widow described feelings of this latter sort:

> In the evening it starts to close in on you. You come home from work, and you are tired, and it starts facing you. Everything is different. I don't like to cook any more. I just don't feel like doing things any more. I feed the children, but kids are kids and they'll eat anything. My oldest said, "You've changed. You're not the same. You're always grouchy, always hollering." I tried to explain, but teenagers are teenagers. Some days you would like not even to come home. I feel as though it is too

much and I can't do it. There's so much facing you, you'd like to keep going in the opposite direction.

Unrelieved responsibility for children appears especially likely to be depleting when there is no one attending to the parent's needs. It is then as though the parent's emotional economy were running at a constant deficit: everything being disbursed, nothing being received. A mother of three children said:

> My mother said to me, when my husband left, that I should devote myself to the children. My mistake. I should have made a life of my own. You get very bitter toward everything and everybody after awhile. They think I should just go on living my life from day to day, home at four-thirty, give the kids supper, get the kids to bed, watch television, go to bed. Well, I have had it. I'm very tired of my life the way it is now. I'm tired of it.

This way of organizing life appears to sponsor depression. Indeed, a formula might be proposed: daily frustration combined with hopelessness about change fosters depression.[1] And certainly depression is a vulnerability of single parents. A mother of two said:

> I just get down. Feel sorry for myself. Sorry for me. I get depressed. I guess that's about the word. Tension headaches, the whole thing. When things get really bottled up in me, that's how things come out. Tension headaches and nerves. And I get depressed a lot over it all.

> I don't really see any goals. The goals that I have would probably be for the three of us just to be all secure, maybe as a family. Maybe remarriage or something like that. Just somebody taking care of me. Not the kids this time, just me. Just saying, "Hey, Charlotte, you don't have to worry about a thing because I'm going to take care of everything." I would like that someday.

The avoidance of emotional overload may require a healthy capacity for self-assertion, for the parent's being willing to claim time and energy for self. Especially vulnerable to emotional overload may be those single parents who are most determined to devote themselves to their children. They may discover only by witnessing their own explosions or depressions that they, too, have needs, including needs for relief from the demands of children and for caring attention to themselves.

The management of new demand

The single-parent household cannot meet from its reserves demands beyond those to which it has become accustomed. The household has no reserves. Help must be found elsewhere, the household must make do with less—less housework, less child care, less income production—or the single parent must accept overload.

Different single parents have different responses to overload. Some try to shed unmanageable demands: they establish priorities and do only what must be done; they insist on time for themselves; they accept no more responsibility than they must. Some call for help when demands become too great. Some keep going as best they can and, if they sometimes feel overwhelmed, hope that tomorrow will be a better day. Here, as elsewhere, it matters that some single parents are more capable than others of dealing with frustration, or have social or financial resources to fall back on that others don't have. But although ways of responding to overload differ among single parents, vulnerability to overload appears to be intrinsic to the single-parent situation.

Let us examine the way in which a two-parent household deals with new demand. A child of one of the married couples introduced earlier had a very minor accident. There were two children in the household, a boy of four and a girl of two. The boy had torn off an entire fingernail while climbing. The mother thought medical attention was necessary. Worth noting here are the sharing of responsibility, the management of tension, and the way in which the task aspects of the new demand were dealt with.

> Yesterday Kenny wanted to go out, because Kenny always wants to go out. And now it was suppertime and I didn't want him to go out any more. But he was going, "Can I go out, Mommy? Can I go out, Mommy?" and Art thought it would be all right. So I said, "Oh, go out." I always give in. And every time I give in, something happens.
>
> He went down for two or three minutes, and then he's yelling, and there's blood all over the place, and his fingernail is hanging. The whole fingernail had come right off. And I said to Art, "Take him to the General." And he said, "Just put on a bandaid." I was hysterical. I said, "I'll never forgive you, Art, if that fingernail grows back funny. I'll never forgive you." I get very emotional. And Art goes along with what I say, because he knows that it is just that at the moment I am so emotional. So he took Kenny to the General. And Kenny came home with a bandaid. The doctor put it on.

The mother shared responsibility with the father for deciding how the accident was to be dealt with. The mother disagreed with the father's proposal but recognized that responsibility was not hers alone. The mother's proposal was then adopted, partly because the father was concerned with the mother's emotional state. Indeed, the father appeared to be as responsive to the mother's need for support as he was to the child's need for medical attention. Finally, with two parents, there was one parent to remain with the second child while the other parent took the injured child to a hospital's emergency clinic.

Now let us turn to the way in which a one-parent household might respond to new demand. The six-year-old only son of a divorced mother became ill enough to require hospitalization. The mother was called at work by her son's babysitter who said the boy seemed ill. She came home early from work, took her son's temperature, and called a hospital clinic that advised her to bring him in. She called a taxi and took him to the clinic. The examining physician thought the boy should remain in the hospital for a while. She agreed, then called the boy's father. She said:

> I desperately had to run back and call his father and share that with him, because it had to be shared with someone else who had the same amount of concern, even though I might be the person who would make the final decision. I wanted someone to support me.

The situation here, in relation to responsibility, tension management, and task performance, is quite different from the situation of the married mother. Here the mother carries sole responsibility, even though she may talk with her former husband. Her emotional state is no one else's concern, not even her former husband's. And there is no one with whom she can share the new task of visiting her son in the hospital—except, possibly, her former husband, for whom it is not clearly a responsibility. This woman went on to say:

> I could go see Perry, but I wanted someone else to be there for him. I wanted his father to come and spend time with him and be with him. I didn't feel there was enough of me to go around for him right then. And when I'd come home and be feeling really bad, I wanted somebody to say, "Oh, boy, I'll bet you feel terrible."

In another instance of new demand, in the family of a mother and four children, one child required a tonsillectomy. The child's father lived in a nearby city but the mother felt he was unwilling to be concerned. The mother, as a single parent, had no one with whom to share responsibility, and no one who might help her sustain her own morale. Arranging substitute child care for the other children, she said, took a good deal out of her. She intensely resented her husband's freedom from her worries and his unwillingness to be helpful in any way. She was, herself, at the limits of what she could do:

> Jeanette was in the hospital this past summer to have her tonsils out. I knew it was not that serious an operation, but I was very worried and upset that my baby was in the hospital and being operated on. It meant getting somebody to watch the other three kids so I could go up to the hospital and spend as much time with her as possible. This took a lot out of me emotionally. And that's when the bitterness starts, that her father won't take any of the responsibility of her being in the hospital or worrying how the operation's going to turn out or what. So I had nobody else to share the worry and the whole emotional thing. If you had somebody else that would take part of the responsibility and the worry it wouldn't be so bad.

The Benefits and the Problems of Raising Children Alone

Single parents seem most often to cope effectively with new demands. A number of examples have been given in previous chapters: the mother whose child was caught smoking in school; the mother who found herself in need of medical attention but who had first to find someone to look after her children; and others. The problem is the cost to the single parent of coping. Almost always, there is cost in anxiety, in a sense of emotional depletion, and in tasks not attended to. Sometimes, there is a cost in children left unattended, as well.

·

The relinquishing of the parental identity

In the one-parent family, there is only one familial role available to the parent. The parent no longer is wife or husband; the parent is only mother or father. This is the role that will have been integrated into the parent's identity, into the parent's image of self that makes sense of his or her life course: "I am someone who got married and had children and, after the ending of my marriage, took care of my children by myself."

What then happens when the children leave? There is relief, to be sure. No longer must the parent worry about children at home, nor always be available to deal with their problems. Now the parent is free to go places and do things. Yet often it turns out that parents who had looked forward to their children's departure, had promised themselves evenings out and vacations in foreign countries, discover that without their children they no longer know who they are:

> When the kids were smaller I felt that they were my responsibility totally, and I resented it, because I wasn't allowed to be me. I had to be mother, mother, mother. My identity disappeared somewhere along the line. If you lose your identity, being involved with your children, you are nothing when the kids leave.

> Now I feel like, Jesus, where have my children gone? My daughter is eighteen, she's going out, so I'm by myself. My son is with his father. What the hell am I doing? I'm a mother, but where are my kids?

With the departure of the children the parent must find new rationales for organizing time and effort, a new image of the self to give life meaning.

There is another issue as well. As has been noted, parent and children tend to be closer in a one-parent family than they would be were they in a two-parent family. Even more than in a two-parent family, the children in a one-parent family augment the parent's life, become fellow family members with whom to plan and to work, and provide a measure of companionship and support. The departure of children means being alone again. It means losing the children just when it is easiest to talk with them; just when they are, perhaps for the first time, less a source of concern and more a potential source of solace. Just when the children are truly capable of functioning as fellow adults, they leave.

These may be the final vulnerabilities in the single-parent life. The parent may for so long have been, as one woman put it, "mother first, me second," that when the children depart there is insufficient "me" left. And the departure of the children, so long anticipated, may leave the parent surprisingly bereft.

CHAPTER 12

Making It Work

THE PREVIOUS CHAPTER pointed out that the single parent is vulnerable to overloads of several kinds because of the absence of a second parent within the household who might provide support on a day-to-day basis and a reserve capability with which to meet new demand. It may be because this second person within the household is so valuable over the long years of child rearing that humans have evolved into a species in which pair-bonding is strong. But what if a pair bond should fail, or if it never came into existence? How then can a parent minimize overload and deal with new demand? One answer, which many single parents have found, is to rely on alternative support systems: family, friends, agencies, counselors, and organizations of or for single parents, along with, if the parent is fortunate, the other parent.

The family as support system

Single parents who live near members of their own families—their parents or sisters or brothers—usually can count on a certain amount of help. Although the single parent retains full responsibility for the children, family nearby can provide an outside-the-household reserve capability. The single parent need not worry quite so much about what would happen to the other children if one child were to become ill, or to all the children if the single parent became ill. As one woman put it, "Just knowing that if I really need my mother, she is there, that helps."

In Chapter Seven we considered the single parent's relationships with kin. Let us here review how kin can be helpful. The children's grandmother may be willing to babysit or to make her house available to the children for the hours between the ending of school and the parent's arrival from work. Sometimes grandparents make themselves available as babysitters of last resort, to be called should alternatives fail, but occasionally grandparents are willing to serve virtually as auxiliary parents for the children, making it possible for the parent to take evenings or even weekends for his or her own pursuits. In all these ways the children's grandparents can provide the relief from child care that permits the single parent to avoid emotional exhaustion.

Grandparents can be helpful in still other ways. They may invite the single parent to dinner when the single parent's supply of cash has neared the vanishing point, provide small loans that need not be repaid, or make outright gifts. Quite regularly grandparents use the children's birthdays as opportunities for providing the children with clothes. They may also make gifts of service, such as helping the parent to settle into a new apartment, preparing dinner for the whole family, or helping put the parent's house in order.

There are limits to what can be asked of the children's grandparents. The grandparents have lives of their own, and more than one single parent has been told something like, "I raised my children; now you raise yours." The grandparents can be aged or so beset by their own problems that they have little ability to help anyone else. Yet most often, even if grandparents have limited resources, single parents can anticipate that they will be concerned, will keep in touch, and will do what they can to help. There is reassurance in this, and some defense against each form of overload. A woman whose widowed mother was able to offer her rather little said:

> My mother goes out shopping once a week or twice a week. She'll stop off here for about an hour when she gets through shopping, because she usually buys a little something for each of the kids. She'll bring it for them and she'll stay for a while. And then she'll go home. And she usually calls me every day.

The single parent's brothers and sisters may also provide auxiliary homes for the children, although if they are raising children themselves or giving energy to establishing themselves, they may be less accessible than the grandparents. Brothers sometimes will act as "man of the family" for a single mother, making repairs around the house, speaking sternly to children who have gotten out of hand, and coaching the children in sports or taking them to games. In the same way, sisters may help single fathers by suggesting menus and places to buy clothes and by helping with housework. While siblings may be less likely than the children's grandparents to have the time to help, they often prove better companions, assuming that the rivalries of childhood have dissipated. And siblings, like parents, can provide reassurance simply by being available should they be needed. A mother of six, for example, said about an older brother who was only infrequently a visitor:

> I don't bother Raymond too much unless I have to. He doesn't see the boys that much, to give them advice. But if anything happened, I know Raymond would be the first one here. He always has been. And if I needed to have him come and talk to the boys, he would come.

Because kin ties are so valuable, single parents may define friends as fictive kin. A mother, when talking with her children, may refer to her closest female friend as "Aunt Barbara." Or a man who is a friend of the mother's family, who may be the mother's boyfriend but need not be, can be presented to the children as "Uncle Bill." The kin term communicates that this is someone who is expected to remain in the children's lives, interested and helpful. Here is what one woman said about an "aunt" she had brought into the family:

> You start picking up relatives that aren't really relatives. My girlfriend Betty is like an aunt to my kids. She comes in here and takes some of this heat off me. She's very good with the children, especially my younger, and I let her deal with them when she is here.

The single parent's kin constitute the most plausible alternative support system to that of the system formed by the two parents themselves. Kin already undersand themselves as obligated to help each other to the extent that they can. Some single parents, when their marriages end, move to be nearer to kin. They often feel later that they were right to have done so.

The other parent as a supportive figure

For those single parents who are separated or divorced, the other parent remains potentially a most valuable supportive figure. The potential can be realized only if the parents are able to continue their parental partnership despite having ended their other forms of partnership.

If the other parent is willing to take the children at times the single parent also finds convenient, and if the single parent can rest easy while the children are with the other parent, then periodic relief from the demands of child care becomes available. Such relief may go far toward preventing emotional depletion. A man who had won custody of his two preadolescent children said:

> Maybe once a month, maybe twice a month, their mother comes and takes them off for the weekend, and I have the weekend off. And that is a great experience of freedom.

It may be possible for the single parent who is separated or divorced to consult the other parent about matters affecting the children. There are not many who manage this, but those who do need not make all decisions entirely alone.

Should a child require hospitalization, the constructive involvement of the other parent is invaluable. The other parent can be with the child while the single parent attends to other matters, perhaps to other children. The other parent can share the single parent's concern. Should there be treatment decisions that the single parent must make, the other parent is available as an equally involved consultant.

A good working relationship with the other parent can be called on whenever there is new demand on the single parent's resources. The other parent can be asked to care for the children if that would make things manageable. One woman, for example, moved to a new city where she had yet to find a place to live. Her former husband cared for their daughter, an only child, until the woman was settled.

Tension and ambivalence are inescapable in the relationship between former spouses. Yet it may be worthwhile for a single parent to seek to set aside negative feelings in the interest of maintaining some degree of shared parenting with the other parent. If this can be accomplished, there may well be benefits to the children in easing the atmosphere of visitation and reducing the sharpness of conflicts of loyalty. There almost certainly will be benefits to the single parent.

Friends as supportive figures

A single parent's friends constitute a kind of community, a social world outside the single parent's home. Work does this as well, but at work the single parent is responded to as someone with skills and job responsibilities, whereas among friends the single parent is responded to as a full person, with a variety of commitments. Friends are enormously valuable in supporting the single parent's activities outside the home, providing ideas and company and now and again the social events themselves.

Friends often can offer a dispassionate understanding available nowhere else. They are marvelous sounding boards, people who will listen without becoming involved, who care but who will not intervene. And friends can be relied on for help in a pinch, although continuing help over an indefinite period may be less assured. Still, in a crisis, friends will help.

Though the single parent, in comparison with the married parent, may have less time for keeping up with friends, he or she has more need of them. A telephone is a necessary item in the single-parent household, not least because it facilitates the maintenance of friendships.

Formal groups as supports

Groups or organizations for single parents can act as supplements or alternatives to the relationships single parents might maintain with friends or relatives. And groups and organizations can have special usefulness. They may become repositories of information about the problems of the single-parent situation and ways in which single parents have met them. By joining such groups a single parent can learn from others in the same situation what their experiences have been and can match those experiences against the single parent's own. It can be reassuring for single parents to learn that their histories are not very different from those of others and that, indeed, they have suffered less than some. It can also be reassuring for them to learn that their reactions, odd though some may have seemed, are by and large like the reactions others have had to similar experiences.

Organizations for single parents, of which Parents Without Partners is a leading example, provide a kind of instant community in which there are people of the same sex who may become friends and people of the other sex who may be potential dates. The attractiveness of these organizations seems to depend largely on whether single parents feel comfortable with the other members they meet. If mutual acceptance is achieved, the resulting sense of membership in a valued community can prove heartening:

A couple of weeks ago I went on a singles' weekend that my church had. There were about fourteen single families. There were three men and the rest women and a lot of kids of different ages. Nobody knew each other, although we were all from around the area. We went on hayrides together, the kids and the mothers and the fathers, and we had prayer services, and we did our own things. And I was just so impressed by it. In the morning, we'd sit and have coffee and start talking. And by the end of the weekend we all felt like we knew each other. Everybody opened up to each other.

Groups and organizations for single parents can effectively allay the isolation that would otherwise be felt by single parents whose friendship network is thin. Should they also provide opportunities for a sense of satisfying social engagement, for fun, they reduce the likelihood of those feelings of depletion that foster emotional overload.

Counselors as supportive figures

Many single parents at some point find it useful to engage the services of a counselor: a social worker, a psychiatrist or psychologist, perhaps a minister or priest. They can take their problems to this person and together work out how to cope with them.

Insofar as a counselor can provide experience and competence that augment the single parent's own and can share commitment to the parent's aims, the relationship is useful. While there is no real reduction in the single parent's responsibility, there is a place to bring uncertainties to, and a forum in which to evaluate them. There is someone else with whom to share worries, someone else with whom to plan, someone to listen while the single parent thinks out loud. It can be useful for single parents just to have a place to go to where, for an hour, they can put into words what is happening to them, describe their feelings, and perhaps step aside to consider their situations objectively.

Sometimes counselors provide advice. Sometimes they help the single parent to make connections between what is happening in the present and what happened in the past. But primarily counselors seem to provide support and guidance and the opportunity to take stock.

A few single parents report having established an understanding with a counselor that they could call whenever things became too much for them. One woman described such an arrangement as lifesaving. When things became too much for her she would call the counselor, who would listen for a bit, perhaps give her advice, and sometimes arrange for an office visit. She said:

> Some days I'll come home and feel as though this is it, I can't face it any more, and I might call him. Usually I don't, but I just might. Any time I need him, he's as close as my telephone.

Some single parents are able to use books as counselors. They can find in books materials helpful to them in sorting out the issues with which they must deal and in deciding on a course of action. And they may find some reassurance from recognition of how widely their problems are shared.

Religion as support

Organized religion can provide support in ways similar to those of both formal organizations and counseling.

A church, for those who are strongly committed to it, is a kind of community. It provides an assured place for people who may feel that elsewhere in their lives they have become marginal. Where it is possible not only to participate as a member of a parish or congregation but also to establish a relationship with the priest or minister or rabbi, the single parent may gain some of the benefits of counseling. The clergyman can serve as a trustworthy yet objective ally with whom the single parent can talk, and whose advice can be trusted. The Catholic Church's practice of confession provides the same opportunity to externalize thoughts and feelings that can, in other settings, be provided by counseling:

> Not that I had that much to confess, I just felt that I needed to tell somebody else who could absolve me of my sins. Not that I'm a pillar of the Church; I'm not. I feel that I should receive the Sacrament more often than I do, but I just can't. I finally went last Monday and I felt a great lift. And my attitude toward my son changed. I was a lot calmer. I didn't lose my temper. I didn't swear.

Religious belief, in itself, is reported by some single parents to be sustaining. The conviction that God can be relied on can combat a sense of hopelessness when one is confronted by overwhelming responsibility or by demands too great to be met. A mother of four children, the oldest ten, said:

> I've become very close to my church. I go to a different church now than I did before. The minister has been fantastic. I used to go to him

for personal counseling. And when I get overwhelmed or really depressed, now what I do a lot is talk to God. I know God is with me and that He is watching over me. And I find I can talk a lot easier to Him now.

Both religious faith and church membership reduce the likelihood of a single parent's feeling like an isolated individual of limited resources, burdened with overwhelming responsibility. They strengthen the parent.

The development of self-reliance

Most single parents who had been married say that their most difficult time was the first year after their marriages ended. This was the time when they were most lost and most worried. Single parents can sustain themselves with the knowledge that if they could survive that, they can survive anything.

> What I've been through the past two years! And until recently I didn't realize how bad the past two years were for me emotionally. I sit down and say, "Think of what I went through, and I survived it." And there was one part of me that knows that no matter what happens, I'm going to make it. So no matter how bad the times get—I still get emotionally upset and depressed—I know I'm going to make it.

Single parents build confidence in themselves as they go. They watch themselves manage the challenges that come along, and their self-confidence is enhanced. They have kept things going so far; they can trust themselves to keep them going indefinitely. A kind of benign cycle is set in motion, in which successful management of responsibility leads to enhanced self-confidence, which in turn makes easier further management of responsibility:

> Sometimes I feel self-pity, defeat: "Why did this have to happen to me?" And I wish somebody would take it away from me. Sometimes I cry. But then it seems like even though there is a lot of responsibility, I've been able to accept all this responsibility and keep everything going. And when you learn to handle it, well, you feel better about yourself.

The single parent, more than a parent in a two-parent household, is a leader within the family. As such, the parent's outlook is absolutely critical to the functioning of the family. The parent who has confidence in self communicates this confidence to the children, and the family as an entity functions better.

Sometimes single parents have a sense of challenge, as though a critical ex-spouse or a doubting family were looking on, waiting for them to fail. One woman said, "My ex-husband thought I would fall flat on my face," and reminded herself of this whenever she was tempted to let things go. And another woman kept herself going through a minor crisis by remembering that her husband did not believe she could manage on her own. There had been a snowstorm and she had to shovel her driveway herself before she could get to her car. Then she discovered she couldn't get her key in the car's door; the lock was frozen. She burst into tears. And then she remembered her husband's saying, "You won't be able to get along without me!" and she went into the house to heat the key.

The following comment was made by a man who was determined he would demonstrate—not to his spouse, but to his family—that they had been wrong in doubting him:

> When I first got the children to myself, my mother told me that I would never be able to raise them. It became a challenge. I'm a stubborn man. I said, "That may be true, but they are going to have to carry me out of here before I quit."

However the determination to manage is reached, it proves most useful.

Not expecting the impossible

Single parents who are working full time do best if they can absolve themselves from guilt for not being with their children as much as they think they should be. They do well to learn to tolerate their realization that their children return from school to an empty house and that, in general, their children are more on their own than other children. They do best, too, to recognize that they cannot themselves compensate for the absence of the distinct contributions that might be made by a parent of the other sex. No single parent can replace a two-parent team.

It is valuable if single parents can establish their priorities. For some single parents, the highest priority may be to be available to the children. This can mean accepting a part-time job and a lower income.

> I work four days a week, and I work until four-thirty every day. I cut down my hours because, even though I needed the money, it was just too much physically and mentally. Plus I wanted to see my kids more. Even on weekends I wasn't seeing them enough; it was always housework and doing things you don't have the time to do during the week.

For other single parents it may be as important to be active in the world of work, to pursue a career, to make a product or provide a service. For still other single parents it may be as important to be active enough socially to have some chance of forming new attachments. There may well be conflict between these commitments and the desires of the children. Yet the single parent, like the children, has the right to a satisfactory life.

Not everything can be done. The single parent who works must accept that housework will be skimped until the children can help and perhaps be skimped even then. Commitment to career or to social life means less time for children. But this need not be damaging to the children. Older children may even profit from the increased self-direction that will be required of them. If everything cannot be done, what goes undone should not be reason for guilt or for sorrow. The following comment exemplifies a useful outlook:

> I used to change my sheets three times a week. That's when I didn't have anything else to do. I don't any more. Now it is every other week. And if it's a month before the sheets get changed, that's what it is, and it's just too bad.

The alternative to realistic expectations of what can be done is a chronic sense of failure. And, because single parents must maintain their morale if they are to continue functioning at near-maximum capability, they cannot afford to attack their own sense of competence.

When there are more bills than money, it is useful to acknowledge that this is the case and to work toward a solution. Some single parents work out systems for juggling the bills. Some tell creditors they are going to need time. Most find it helpful to be realistic, without worrying obsessively, and not to let troubles accumulate before doing something about them.

Single parents sometimes find that if they are to avoid task overload they must hire help. Some, despite a tight budget, hire an adolescent from the neighborhood who will mow the lawn and keep the yard in order and, in the winter, shovel snow. One single mother employed a fifteen-year-old girl to help her with housework partly because she needed the feeling of not doing it all alone:

> I hired a girl to come in every week for a couple of hours. It's a neighborhood girl and I'll pay her four dollars. I can't afford it; there is no way in hell I can afford it. But she works with me, she helps me change the beds, while I'm vacuuming or dusting she'll vacuum or dust the other room, so we get it done a little bit quicker. It makes me work a little better. And then if I feel like sitting down for a cup of tea, she'll fold the wash. So every two weeks my house is really clean.

Balancing the personal and the parental

Total devotion to children, while admirable, can produce a barren life and, sooner rather than later, resentment of the children for whom so much is being sacrificed. A life entirely devoted to responding to the demands of others, even one's children, can be more than most emotional systems are able to bear. If single parents are to make their lives work, they would do well to provide themselves with both time off and attention to their own needs.

Single parents find it useful to establish breaks for themselves during the evening when they are not at their children's bidding: to take ten or fifteen minutes after supper to relax and read the newspaper. We have already noted the importance to working parents of the hour at the end of the day, after the children are in bed. Some single parents say that when they come home from work they require their children to give them time to catch their breath before the children confront them with their problems or needs or stories. One woman, a mother of four children, said:

> You come in from work and everybody wants to tell you everything that has happened to them all day long. Sometimes you just have to say, "Hey, cool it for a while until I get my train of thought together."

Single parents will also need some evenings off. Just how many varies, but most single parents find that one evening a week away from the children is almost necessary. To avoid the children's objecting, the parent may try to work out an arrangement acceptable to them. One mother, not working outside her home, attended evening classes two nights a week. She said:

> At the time my children were four and six, I felt the need to get out of the house at night to keep my sanity. The children resented it. So I sat down with them and I said, "Okay, I'll make a deal. I'll be in four nights a week, and I'll go out three. Therefore, I'll spend more evenings with you." And that seemed all right.

In addition to needing time off during the day and an occasional evening in the week, single parents sometimes need a vacation during the year. The separated and divorced are fortunate if they can permit their children to spend a week or two with the other parent and the other parent will have them. One woman, mother of a nine-year-old only son, reported:

> This summer Nick went away for three weeks. I had a lot of misgivings about that. But once he got on the plane I had the best three weeks in

the world. I went lobstering with some friends, I played tennis, I went away for a weekend with my boyfriend.

The widowed and those single parents who, though the other parent is living, cannot ask the other parent to care for the children may have to find other ways of giving themselves a vacation. Sometimes relatives will take the children for a week or so. Sending the children to camp in the summer, if the children are old enough, can be as desirable for the parents as it is for the children.

One problem many single parents experience in connection with their own needs is guilt because they believe they are depriving their children by caring for themselves. The children may, indeed, play on their guilt: "Oh, Ma, you went out two nights already this week." Single parents might keep in mind that in order to be giving and loving as parents, they cannot be resentful of their children, and it helps if they are content with their lives. It is entirely justifiable, even from the perspective of the children, for single parents now and again to be self-indulgent. Single parents who appear most effective in fending off emotional overload occasionally take their children for a meal out and sometimes splurge on an article of clothing for themselves or a ticket for a play. Maintaining a personal life that is active and gratifying—although not so hectic that it is itself a source of overload—appears the best of all supports for the single parent's continued functioning.

A matter of attitude

Managing well as a single parent seems partly to be a matter of supports, partly a matter of the single parent's attitude. And the latter may be aided by focus on what is positive and constructive in the single parent's situation, rather than on ways in which the situation is undesirable. Some positive factors were noted in the preceding chapter. Here is a shorter list.

To begin with, the single parent is not alone; there are the children. One widow said:

> I thank God that I have the children, because if I didn't, God knows what might have happened. My uncle thinks that the answer to everything is to have a drink so, who knows, I might be an alcoholic if it weren't for the children. Sometimes it gets rough, and you just want to say, "The heck with everything." This is how I feel sometimes. But then I say, "No. I have the kids." I thank God for the kids.

Making It Work

It can be helpful to observe that marriages are not unmixed blessings. One woman said, "Sometimes I see a married girlfriend of mine going through hell with her husband, and I sit back and I feel good because I don't have to cope with all that."

If the children seem to be doing better as a result of the ending of one's own unhappy marriage, then parenting alone can feel quite worthwhile. Here is a comment made by a mother of four:

> My children are more relaxed and are doing better in school. And they're more mature. Because they've had to cooperate more, they are a little more thoughtful. We're just as close in the family. They are always home. They can see their father often enough. They have his love. They have love from me, they have my brother, they have my boyfriend— and he is a man who loves children. In many ways they are in a fortunate situation.

And if the children are recognized by others as on their way to becoming responsible, attractive adults, the single parent can take pride in having accomplished so much alone. A mother of three, the oldest now sixteen, the youngest eleven, had been on her own for five years. She said:

> It is a sense of satisfaction to know that I did it myself. I get the biggest kick out of it when people say, "I've met your kid." There's this old man who sells papers. I buy a paper from him every night. He saw me with Christopher and he said, "Hey, is that your kid?" I said, "Yeah, that's one of them." And he said, "He's got two sisters, right? One with long hair and one with blond?" He says, "I got to tell you what good kids they are. They are darned good kids. This kid helps me out one night. I was having trouble with the papers and I was in a rush, and I spilled everything all over the floor, and this kid took time out to stop and pick everything up."

> And that gives me a big kick. Somebody that doesn't know you notices the kids and says that they are good kids. If you bring them up yourself, you have to take pride in it: this is what I produced, and it is worthwhile.

There is no question but that single parenthood is sometimes hard going. But single parents can take heart from recognition of the importance of what they do. For, ultimately, there can be little else in life as worthwhile as having been faithful to one's children.

NOTES

Preface

[1] Paul C. Glick and Arthur J. Norton, "Marrying, divorcing, and living together in the U. S. today," *Population Bulletin* 32, no. 5 (Population Reference Bureau, Inc., Washington, D.C., 1979): 28, 40.

[2] Heather L. Ross and Isabel V. Sawhill, *Time of Transition: The Growth of Families Headed by Women* (Washington, D.C.: The Urban Institute, 1975), p. 22.

[3] Paul C. Glick and Arthur J. Norton, "Marrying, divorcing, and living together in the U.S. today," p. 28.

[4] Mary Jo Bane, *Here to Stay: American Families in the Twentieth Century* (New York: Basic Books, 1976). Paul C. Glick and Arthur Norton estimate that 45 percent of all children born in 1977 are likely to live for a period of at least several months as members of a one-parent family. See their "Marrying, divorcing, and living together in the U.S. today." p. 29.

[5] Table 5, "Presence of parent, by marital status of parent, for persons under 18 years old living with only one parent, by age and race: March, 1976," in U.S. Bureau of the Census, *Current Population Reports*, Series P-20, no. 306, U.S. Government Printing Office, 1977.

[6] Table 4, "Family relationship and presence of parents, for persons under 18 years old, by age and race: March, 1976," in U.S. Bureau of the Census, *Current Population Reports*, Series P-20, no. 306, U.S. Government Printing Office, 1977.

[7] Bernice Eiduson, *Scientists, Their Psychological World*, (New York: Basic Books, 1962), p. 22. See also C. Janet Newman and Jeffrey S. Schwan, "The fatherless child," in Joseph D. Noshpitz, editor, *Basic Handbook of Child Psychiatry, Vol. One*, (New York: Basic Books, 1979), pp. 357–372, especially pp. 369–370.

[8] The materials on which this book is based have also given rise to several other publications. These include the following by the author of this book:

"Couple relationships," in *The Couple*, Marie Corbin, ed., (London: Penguin Books, 1978), pp. 137–154.

"The emotional impact of marital separation," *Journal of Social Issues* 32, no. 1 (1976): 135–143.

"Growing up a little faster: The experience of growing up in a single-parent household," *Journal of Social Issues*, forthcoming.

"Helping relationships: Relationships of clients with physicians, social workers, priests and others," *Social Problems* 20, no. 3 (Winter, 1973): 319–328.

Loneliness: The Experience of Emotional and Social Isolation (Cambridge, Massachusetts: M.I.T. Press, 1973).

Marital Separation (New York: Basic Books, 1975).

Also, by the author, Ira O. Glick, and C. Murray Parkes, *The First Year of Bereavement* (New York: Wiley-Interscience, 1975).

Chapter 1

[1] Table 5, "Marital Status and living arrangement: March 1976," in U.S. Bureau of the Census, *Current Population Reports*, Series P-20, no. 306, U.S. Government Printing Office, Washington, D.C., 1977.

[2] Nicholas Zill, "Divorce, marital happiness and the mental health of children: Findings from the Foundation for Child Development National Survey of Children," a working paper prepared for The National Institute of Mental Health Workshop on Divorce and Children, Bethesda, Md., February 7–8, 1978 (New York: Foundation for Child Development, 1978). It may be that it is the youth of the mother, rather than her marital status, that determines her susceptibility to misuse of her children: widowed mothers tend to be older than the separated and divorced, who in turn tend to be older than unmarried mothers. And it has been reported elsewhere that very young married mothers are about as likely to be hard on their children as are unmarried mothers of the same age. However, in interviews with mothers, a sense of having been trapped by motherhood appears more important than some such characteristic as "immaturity" in explaining irritation with children.

[3] For a sensitive discussion of families in which the children's parents were not married, see Carol Stack, *All Our Kin* (New York: Harper and Row, 1974), ch. 4. Stack quotes one child as saying, "Take my father, he ain't my Daddy, he's no father to me. I ain't got but one Daddy and that's . . . the one that raised me" (p. 45).

[4] Saul Hoffman and John Holmes, "Husbands, wives and divorce," in Greg J. Duncan and James Morgan (eds.), *Five Thousand Families: Patterns of Economic Progress*, vol. 4 (Ann Arbor, Mich.: Institute for Social Research, 1976), p. 43.

[5] Robert S. Weiss, *Marital Separation* (New York: Basic Books, 1975); Ira O. Glick, Robert S. Weiss, and C. Murray Parkes, *The First Year of Bereavement* (New York: John Wiley, 1975).

[6] It has been speculated that black mothers or fathers may be better prepared to assume sole responsibility for a family because the more frequent occurrence of single parenting among blacks gives rise to a supportive network. See Carol Stack, *All Our Kin* (New York: Harper and Row, 1974).

Chapter 2

[1] Greg J. Duncan, "Unmarried heads of households and marriage;" in Greg J. Duncan and James N. Morgan (ed.), *Five Thousand American Families: Patterns of Economic Progress*, vol. 4 (Ann Arbor: Institute for Social Research, 1976), Table 3.4, p. 87.

[2] June 1975 *Current Population Survey*.

[3] National Opinion Research Center General Social Service Survey, 1970–1975. Data analyzed by the author and Mary Jo Bane.

[4] Thomas W. Rodes and John C. Moore, *National Childcare Consumer Study: 1975*, vol. 3, "American consumer attitudes and opinions on childcare" (Arlington, Va.: UNCO, Inc., 1977).

[5] Rodes and Moore, *National Childcare Consumer Study: 1975, Vol. 3*, Tables 3–10 and 3–11.

[6] Based on statistics in Lee Rainwater, "Work and welfare experience of wives who become solo mothers," unpublished memorandum, Harvard-M.I.T. Joint Center for Urban Studies, Cambridge, Mass., 1979. In this memorandum Rainwater reports findings from his analysis of data collected in the University of Michigan Panel Study of Income Dynamics.

[7] Rainwater, "Work and Welfare."

[8] Among those who do not receive welfare assistance in the first year after the dissolution of their marriages, only about 5 percent receive welfare assistance thereafter. Rainwater, "Work and Welfare."

[9] Carolyn Farley Maricq, "The support choices of female-headed families." Unpublished working paper sponsored by the project on family policy directed by Lee Rainwater and Martin Rein, Harvard-M.I.T. Joint Center for Urban Studies, Cambridge, Mass., 1978 (Table 3G, p. 67). Maricq has also analyzed data from the University of Michigan Panel Study on Income Dynamics. She took as her sample

Notes

women who had been married for three years before their marriages ended. Many in her sample moved out of the single-parent status because of remarriage. Rainwater shows that among those who remain single parents, welfare utilization drops off less dramatically.

[10] Maricq, "Support choices."

[11] Summary of statistics from reporting states, *First Annual Report to the Congress on the Child Support Program* (Office of Child Support Enforcement: Department of Health, Education and Welfare, June 30, 1976).

[12] *Child Support Enforcement*, Supplemental Report to the Congress for the Period Ending September 30, 1976 (Office of Child Support Enforcement: U.S. Department of Health, Education and Welfare, June 30, 1977).

Chapter 3

[1] For a description of the more traditional family organization, see Robert O. Blood and Donald Wolfe, *Husbands and Wives* (New York: Free Press, 1960). For the more nearly symmetric family organization, see Michael Young and Peter Willmott, *The Symmetrical Family* (New York: Pantheon Books, 1973).

[2] Joseph H. Pleck, "The work-family role system," *Social Problems*, vol. 24, no. 4 (April 1977), pp. 417–427. Reports of time–budget studies include Kathryn E. Walker, "Time spent by husbands in household work," *Family Economics Review*, vol. 4 (1970), pp. 8–11; and John Robinson, Thomas Juster, and Frank Stafford, *American's Use of Time* (Ann Arbor, Mich.: Institute for Social Research, 1976).

Chapter 4

[1] Robert O. Blood and Donald Wolfe, *Husbands and Wives* (New York: Free Press, 1960).

[2] Erving Goffman, *Asylums* (New York: Doubleday, 1966).

[3] Other comments on early maturity among children in single-parent situations may be found in Victor George and Paul Wilding, *Motherless Families* (London: Routledge and Kegan Paul, 1972), p. 73; and Richard A. Gardner, *Psychotherapy with Children of Divorce* (New York: Aronson, 1976), p. 169 ff.

[4] E. Mavis Hetherington, Martha Cox, and Roger Cox, "Divorced Fathers," *The Family Coordinator*, (October 1976), pp. 417–428. On page 425 the authors say, "The divorced mother tries to control the child by being more restrictive and giving more commands which the child ignores or resists. . . . However, by the second year her use of negative sanctions is declining. . . . The divorced mother decreases her futile attempts at authoritarian control and becomes more effective in dealing with her child over the two year period." Children in this study were attending nursery school at the time of the parents' divorce. The "second year" referred to here is after *divorce*, not after separation.

Chapter 5

[1] The material of this section is based in part on a pilot study conducted by the author, Dr. Mary Howell, and Dr. Esther Gottstein of the impact on children of growing up in a one-parent family. I am also indebted to the growing literature on the impact on children of parental separation and the death of a parent, especially the work of Judith Wallerstein and Joan Kelly, and to the theoretical contributions of John Bowlby.

Notes

Chapter 6

[1] Susan E. Anderson-Khlief, *Divorced Fathers and Children: a Study of Interaction, Support and Visitation in One-Parent Families*. Dissertation submitted to Harvard University, Department of Sociology, 1976.

[2] Corroborating materials are presented by Anderson-Khlief, *Divorced Fathers and Children*.

[3] Weiss, *Marital Separation* (Basic Books, 1975).

[4] Rhona Rosen, "Children of divorce: What they feel about access and other aspects of the divorce experience," *Journal of Clinical Child Psychology*, vol. 6, no. 2 (1977), pp. 24–27.

[5] Joan Kelly and Judith Wallerstein, "Part-time parent, part-time child: Visiting after divorce," *Journal of Clinical Child Psychology*, vol. 6, no. 2 (1977), pp. 51–54.

Chapter 7

[1] Mark S. Granovetter, "The strength of weak ties," *American Journal of Sociology*, vol. 78, no. 6 (1973) pp. 1360–1380.

Chapter 8

[1] John Bowlby, *Attachment and Loss: Volume II, Separation* (New York, Basic Books, 1973).

[2] Useful discussions of loneliness include Carin M. Rubinstein and Phillip Shaver, "Loneliness in two northeastern cities," in J. Hartog and R. Andy (eds.), *The Anatomy of Loneliness* (New York: International Universities Press, 1979); and Letitia Ann Peplau, Dan Russell, and Margaret Heim, "An attributional analysis of loneliness," in I. Frieze, D. Bar-Tal, and J. Carroll (eds.), *Attribution Theory: Applications to Social Problems* (San Francisco: Jossey Bass, 1979).

[3] Robert S. Weiss, *Loneliness: The Experience of Emotional and Social Isolation* (Cambridge, Mass., MIT Press, 1974).

[4] Data are from the National Opinion Research Center General Social Survey, 1970–1975. Data analysis is by the author and Mary Jo Bane.

Chapter 11

[1] George Brown's work suggests that experiences of loss or disappointment, particularly if they lead to a questioning of identity, together with absence of an intimate relationship, foster hopelessness, and this in turn is central to development of depression. See George W. Brown and Tirril Harris, *Social Origins of Depression: A Study of Psychiatric Disorder in Women* (New York: The Free Press, 1978).

INDEX

Index

Cox, Martha and Roger, 94
Cub Scouts, 125
Custody fights, 147, 154, 206

Dating, 215–21; children and, 234–41; hesitancies about, 201–6. See also Social life
Dating bars, 215–17
Daughters: fathers raising, 125–28; only, and mothers, 117–19. See also Children
Day-care centers, 26–28, 64. See also Child care
Daydreaming, 200–201, 254; by children, 69
Decision-making: and age, 8; alone, 261–63; and authority, 90; in one-parent families, 74–78; and priorities, 67–68; and responsibility overload, 269–70; in two-parent families, 73–74
+Dependency: and children, 84–85; and support money, 20–21, 64; and welfare assistance, 34
Depression, 41, 145; among children, 130; from emotional overload, 275–76; and loneliness, 195; and sexual frustration, 199
Desertion, 183, 271
Discipline, 48; fathers and, 58; by the parent's boyfriend or girlfriend, 247–48; mothers and, 12; in single-parent families, 89–96, 264
Discrimination: in credit, 10–11; in renting, 39
Divorce, 3–4; and difficulties with former spouses, 141–48 (see also Former spouses); and investment in parenthood, 66; relationships following, 133–41, 148–63; and remarriage, 201–6
Double standard, 222–23, 244–45
Drinking, 107, 127, 207
Drugs, 107, 109, 127, 145

Echelon structure, 73–82
Emergencies: and friendships, 182; and overload, 276–79; resources needed for, 167–68
Emotional overload, 274–76; and counseling, 286–87
Emotional problems, 129–32. See also Depression
Emotional support: from children, 6–7, 86–88, 90, 103; from counselors, 286–87; from former spouses, 59–61, 283–84; from friends, 173–83; from groups for single parents, 285–86;

insufficient, 265–67; from relatives, 169–73, 281–83; from religion, 287–88; among siblings, 122
Employment. See Work
+Expenses: unexpected, 268; and welfare grants, 33. See also Finances

Family, 281–83. See also Relatives
Fathers. See Single fathers; Single parents
+Finances, 11–12; children and, 83–84; coping with, 290; family help with, 35–38; and marital separation, 15–21; and new relationships, 249–54; responsibility for, 268. See also Income
Food stamps, 33
Former spouses: attitudes toward, 5; children's relationships with, 156–60; negative feelings toward, 151–56; positive feelings toward, 149–51; relationships with, 134–41; as supportive figures, 283–84; support money from, 18–21 (see also Support money); trouble from, 141–49
Friends, 14, 173–83; defined as kin, 283; introductions from, 211–13; as supportive figures, 284–85
Fringe benefits, 24

Gender: and chore distribution, 124; and discipline, 93–94
Gifts, 18, 143, 249; from family, 282
Goffman, Erving, 74
Grandparents, 36–38, 282. See also Relatives
Groups for single parents, 285–86
Growth, 263
Guilt: and children's roles, 78–79, 88, 92; and dating, 204; and rage, 100; and self-expectations, 289–90; of working parents, 63, 70–71

Hetherington, E. Mavis, 94
Holidays, 196
Homosexuals, 203
Hospitalization, 3, 284
Household management, 47–54, 290; children's role in, 74–85; and new relationships, 246–54; and work, 54–65
Housekeepers, 61–63
Housework, 22, 52–55, 59–65; skimping on, 290. See also Household management
Hyperactivity, 130–31

300

Index

Index